PARADISE HOTEL

and other plays

ALSO BY RICHARD FOREMAN

Plays and Manifestos
Reverberation Machines
Love and Science
Unbalancing Acts
My Head Was A Sledgehammer
No-Body

PARADISE HOTEL

and other plays

RICHARD FOREMAN

THE OVERLOOK PRESS
WOODSTOCK & NEW YORK

First published in the United States in 2001 by
The Overlook Press, Peter Mayer Publishers, Inc.
Lewis Hollow Road
Woodstock, NY 12498
www.overlookpress.com

Pearls for Pigs and *Benita Canova* were published in earlier versions
separately in "Theatre Magazine" and "Lacanian Ink," respectively.

Library of Congress Cataloging-in-Publication Data

Foreman, Richard.
Paradise Hotel : and other plays / Richard Foreman
p. cm.
Contents: Paradise Hotel—The Universe—Permanent brain—
Pearls for pigs—Benita Canova—On the plays—Rules.
PS3556.O7225 P37 2000   812'.54—dc21   99-087849

PHOTOGRAPHS © PAULA COURT
BOOK DESIGN AND TYPE FORMATING BY BERNARD SCHLEIFER
Manufactured in the United States of America
ISBN 1-58567-004-9 (hc)
ISBN 1-58567-015-4 (pb)
1 3 5 7 9 8 6 4 2

CONTENTS

ON THE PLAYS

In the plays I write, there is no "story" in the normal sense. But there is definitely a SITUATION.

There is no story, because IMPULSE is set free to deflect normal linear development. Linear, narrative development in the theater always ends with a denouement that delivers a "meaning"—i.e., a moral.

Perform in such and such a way, and such and such are the results. This kind of a narrative, this kind of logically arrived-at "moral" conclusion, is in fact a way of reinforcing the spectators' behavioral conditioning—conditioning provided by the world which exists as we have been conditioned to perceive it by physical reality, society, inherited psychological patterns, et cetera.

Such a world disciplines, orders, and imprisons a wide and potentially fruitful range of human impulses towards diversity and invention. My theater is a theater of SITUATION and IMPULSE.

To the extent that impulse is policed and suppressed (by society or by the superego) we suffocate. Ah—do I propose that a good society (or a good way to live one's personal life) is to let impulse run free? No, I do not. But I do propose that the most desirable human condition is that where one is able to avoid stasis—spiritual and emotional—by continually subjecting oneself to the nonstatic unbalanced state, where impulse is continually permitted to introduce a creative wobble to the straight and narrow of well-disciplined mental life.

IMPULSE, of course, need not just mean hitting someone on the nose—it may also mean reaching for an unsettling idea, or letting words surface from the unconscious. The point is: ART IS THE PLACE TO ALLOW THAT WHICH CANNOT REALLY HAPPEN IN LIFE, TO HAPPEN IN ITS FULL, RICH, RADIANT, ABUNDANT GLORY.

But—HERE'S THE MOST IMPORTANT PART—in my plays, the manifestations of impulse are not just narrated, but rather THE SAME IMPULSE THAT PUSHES THE CHARAC-TER INTO "ACTING OUT" ALSO TWISTS AND CONTROLS THE ARTISTIC STRUCTURE, so that the form and sequencing of the play itself reflects that impulsive, usually suppressed, energy of the human mental/emotional apparatus. And it's this isomorphic relationship between form and content that often perplexes people about contemporary art.

Why not—for easier comprehensibility—show charac-ters acting impulsively within a normal narrative structure? Of course, that happens all the time in drama and film and the novel. But there now exists a large group of so-called dif-ficult, or transgressive, artists who believe that such a strat-egy no longer suffices to introduce powerful and effective "impulse" therapy to audiences desperately trying to control their own impulsive tendencies—for fear they will interfere with their ability to lead efficient lives in the industrialized world's highly organized and demanding society. So artwork that presents impulsive behavior within a normal narrative allows the spectator to maintain control, as it were—godlike in his/her ability to set the "other" of disruptive impulse within the safe prison of moral-delivering, meaningful nar-rative. But narrative and meaning themselves churned up and fragmented by impulse hopefully provide the spectator with a"'disorientation massage" that perhaps brings him/her back into contact with a deep part of our mutual human self.

One might object: But what you propose sounds like a recipe for "anything goes"—so might the results be nonsense rather than the therapeutic aesthetic you describe?

Ah well—history, I suppose, will decide. (Does it always tell the truth?) It is as difficult, finally, to justify one's art to someone who has no taste for it as it is to justify one's choice of a beloved to those who "can't see what he sees in such an uninteresting person"! I can assure you only that "anything goes" is as far from our procedures as one can imagine. Ten weeks of maddeningly slow and deliberate rehearsals, changing and changing everything dozens of times until each "irrational" cell seems to me to have a coherence within the overall structure that is as firmly in place as a successful string quartet. Believe it or not, lucidity is my overriding concern—lucidity in the framing and ordering of each impulsive, and disruptive moment of dialogue and action until—for me at least, this "impenetrable" piece of theater sparkles like a diamond.

RULES

(For myself only. By what right could I make rules for anybody else? Except my own rules came from someplace else, of course—can I remember where? But I made some of them mine, no doubt distorting them in the process. So perhaps somebody else can pick up and distort usefully some of my own rules . . . ?)

If the process is right, I think the writing is right.

I grew up in a theatrical world where the ideal was to convince the audience—convince them of the reality of the characters, of the truthfulness of observed reality, of the logic in plot development, et cetera.

I now think the task is rather to notate the ways in which one's own mind, in the writing of the text, surprises oneself. Careful: This is not to ask itself "What will surprise my audience?," but simply to notice and be true to the inevitable jumps the mind is hungry to make as soon as it's activated. Careful: These are not plot jumps or idea jumps, not free association or imagination, but the little voice inside the voice that is doing the writing—in other words, the jumps in language; and the smaller the unit within which the jump occurs, the better. Tiny little "spark gaps" inside the language itself which must never be invented, but simply noticed. In other words—write fast enough to catch those jumps, those hitches and swerves in language.

This is not to say rewriting is out—but rewriting as often as not suppresses what is idiosyncratic and alive in a text as it clarifies.

Of course, the best rewriting is cutting. Always try to turn a hundred pages into fifty pages. Break all rules, but know that the theater is not really about conflict (which can be very boring if the terms of that conflict are self-evident), but about misunderstanding. Write moment-by-moment misunderstandings—one character misunderstands *part* of what the other character is saying, and the enactment of that misunderstanding leads to new misunderstanding, and then new misunderstanding, and then new misunderstanding— and then even the characters forgetting and misunderstanding what he/she has semi-said.

Language always slides—is always slippery—but don't love the language too much. The minute you notice its inevitable slippage beginning, register that (let another character register that in some way) rather than falling prey to the delirious "go with the flow" that can seduce a writer into falling in love with his/her own voice and boring the audience to hell.

Write only to get lost. Only then is there hope that you'll end up saying what you didn't know you wanted to say, and only if you end up surprising yourself will the writing be alive. It will be the greatest gift that writing will bestow on you, if your play ends up saying the opposite of what you thought you believed—because then the writing has been alive as it came through you, instead of your own pre-programmed dead writing that was only "going through the paces" in order to prove or demonstrate your own private, passionate, "flavor-of-the-month" belief.

Write in such a way that your play falls apart. Then—can you do this?—find the way in which it hasn't fallen apart. Rebuild it around the very thing that, because you didn't expect it to be there, made it fall apart.

There is no way to write a play or anything else, until you learn to stop worrying about how you write—and *then* you learn to cut. Cut out all your best stuff. Hemingway, in an interview, claimed his greatest talent as a writer was his own built-in shit detector; he knew what to throw out.

The task is to make the writing isomorphic with a certain urge in the body. Never say what you think should be said next, but emote what rushes through you—then IMMEDIATELY, let that be interrupted. Contest at every moment what you want to say, because anything you want to say is being contested at every moment by another "you" deep inside yourself. Look deep—that's the true fact of being human, the fact that every impulse gives rise at the same moment to its counterimpulse. When Aristotle said irony was at the root of the dramatic experience, he was correct. Only today, as we dig deep inside human being-ness with different (not better) tools than the tools in favor in Aristotle's day, we locate that irony on a different level. No longer on the level where one character doesn't know what the audience knows (how dull by now—we've seen all the moves in *that* particular game a hundred times over)—but on a level where the things we say, as we say them, are known by ourselves to be at best half truths because nothing else is possible. This knowledge, this irony, is what plays today must be built out of.

Somebody disagrees? Fine. Prove it. By writing a differently based play, of course. But don't prove it by trying to write a play that persuades to some other point of view. (Oh well, if you want to write for the movies or TV, okay.) Prove it by investing such authority in your way of making a play that it cannot be denied, even if it doesn't convince. Have the courage at every moment to believe on the deepest level, this is the way this play must be. Not because you decide, but because the language that comes out of you does the deciding.

These thoughts can't be rules to follow. There are no rules to follow, only a kind of music whose beat and tonality one can tune to, if one so chooses.

That's it, finally. Build a world around yourself that is composed of the things you thrill to (you needn't tell anyone else what those thrill provokers are)—bathe in that private world, and then—NEVER NEVER NEVER try to copy or even evoke that world in your own work—just trust to the fact that your rigorous (oh so rigorous) orientation will do its work inside you—and let come forth from inside you what has to come forth, without trying to twist it so it resembles something different (or even better) than what it REALLY IS!

Never try to make things better. Only make them more clearly what they already are.

NOTES ON PRODUCING THE PLAYS

I always insist that one good way to stage these plays is to erase all the stage directions, even the assignment of characters, and use the naked text to then reimagine a new scenario—whatever the pure dialogue suggests to the director. These texts include complete notations of what my own productions were like and may hopefully convey some of their flavor.

I write the original text with no speakers or stage direction indicated. Then I start imagining scenarios for the text. For instance, my original idea for *Benita Canova* was to stage it as if a group of fashion models were on a shoot in some poverty-stricken South American country, with Madame being a witchlike, elderly shaman. Obviously, that's not the way I ended up staging it. But perhaps somebody else should—or imagine whatever the text suggests. If the play is staged in some new way, the director should feel free to make the obvious minimal changes to justify a shift of locale and character. I do not want the order in which the dialogue is spoken changed—but the dialogue can be reassigned; with more or fewer characters, different genders, or a run of dialogue spoken by one character instead assigned to several, or vice versa.

(Perhaps I should also state that in all my productions the actors use radio mikes, so that they can exploit a quiet and intimate vocal delivery which I believe serves my texts very well—even when they are being intense and emotional. Obviously, not all theaters will be able to afford this, but I would suggest it as one aspect of my staging technique that those who can do so might consider.)

All this is not to say I am against productions that observe many of my own directorial decisions indicated in these printed texts, but it is to proclaim my openness to an alternative style of mounting them.

THE PLAYS

THE UNIVERSE

The Universe. Produced by the Ontological-Hysteric Theater at the Ontological Theater at St. Mark's Church, New York City. January–March 1995. Written, directed, and designed by Richard Foreman.

With: James Urbaniak, Tony Torn, and Mary McBride

And Servants: Cradeaux Alexander, D. J. Mendel, Julie Mullen, Karen Williams, and Leigh Withers

A room, dominated by a long table downstage, running parallel to the footlights. From the rear, TONY runs on, carrying a suitcase that he throws to the floor, which is immediately cleared by five SERVANTS in tuxedos, dark glasses, and conelike hats. TONY himself is dressed in a business suit with a floral tie, but he also wears glasses with one lens blacked out and a giant, elaborate eighteenth-century white wig.

The SERVANTS are present through most of the play, performing somewhat aberrant, carefully choreographed actions, delivering props to provoke the actors which are sometimes used and sometimes rejected— any future directors of the play should feel free to fully develop interaction between the three main characters and the servants.

As the SERVANTS hurry off, JAMES appears from the other side of the stage, moving slowly to the table, balancing a glass of milk on a round serving tray. He is dressed in a dark suit, and his head is bandaged; plus, a small bandage covers a cut on his face. The rhythm of a soft repetitive music fills the stage and continues throughout the play.

TONY: *(Leaning over the table toward JAMES)* This doesn't make any sense.

JAMES: None at all?

TONY: None at all. When I left—you were on the planet of the disturbed people.

JAMES: Yes, I suppose I was.

TONY: Now I find you here—

JAMES: Where else should I be?

TONY: Acting almost normal.

JAMES: There's nothing normal about the way I'm acting.

TONY: Of course there is. The milk in that glass is real milk.

JAMES: I'm not ready to deny that.

TONY: Of course not, because it wouldn't make any sense.

JAMES: Do you see me drinking this milk?

TONY: Not right now.

JAMES: Of course not. You're welcome to hang around watching me all night—

TONY: No, thank you.

JAMES: I don't think you'll see me doing anything special with this milk.

TONY: It's a kind of drug.

JAMES: Of course. It calms me.

TONY: Which is why you avoid tasting it?

JAMES: I don't avoid tasting it, it just never happens that I have such an urge.

TONY: Then why are you holding it, my friend?

JAMES: This can't be answered.

TONY: You don't know?

JAMES: I can't answer.

TONY: This is weird.

JAMES: This is your perception of something weird.

TONY: I agree.

JAMES: To me it doesn't seem weird at all.

TONY: That could be your particular perspective.

JAMES: Exactly. That could be my perspective.

> *(As the music rises, JAMES and TONY and the SERVANTS are running around the room, exchanging glasses of milk. JAMES offers his glass to TONY.)*

TONY: Are you trying to make me drink milk?

JAMES: Maybe I am . . .

TONY: This doesn't make any sense. Why would you offer me your milk?

JAMES: I already explained.

> *(There is a crash, and the lights change to reveal MARY, leaning against a wall, her face masked, exposing a naked breast. JAMES looks, then turns away to think.)*

What do you know. Am I acting normal? No, there's nothing normal about the way I'm acting.

TONY: At the same time, you say there's nothing weird.

JAMES: Do I say that?

TONY: Put those together, they don't make any sense.

JAMES: I put them together.

> *(MARY has disappeared.)*

They make perfect sense.

TONY: This is very weird.

JAMES: Of course it is, my friend!

> *(SERVANTS have grabbed TONY and are pulling down his pants.)*

TONY: Hey, you still think of me as a friend?

JAMES: *(As TONY bends down to lift his pants)* You entered a room with no back door—

TONY: Did I do that?

JAMES: —and somebody else, here already with a glass of warm milk, so *your* head goes into some kind of terrible spin. I.e., "I can't open the door to my own mind, so how can I find the way out?"
  That's not you speaking, of course.

TONY: Hey, I'm not speaking.

(The SERVANTS are rear, watching.)

JAMES: I'm just featuring the unrecognizable tone of voice somebody else is good at using like I'm good at using.

TONY: We're not alone, I'm afraid.

JAMES: Right. We decide to go partying in some of the very best places—says the man who pops in with the funny crossed eyes.

TONY: The eyes is off limits.

JAMES: But the minute he's really *drunked up* his glass of milk . . .

TONY: It must have been really good stuff.

JAMES: . . . he goes into other areas fast.

TONY: I wish it could always be like that—

JAMES: Which means you're thinking about yourself first, instead of that ex-cross-eyed milk drinker—right?

TONY: Right.

JAMES: Right. But I do notice you haven't asked for much in the way of explanation. Then again, who knows much about tailspins or other things worth talking about, so,

(Everyone collapses to the floor.)

Just drop in on me like you did, and we'll all have a good laugh about this—

Except as of yet—nobody else is here. So "who's really laughing" is my next logical question.

(JAMES rises, runs into a wall, and staggers back from the collision; he ends up bending over as a SERVANT prepares to hit him with a small paddle.)

Ah—that famous back door—

(The SERVANT whacks JAMES.)

There it is!

TONY AND JAMES: *(Both with a delayed reaction, even though only JAMES has been hit.)* Ow!

TONY: I don't see anything.

JAMES: It's a question of getting a little more information to surface.

TONY: You can make that possible?

(SERVANTS carry onstage a small table piled with books.)

JAMES: You tell me.

TONY: How do we do that? How do we get more information to surface than is surfacing right this minute?

JAMES: A better idea.

TONY: *(Tearing up pages of a book)* Better than this?

JAMES: We could have a séance using this very table.

TONY: Just two of us isn't enough.

JAMES: Let's try—

TONY: Well, you may try, but—

(The table falls over by itself.)

TONY & JAMES: Holy shit!

TONY: Maybe this means—the table doesn't want to be used for a séance.

JAMES: *(Lifting the table.)* I don't like recalcitrant tables.

(He sets it down and straightens a tablecloth the SERVANTS *have provided. The* SERVANTS *lay down two place settings, and* JAMES *gives the silverware a final adjustment.)*

That should calm it down, don't you think?

TONY: I wonder what it was afraid of revealing.

JAMES: Maybe it just wanted to eat something.

TONY: How many unpleasant aspects of this shared universe should we uncover please?

JAMES: Ah! Food for thought—

(There is a crash, and a SERVANT *places a framed window against the wall.)*

This window you thought was a window onto the world outside?

TONY: *(Seizing the window)* Wait a minute. I never noticed these windowpanes were in fact false.

JAMES: That's impossible.

TONY: It was already night when I arrived, so I never realized they were black, opaque material.

JAMES: Maybe it's a blackboard.

TONY: Blackboards are supposed to be transparent.

JAMES: You can see through *me*, apparently? In fact, I'm not necessarily in this room.

(Some SERVANTS shoot him with bows and arrows— cupids aiming at his heart, as MARY passes through in the rear.)

Ow! Total transparency means—you know a great deal about me already.

TONY: A great deal?

JAMES: A great deal. Am I acting normal?

(He hits TONY on the shoulder.)

Hey! Why did you fly into a panic when you saw me carrying my milk?

(Several SERVANTS present several glasses of milk.)

TONY: I was expecting something like this to happen.

JAMES: Here's an idea—*(Offers his hand in friendship.)*—let me introduce myself.

TONY: Skip it.

JAMES: You seem frightened.

TONY: I have every reason to be frightened, but I keep it bottled up inside.

JAMES: That's where it shows.

(A suitcase has been left on the long table. TONY opens it.)

TONY: Inside?

JAMES: *(As TONY extracts a bloody apron from the suitcase)* Outside.

TONY: *(Putting on the apron)* You assume a great deal about me, sir. But since I'm not obligated to participate in non-verifiable assumptions, I'll just reclaim my belongings and vanish like before, thank you.

(He picks up the suitcase and starts to leave as JAMES blocks the exit.)

JAMES: The only exit is on my side of the room, you big tough palooka.

TONY: I was thinking about the back door.

JAMES: You were thinking about an impenetrable window!

(A crash, and the lights go out, and we can see MARY and the SERVANTS in the shadows, all appearing with eye masks and long carrot noses. MARY is leaning against the wall and massaging her breasts.)

Why do you suppose neither of us is moving?

TONY: Did we succeed in changing an unpleasant subject?

JAMES: Ah—doesn't the table look inviting, bedecked with flowers?

TONY: I already picked up on that.

JAMES: It's as plain as the nose on my face.

TONY: What's wrong with my nose?

(A SERVANT has placed a realistic-looking human head on the long table.)

JAMES: Who knows?

(JAMES removes the nose from the human head. He studies it.)

Is there something funny about his or her nose?

(It makes him sneeze violently into a hankerchief, which he tosses on the table. The SERVANTS collect the hankerchief and display it against a picture frame. The blood residue of the sneeze resembles a cosmic display of the Milky Way.)

TONY: Remind me what planet is this?

(Pause.)

JAMES: Difficult to decide.

TONY: Okay, what meal is this table set for?

JAMES: Even more problematic.

(A SERVANT pours some cereal into a bowl.)

TONY: Wrong, breakfast, apparently—which is not very appropriate.

JAMES: Why not?

TONY: Oh please, I've been around. Time for breakfast is long since gone.

JAMES: But it's my favorite meal.

TONY: What's on the menu that's so special?

JAMES: See for yourself.

(He digs into the cereal enthusiastically.)

TONY: How can you justify eating that tiny stuff?

JAMES: You can't be serious.

TONY: Why shouldn't I be serious?

JAMES: Listen to me carefully, you big tough palooka. Hidden inside each small, perfect grain of wheat, a vast store of energy is waiting to be released.

TONY: No.

JAMES: *(Holding a flake of cereal up to the light)* Yes!

TONY: Where do you get this information?

JAMES: This! This! This is why I have breakfast, many times over—in search of what never arrives? Maybe, but maybe it does; and each time, I'm just royally fooled as usual.

(MARY has appeared behind JAMES, and is refilling his bowl with cereal.)

TONY: Apparently more wheat flakes are being heaped on for a better breakfast.

JAMES: With no real possibility of satisfaction, of course.

(He turns and sees MARY. Their eyes meet; they both stagger back and simultaneously explode with a loud sneeze. MARY runs from the room and JAMES grabs the cereal and begins shoveling it down, scattering cereal over the carpet as he does so.)

TONY: You wolf down your breakfast with amazing enthusiasm—

JAMES: Wolf? The animal? Well, hungry indeed I am—but never satisfied.

(A crash, and the SERVANTS run to hold another window against the wall.)

TONY: Holy shit!

JAMES: It's okay. That window is only a mirror.

TONY: Not for me personally, I hope.

JAMES: Let me invite you to share my most intimate experiences. Come to me. Eat.

TONY: We're still not in sync, I'm afraid. What time is it?

JAMES: Nighttime.

TONY: I thought this was breakfast?

JAMES: Right again.

TONY: Ah, you want the feeling of a new day beginning again and again and again—

JAMES: *(Interrupts)* Notice?—Notice anything about my mouth in particular?

TONY: *(Turns away)* I can't bear to look at it.

JAMES: *(Runs to the other side of the room)* Can you see it better over here?

TONY: Yes.

JAMES: What's special about it?

TONY: It always wants to be eating things.

JAMES: How can an invisible desire be so visible? Wait a minute—what desire am I talking about?

TONY: What desire are you talking about?

JAMES: I don't think this is the right time for an extended philosophical discussion.

TONY: Use a finger, point to something.

JAMES: What happens if the thing I'm pointing to isn't visible?

TONY: Turn around three times fast, close your big blue eyes—open them, the person you see standing in front of you is somebody different.

JAMES: Smiling?

TONY: Maybe.

JAMES: In close physical proximity?

TONY: What desire are you talking about?

JAMES: Well, let's just say—breakfast, apparently. I'm imagining it.

TONY: I find it hard to imagine that desire.

JAMES: To reestablish our relationship on a less emotional basis.

TONY: Emotion?

JAMES: *(Holding up a flake of cereal)* Yes, I offer you in friendship a single, administrable dose of energy.

TONY: Where is it?

JAMES: In my breakfast cereal.

TONY: It's an acquired taste.

JAMES: Not by choice.

TONY: You do eat sloppily, however—so what's necessary is attire that appropriately guards both of us from such sloppy eating habits.

(He pulls off the tablecloth from the small table, scattering cereal and plates, and puts the tablecloth around JAMES's neck to serve as an apron.)

That seems satisfactory.

JAMES: *(Studying his improvised apron)* How do we use this thing?

TONY: We stay wrapped up in it, so food of obscure derivation, even though it misses the mouth, never reaches what's underneath.

(They have acquired skirts as well as aprons, and they prance across the stage, whirling, trying them out.)

JAMES: Perhaps I'd rather go outside for breakfast after all.

TONY: I haven't spoiled it for you here, I hope?

JAMES: Oh, no! I'm making a quick mental comparison between this room, limited in its appeal, and the wide avenue I remember downstairs, lined with trees and white café tables sparkling in the sunlight.

TONY: I remind you, it's night.

JAMES: Here's an idea. For extra money, breakfast can be served at night.

TONY: But that frustrates your particular lust for the ambiance of a day just beginning.

JAMES: Which never lives up to my expectations—

TONY: Let me show you something that does—

JAMES: What?

TONY: The sun.

> *(The lights change suddenly, and JAMES stares into very intense light, pouring from offstage.)*

JAMES: *(Softly)* I see it one hundred percent.

TONY: And having seen it?

JAMES: It's enough. It's . . . everything.

> *(Pause, then he takes off his apron and turns to TONY, who is spinning in ecstacy.)*

Do me a tremendous favor, please.

TONY: Yes.

JAMES: You say 'yes', without knowing what I'm going to ask.

TONY: Yes, yes!

> *(He stops spinning.)*

JAMES: First, collect these flakes of my breakfast cereal accidentally scattered over the carpet—

TONY: You don't plan on eating them, I hope?

JAMES: I'm not sure yet.

TONY: They're very soiled by now.

JAMES: I'd like to examine each one of them for myself, thank you—

> *(TONY bends down to pick up a flake.)*

Careful! Careful! There's tremendous energy in each individual flake!

TONY: I'll collect just a few at a time. You start examining these while I move on to others.

(He holds some out to JAMES.)

JAMES: Just . . . put them on the table.

TONY: "Just"?

JAMES: Just.

TONY: I think "put them on the table" were the only words necessary.

JAMES: "Just"?—Yes. My mouth certainly moves to excess, which I let happen in anticipation of energy yet to come—

TONY: *(Seething inside)*—You made me lose my train of thought!

JAMES: It's a conspiracy, in fact—so much extra energy floating around in my head it overflows—

TONY: *(Exploding in terrible rage)* You don't understand! When I lose my train of thought, it's like losing contact with EVERYTHING! You can't IMAGINE how irrationally UPSET I GET!

(The music builds, while the enraged TONY has acquired a handsaw with which he tries to destroy the furniture. JAMES tries to stop him several times, and each time, they both lose their footing and fall down— as the deafening music continues, and they scream out in terror, "Oh my God! Oh my God!" Then TONY somehow gets his saw between JAMES's legs, and JAMES screams in pain and pulls away.)

TONY: Okay. This may hurt somebody, but pain is the way in which people get knowledge, so hurting isn't what happens. So it won't hurt.

JAMES: This is amazing. I thought you were going to saw wood, but now I realize you're going to saw my arm, so I'm in the process of detaching myself from that extremity—

TONY: *(As he tosses a stuffed arm onto the table)* Here it is.

JAMES: Is that real?

TONY: The only problem is—it's already been sawed off apparently.

JAMES: You were perfectly right. It didn't hurt. Shit.

(A beam of wood suddenly appears from offstage.)

TONY: What should I do with this stick?

JAMES: That's your problem—

TONY: Which of us should receive a blow from this stick?

(He whirls it, and it falls to the floor.)

JAMES: Why're you putting it down?

TONY: Why do you think I picked it up?

JAMES: The effect was comical.

TONY: I'm not sure the result is comical—

JAMES: *(As another beam of wood appears)* Holy shit! Here it is again—

TONY: So which one of us gets hurt?

(JAMES whirls with the beam, and crashes it into the wall, at the same time that MARY appears on the other side of the room and TONY covers her face with a phonograph record, hiding her from JAMES's sight.)

JAMES: No. Here's what really happens. Somebody—

TONY: Me?

JAMES: No.

TONY: You?

JAMES: *(Indicating the hidden MARY)* Don't do this to me.

TONY: I'm about to do it, but I haven't done it yet.

JAMES: That's why nobody should move.

(He drops the beam, which accidentally hits his foot, making him howl in pain. MARY ducks out from behind the record and laughs at him.)

MARY: I apologize for laughing.

JAMES: *(Glancing at MARY, then turning away)* This is not something I need in my life!

TONY: I pick up on a certain electricity between you two people.

JAMES: Why should I believe something nobody can verify?

MARY: Suppose a man with whom I've never had a proper conversation before says "I can bring you the dreams of a lifetime," and he smiles. Should I believe him?

JAMES: I never smile.

MARY: Then what could I possibly be remembering?

TONY: *(Holding out a book)* Look twice.

MARY: I've never read that kind of book before.

TONY: But you recognize the smile—?

MARY: What smile?

JAMES: I never smile.

TONY: Let me give you something that will put a smile back.

MARY: Where?

TONY: On your face, sweetie.

MARY: *(Opens the book, then throws it away)* I can tell—this book says it all.

(She runs from the room.)

JAMES: What book were you letting her read?

TONY: *(Snatching the book away so JAMES can't see it)* Nothing.

JAMES: You're hiding it from me?

TONY: *(Putting it into a suitcase)* Storing it for future reference.

JAMES: I'll carry my own baggage, thank you.

TONY: You won't find it as interesting as she did.

JAMES: Show me the book.

TONY: *(Opening the suitcase)* It's in the suitcase.

JAMES: I see it.

> *(Pause. Then he grabs the book and leafs through its pages.)*

I can't make heads or tails of this thing. Read it to me.

TONY: Out loud?

JAMES: If I hear it, I might comprehend better than just reading.

TONY: All the words are run together, so it's just letter after letter—ad infinitum.

> *(JAMES makes a gibberish noise.)*

I don't know how to pronounce that.

JAMES: But you read it to yourself?

TONY: That way I can project my own meanings into it.

JAMES: You must have a lot of secrets.

TONY: I don't think so.

JAMES: Secrets! That's why I left a minute ago, and that's why I'm about to repeat myself.

TONY: Everything I do is perfectly normal.

JAMES: One more chance.

TONY: To do what?
JAMES: Time's up.

> *(The SERVANTS have assembled in the rear. One holds up a clock. Another has a silver tray on which JAMES places the book.)*

Find what I just hid in plain sight.

TONY: *(He looks under the table, then runs about the room, avoiding the silver tray and singing under his breath)*
I'm looking high
I'm looking low
I'm gonna find where did you go
I'm looking up
I'm looking down
I'm gonna look all over town.

(He comes back and confronts JAMES.)

You win.

JAMES: No I don't.

TONY: Why?

JAMES: I don't know where I put it!

(Both close their eyes and whirl as the music rises. JAMES runs and grabs the clock, which he holds in front of his crotch. He starts rubbing the clock face, moans, and collapses to the floor. Everyone assembles to study him.)

TONY: Did you think getting dizzy would help? Well, it doesn't.

JAMES: I'm just as dizzy as before, you son of a bitch.

TONY: Then maybe it helped.

JAMES: Right. Acting almost normal—looking into somebody's eyes and suddenly realizing somebody's looking back. So going public with no real place to do that because after all, I can't just sit down in the middle of the carpet—I mean I could, but I don't. *(Slowly rises.)* And I can't help thinking, a story with powerful emotional content, begun but then dropped midway, makes no sense in the sense of—why begin even?

(MARY sneaks in behind him and slowly puts her hands under his arms, reaching around to massage his chest.)

But then plunging a little more deeply into the relevant matter, I begin glimmering for myself a very desirable self-turbulence with no escape routes that seem particularly desirable to me.

MARY: *(Whispering into his ear)* What desire are you talking about?

JAMES: *(Whirling as she runs away)* Who's talking!?

TONY: I think there's somebody you should turn around and meet.

JAMES: Oh, in principle I know who that person is, but I don't want to meet that person!

TONY: Why not?

JAMES: Don't you get it?

(The SERVANTS have cymbals, which they clash in accompaniment to the speech of the excited JAMES.)

I don't need any of this in my life!

MARY: Well, I don't see any of this in my life either.

TONY: Take the risk.

(The SERVANTS are now on the floor, bowing down to JAMES.)

Try acting normal, like the vast majority of the human race.

(The music rises, and the three characters bang crazily into the walls as the SERVANTS hold hands and dance once around the room, then exit.)

MARY: *(Very excited by all the turmoil)* Okay, okay, okay, is it gonna happen? What the hell—or isn't it gonna happen?

TONY: There's somebody special I think you should meet.

JAMES: I know who it is, but I don't want to look.

TONY: Why not?

JAMES: It would be too intense.

MARY: That's what I say, it would be too intense.

TONY: I thought both of you would like that.

MARY: Sometimes she would.

JAMES: Sometimes he would not.

TONY: Accept emotional reality, please—pivot on the tiniest hint of information.

MARY: Pivot?

TONY: Ah, the lady's asking for a definition.

JAMES: A nonlocatable point that hurtles me into emotional turmoil.

TONY: Just write down "pivot."

JAMES: Just?

TONY: Just. No more. no less. Everybody pivot.

(SERVANTS put a white cloth over JAMES's head.)

MARY: I don't want to pivot.

TONY: Why not?

MARY: I can imagine the results.

JAMES: *(From under the cloth)* Wait a minute. Do I know that voice?

MARY: Hello? The only way you can find out for sure is by taking a big risk.

(The cloth is removed. JAMES and MARY stare into each other's eyes for the first time, staggering backwards from the shock.)

MARY AND JAMES: You! You!

(They collapse and rise quickly.)

MARY: *(Trying to collect her thoughts, spinning to the music)* This is me. This is Mary from someplace very far away. This must be something that's happening to me.

JAMES: How the mind works—it reaches for something that glows in the dark—

(He reaches out towards MARY, accidentally looks into her eyes, and turns away screaming.)

Ow!

TONY: That must have been the sun.

JAMES: It's midnight, goddamn it, I don't think it was the sun.

TONY: But the sun's always shining.

JAMES: Okay, so somebody's eyes burn through my head while the mind clouds the experience with something different—

MARY: I turned around as fast as I could—

JAMES: *(Putting the cloth over his head again, as protection)* Present but hard to notice, because the mind is more efficiently distracted elsewhere.

TONY: Does somebody's mind really work like that?

JAMES: One more distraction, please!

MARY: I don't see anything different.

JAMES: A painting about pain, I believe.

MARY: A painting about pain?

TONY: A painting about pain.

MARY: I never imagined there could be such a painting.

(A SERVANT carries in a six-foot-tall blank canvas, and MARY goes to examine it.)

JAMES: I'm about to reveal it—turn around, of course.

MARY: Really?

JAMES: Perhaps I'm just talking to myself. Turn around, of course!

(He pulls the cloth off his head as MARY turns to face him, and once again the shock of looking into each other's eyes knocks them to the floor.)

JAMES AND MARY: You!

JAMES: Why do I fall down?

MARY: Okay, me too I fell down!

JAMES: *(As both regain their feet)* Okay. A big disappointment.

MARY: *(As she gets on the table to lie on her back with her legs in the air and show her hindquarters to JAMES.)* See?

JAMES: Human beings never get inside each other.

MARY: I don't know how—

JAMES: No way exists for one human being to get inside another human being!

MARY: Let's try again.

JAMES: Every *conceivable* way has been tried—nothing works!

(He turns away in desperation.)

Give up, please.

MARY: I do give up.

JAMES: You haven't given up.

MARY: Yes, I give up.

JAMES: *(Falling to the floor in anguish)* Give up, change both of us completely.

MARY: Please . . . touch me?

JAMES: Where?

MARY: *(Swinging her legs down, sitting on the table)* One my arms, two my knees, three my thighs, four my breasts, five my fingers, six between my legs, seven under my arms—

JAMES: Give up!

MARY: I do give up.

JAMES: You haven't given up!

MARY: Have you?

JAMES: Not yet.

MARY: Why not?

JAMES: I don't think it's something you can do on purpose.

MARY: It's like an accident.

> *(There is the sound of a crash, and a startled MARY and JAMES run to hold each other, then, realizing they are in each other's arms, break away and run to opposite walls.)*

That was scary.

JAMES: I don't know what it was—

MARY: That's what makes it scary!

JAMES: *(After a pause, whispering)* Please, get undressed.

MARY: *(Laughs)* I apologize for laughing, smack me.

> *(She holds out her hand and slaps it herself.)*

You get undressed.

JAMES: *(He considers, then whirls around and crosses to her without looking at her, begins to undress, then notices the SERVANTS lined up behind the table, with lifted cymbals held in the air, waiting to clash them together. He whirls towards them.)* Excuse me?

MARY: Hey, say something nice to me.

JAMES: I'm the idea man. I don't have any!

> *(The SERVANTS clash the cymbals.)*

I don't really need this in my life!

> *(They do it again.)*

MARY: I don't really need this in my life either.

> *(The SERVANTS exit, and JAMES stands rooted to the spot, staring at MARY. A battle is going on inside him, and finally, with his face distorted in agony, he shouts at her.)*

JAMES: Go away!

> *(She hesitates, not knowing what to do. Then she whirls and dashes out of the room. There is a pause as JAMES stares after her. Then he shouts after her in anguish.)*

Come back!

> *(She runs back into the room. They stare at each other. Then he again bellows at her.)*

Go away!

> *(She hesitates, runs off. He starts to go also, then stops, turns back to look where she has disappeared and again shouts.)*

Come back!

> *(He dashes from the room and a second later she reappears. As she reenters, TONY comes up behind her and offers her a crown.)*

MARY: Is that for me?

TONY: Do you deserve it?

MARY: *(She holds it, considers it, then plops it forcefully upon her head)* This is about time! Me—!

(She screams to express her frustration, running out of the room.)

Erghhhhhhh!

TONY: *(Calling after her)* The sun's always shining my dear.

MARY: *(Reentering immediately)* Looking for a respite from this pressurized psychological turbulence I decided to go outside. Well, I decided to go to—well—I know! The classical record music store, yeah!

(She has run around the table as the SERVANTS clash cymbals.)

—and buy myself a record, violins and harpsichordings—because I was in such a turmoil after all this stuff happening—I needed a little majestic something in my life to make me feel better. But my eyes hurt.

TONY: *(Pointing to his blanked-out eyeglass)* Hey, the eyes is off limits.

MARY: Okay. I felt inside a shell, like a big red lobster that was my own body maybe, with my head clogged up—ah, ah, ah . . .

(She is fighting a sneeze.)

—excuse me—ah-choo!

(Cymbals clash, and she runs around the table once as the music crests. Then she stops, and a faraway look comes into her eye.)

What would happen to me if I opened my ears to this musical majesty I'm imagining? Either I myself would find some way to fuck it up, or it would kill me instead.

TONY: Ah, killed by great music.

MARY: Hey, we're talking Mr. Mozart here, really great stuff. Oh! I wish I was on some other one of the millions of millions of planets in the whole Milky Way in the skies.—Who am I kidding? I'd still have the same problems, still be bored, bored, bored in every inch of my body—let's see what I mean by that—eyes, brain, inner nose, inside the ears,

(The SERVANTS have come and are climbing over the table; all freeze in place, with their rear ends facing the audience.)

—plus lots of amazing body orifices I can't locate or choose to name, that's what the beautiful music would have to go to work on, but would it be effective?

(The SERVANTS have come down on the other side of the table and collapse.)

I don't think so. But you know, inside me still is such a powerful, powerful need, I have to get out and purchase some shitty worn-out record. Some shitty morsel of worn-out Mozart or something, because you know what? This is the only thing that can be background music for my whole life, which up until now is something that I have to call—deep shit in the middle. But this way of fixing things is not something I believe in. No more atmosphere, please! No more worn-out Mozart nostalgia shit for me. Shit!

(She starts giggling with pleasure.)

—But I like it, I like it, I like it! But this is not something I *should* like. You see, when I look in a mirror— this is very "now" for me—what do I see?

JAMES: *(Lurking in the shadows, wearing dark glasses to protect his eyes from MARY)* You see me?

MARY: I see myself.

JAMES: Shit. We have lots in common after all.

MARY: *(As she leaves the room in disgust)* Come back into my life so it can be more terrible than ever.

JAMES: *(Calling after her)* Sure thing, "sweetie"! Did I hear somebody just put the two of us into a very precarious position?

(The SERVANTS have all lined up behind the table.)

MARY: *(She slowly returns, wearing dark glasses to protect her eyes from JAMES. A lit cigarette in her hand.)* I don't know if I should believe anything you tell me.

JAMES: That's because things pop out of me with a certain violence.

MARY: I don't doubt that violence.

JAMES: Can't you tell—deep inside I'm not a violent person.

MARY: Then why are you trying to provoke me?

JAMES: I have a confession to make.

MARY: So do I.

TONY: I don't believe either of you comedians.

MARY: Believe this comedian. I'm part of a very secret organization. A group of people who seem, on the surface— well, how do I seem?

(She puts her cigarette between the lips of the most attractive SERVANT. After he takes a puff, she takes it back and puffs on it.)

Normal? Or rather, "disturbed"?

(There is a crash, and she waves it away with a flick of her hand.)

Yeah, yeah. I'm talking about a group of people, some of them very, very good friends of mine, who spend their lives developing techniques to disrupt the lives of other people.

JAMES: You just told me about it, didn't you?

MARY: Did I?

JAMES: So how could it be secret?

MARY: I broke the rules.

JAMES: I, too, have a confession to make.

MARY: What?

TONY: I don't believe either of you comedians.

JAMES: Believe this comedian. I'm part of the same organization.

MARY: That must be why you have this terrible effect on me.

(She thrusts at him with an accusing finger.)

—I curse you!

JAMES: *(Collapsing to the floor)* I curse you!

MARY: *(Collapsing also)*—I curse you! I curse you again! I curse you once more on top of that!

JAMES: I wasn't protected, but I looked into your eyes for the first time, and my eyes hurt and my legs collapsed under me—

MARY: I didn't see you fall down.

JAMES: Of course not! Because you fell down at the exact same moment.

MARY: I don't remember.

JAMES: Yes, yes, yes—that was because I fell down at the exact same moment.

MARY: What happened?

JAMES: *(Taking a deep breath)* You looked back at me.

MARY: Oh, no—you looked at ME!

JAMES: We started bleeding from the eyes!

MARY: I don't see blood.

JAMES: This is possible! Take a knife and cut out from two heads belonging to us two times, two eyes between the two of us, and grind them into one another like four pieces of broken glass.

MARY: *(As JAMES is crawling towards her on all fours)* Stop that! STOP THAT!

JAMES: Listen to this, please. If your beautiful face gets pressed up really TIGHT against my own so four eyes glue into one another—then you're so CLOSE I can't see you, and everything between us goes dead.

MARY: Why does it go dead?

JAMES: Dead dead dead dead.

(He has rolled on his back, and a SERVANT drops a large white globe onto his chest.)

MARY: I don't know if it's supposed to go dead.

(He sits up, and stares at the globe he now balances on his knees.)

Hey, what are you looking at?

JAMES: Whatever direction I'm facing, that's what I'm looking at . . .

MARY: Look at me.

JAMES: Why not?

(Turns his head to look at her from behind his dark glasses.)

MARY: *(Looking away)* Didn't you forget something?

JAMES: Nothing. Not my dark glasses to protect my eyes, or my handkerchief to clean up my mess afterwards, or my ability to maintain self-control.

(There is a pause, then he explodes.)

Hey, I'm still here, I'm still here!

MARY: —Hey, I have an idea.

JAMES: What?

MARY: *(Very quiet)* Let's see if kisses work.

JAMES: What do you mean, "work"?

MARY: Let's see if they give us sexual arousable.

JAMES: It's unavoidable. It works automatically.

(He comes and gives her the white globe.)

MARY: Don't you think I know that? Please. Get undressed for me.

JAMES: No. You get undressed.

MARY: What will happen afterwards?

JAMES: Look, Mistress Mary. I don't want to be sick!

MARY: Look, Mr. James Full-of-Himself! I don't want to be sick either.

(She throws the ball to JAMES and runs across the room, where others surround her with a protective hospital folding screen. She calls from behind.)

Okay. I take that back!

(JAMES throws away the globe, rips away the screen, grabs her shoulders, then plants a big kiss on her lips. Pulls back to watch her, and, when she doesn't indicate a response, shouts at her.)

JAMES: That was a kiss!

MARY: *(Turning and exiting)* How you get on my nerves when you don't answer my questions.

(JAMES watches her go, baffled. Then turns to the audience.)

JAMES: Okay, folks, I didn't know the real identity of this woman, so I dredged up a whole range of experience in the hopes of a more genuine relationship, but—nothing! NOTHING!

(He exits.)

MARY: *(Reentering)* I think my way back into an empty room that a couple of us filled once upon a time with a couple of ill-assorted twitches.

TONY: *(Crossing at the rear)* I psych out parallel trains of thought.

MARY: Where, when, and how often—

> *(SERVANTS are crossing with glasses of milk on silver trays.)*

> Somebody offers me a glass of warm milk, and I think— sleep means either good dreams or bad dreams.

JAMES: *(Has reentered and taken one of the glasses of milk)* I don't need this in my life.

MARY: I don't need this in my life, either.

JAMES: *(As a SERVANT grabs the glass of milk out of his hand)* Haven't I seen this hand do major flying in a category I couldn't count on once—?

TONY: *(Placing a book in JAMES's hand to replace the milk)* Read a book—

JAMES: Do they still write important stuff in here?

TONY: Levitate into an easily forgettable direction.

JAMES: *(As if performing a music hall number)* Once upon a time I thought I could enlighten myself with a good read—

> *(Tosses away the book.)*

> BUT OW!—

> *(He holds his head in pain and whirls once as SERVANTS who were lined up behind with books fall to the floor at his cry of pain.)*

> All I can see is her eyes shining—and I didn't expect to be upended like this

when I tried to hold on to the invigorating experience of
    language
so I could vent the necessary ventilation,
but no such luck—
with the brain heavier still—like a disappearing hot
    plate,
Ow!

*(SERVANTS have crept up behind him and hit him on the
head with books, and he falls under the blow.)*

Guess what I've done?
I glued all my valuable pages together!
But I'm not being saved—notice?
I'm just turning a LAYERED self
into a self that sucks its own funnel
into this amazing piece of shit that learns how to do
the amazing maneuver called butterfly strokes run
backwards
—but call that a substitution
in which all points circulate in multiple directions
with a very distinct aroma of impossible blends
appealing to certain noses that know how to turn a twitch
into a message.

MARY: Beep, beep, I hang up on you.

(She turns and dances out of the room.)

JAMES: Scraped out on sandpaper provided
    the minute a really profound idea
    starts doing its toilet training
    which is always too late
    for anything but a big—

MARY: *(Reenters, holding her nose)* Go away!

JAMES: NO! I CAN'T SAY IT!
    I CAN'T SAY IT!

But here's a hint!
It goes out for a secret walk
in a pair of cut tight to the bounce
SEAT OF MY PANTS!

MARY AND TONY: *(Banging on the table)* Ants! Ants!

JAMES: *(Bending over as SERVANTS paste loose pages of books on his rear end)* SEAT OF MY PANTS!

MARY AND TONY: Ants in pants!

JAMES: Now wait a minute, folks—dare I bend over?

TONY: That's a perspective in which I choose non-participation.

JAMES: *(Trying to sit on a presented bucket, he tumbles to the floor)* Of course—Lost as I am—

MARY: *(Running from the room)* Please, I never spank somebody just because they get kissed.

JAMES: *(Rising)*—Did somebody say "bend over"? *(Falling again.)* Ow! What I still feel the need for is peripheral reading matter.

MARY: *(Returning with roses, which she drops)* Ow! There are thorns on my roses.

JAMES: So what, you hurt my eyes!

MARY: You hurt my eyes!

TONY: *(Taking off his own glasses)* When somebody's eyes hurt, he knew it was time to clean his glasses—not that I'm wearing any—but whenever a door swings open? *(Bangs into a wall and recovers.)* Nothing much see-able.

MARY: Thank God for a misdirected attention span.

JAMES: Maybe that's my way of transcending difficulty with people who try to be polite, but let's face it—still wear their aura bisecting the physical body in a blur that always seems to be WHISPERING to me—careful, my friend—this is really a test.

MARY: You hurt my eyes.

JAMES: But I have this need to look at you again and again and again.

TONY: Nobody move. Why not? Is this possibly one of those embarrassing moments that get engraved in the memory because nothing else is happening?

(There is a crash.)

Right, almost by accident. So gruesome you can't tear yourself away. Isn't that the by-product of a genuine accident?

(Everybody but JAMES and MARY leaves the room.)

MARY: You hurt my eyes.

JAMES: I know that.

MARY: The minute I turn to look at you, I see you looking back into my eyes.

JAMES: Don't look back at me!

MARY: Never?

JAMES: *(Smiles bitterly to himself)* That's not possible.

MARY: I can try.

JAMES: *(Pause)* Didn't you read today's newspaper?

MARY: What newspaper?

JAMES: If you look at today's newspaper, you'll find information concerning the new law.

(SERVANTS run in and stuff newspapers into the drawers of a cabinet.)

MARY: What new law? What new law? I read the newspaper, and I don't see anything about a new law.

JAMES: *(Retrieving a newspaper from the drawer)* There's a new law from now on that all emotional-type conversations have to take place with the conversing participants each looking directly into the eyes of the person with whom they are in conversation.

MARY: That's an impossible law to enforce.

JAMES: It's the law.

MARY: I don't believe you.

JAMES: It's the law!

(He has been tearing the newspaper pages to pieces and now throws them in her face.)

As difficult as it may be—if the law of looking into the other person's eyes is broken—

MARY: What then?

JAMES: *(Pause)* What am I looking at?

MARY: Me, myself.

JAMES: I'm looking into a hole.

MARY: My eyes.

JAMES: Right, a hole straight into the brain.

MARY: Me, myself!

JAMES: Nothing!

> *(She backs away from him, frightened, and hits a wall by accident, uttering a little scream and falling down.)*

I mean a HOLE is nothing!

> *(There is a pause; they look at each other.)*

Please, go away.

MARY: No.

> *(Another pause.)*

JAMES: Come back!

MARY: No.

JAMES: *(As the music rises in volume, shouts)* Go away!

MARY: No!

JAMES: Come back!

MARY: No!

> *(JAMES, frustrated, turns away. Then whirls back to her and, strumming his lips with his fingers, makes gibberish noises, falling to the ground as he does so.)*

MARY: Stop that, stop that! What are you, some kind of Indian in a powwow?

JAMES: *(His gibberish has changed to bitter laughter)* I apologize for laughing—was I laughing? *(He gets on all fours and starts towards her.)* Blind me! Please. Sweetie pie?

MARY: That's sick. Don't say that.

JAMES: Blind me, so I no longer have to see those eyes looking back at me and feel terrible.

MARY: Stop looking at me.

JAMES: I can't help it.

MARY: *(Nervously laughing)* Okay, then look at me.

JAMES: Blind me!

MARY: My God—stop saying that!

JAMES: Blind me! I don't care if it hurts!

> *(The music is deafening. JAMES runs from the room and we hear him shouting next door.)*

Goddamn it, I can never find anything when I need it!

> *(He returns carrying a canvas and a paint brush. Some of the SERVANTS have set up easels in the rear, and peer out from behind them. MARY rises, and sits on the long table, having calmed herself a bit.)*

MARY: See, that was just trying to scare me. What is everybody doing?

JAMES: I don't know what everyone is doing, but I know what I'm doing. If I paint your image, maybe I'll be able to destroy your power over me.

> *(He attacks his canvas, scratching at it with his brush while MARY acts totally uninterested, wiggling her feet and staring at the sky. Finally, JAMES seems to lose*

hope. His body droops, and he lets his canvas fall to the floor. He speaks very quietly to himself, but with great bitterness.)

It has the opposite effect. Shit!

(He seems crestfallen. But MARY *laughs at him, then jumps down from the table and, mockingly, kisses her own hand while posing provocatively. Then she waits.* JAMES *can't think of what to do, and the music gets louder and louder. Then, with insane determination, he unbuckles his belt and lets his pants fall to the floor.* MARY *crosses, looks at him, and bursts into laughter.* JAMES *pulls up his pants as* MARY *crosses behind the folding hospital screen.* JAMES *deliberates, then goes and opens the screen, seizes* MARY, *and starts planting frantic kisses over her face as the* SERVANTS *gather round to watch. The kisses make* JAMES *dizzy, and he tumbles from amidst them all and crashes to the floor. He lies there for a long moment, then screams over the music.)*

JAMES: Come back!

*(*MARY *crosses to him. Nothing happens.)*

Go away!

(She returns to the screen.)

Come back!

(She comes to him again. His face is now distorted with anguish.)

Go away!

(She doesn't move.)

Go away! Go away! Shit!

(He rises, faces her. Then, again, he undoes his belt, and his pants fall to the floor. They stare at each other.

Then she goes away. JAMES screams after her, his voice distorted into an animal howl.)

Come baaaaack!

(A pause as he thinks about things. Then he pulls up his pants and moves to a cabinet at the rear. As the SERVANTS start doing a controlled but jaunty jiglike dance step to the loud music, JAMES takes a plate holding scissors and bandages from the cabinet. He places it on the table. The SERVANTS are joined in their dance by TONY and MARY. It amounts to a rhythmic walk, everyone snapping their fingers in rhythm, looking terribly cool, and seeming to ignore JAMES as he wraps the bandage around his hand to protect it, then takes the scissors and plunges them into one of his eyes. With a howl of pain, he disappears behind the table. He screams again and again over the loud music, while the dancers seem to ignore him totally, circling the table, smiling, and snapping their fingers. Finally JAMES reappears with a bloody rag held to his eyes.)

JAMES: *(Laughing crazily)* Okay,—one hundred percent okay.

(He lowers the rag, revealing eyes encased in blood. He seems manic, energized, and totally crazed.)

Hey—why do I get the feeling nobody believes anything I say?

TONY: I believe everything you say.

JAMES: Oh no, I believe everything YOU tell ME.

TONY: That I don't believe.

JAMES: Okay, okay, for instance—my name is still James. How many fingers does James have?

(MARY plops the stuffed arm into JAMES's hands. The SERVANTS point to it with golden sticks.)

Come on now, don't be shy, how many fingers does James still have?

TONY: Five.

JAMES: Right, and how many circulatory systems does James still have feeding the brain?

TONY: Two.

JAMES: Right, and how many eyes do I have?

(TONY turns away, troubled.)

Well, if there were more than two of them, I wouldn't be a normal human being, would I?

TONY: I don't think the number of fingers or circulatory systems or eyes is central.

JAMES: How many eyes do *you* have—to help you stumble through life?

TONY: Two.

JAMES: You're still normal.

TONY: In some ways.

(With a wide grin on his face, JAMES starts flailing about with the stuffed arm, occasionally hitting TONY and yelling, "Pow, pow, pow!")

MARY: Stop that, stop that! Why are you hitting people?

JAMES: I didn't know I was hitting people, I was having fun.

TONY: Fun? Then I apologize for complaining.

JAMES: Oh, nobody's asking you to apologize.

MARY: I apologize for laughing.

JAMES: Please, never apologize!

TONY: She wasn't laughing.

JAMES: *(Popping his eyes wide)* Was that—ME laughing?
   (He breaks into hysterical laughter.)

MARY: This is for you.
   (She holds a piece of pie on a plate.)

JAMES: What is it?

MARY: It's a piece of pie.

JAMES: Is it a reward?

MARY: I don't think so.
   (The SERVANTS enter and line up behind JAMES, single-file. The last one in line carries a little roly-poly doll-man in a red suit and a crown, who holds another plate with a pie in his extended hands.)

JAMES: But is this piece of pie really for me?

MARY: Yes, but you have to promise not to wolf it down.

JAMES: Why? Why isn't that permitted?

TONY: Because in spite of your predilection towards violence—

JAMES: Right, I'm a relatively violent animal!

TONY: You're not a wolf, sir, but a veritable human being.

JAMES: Ah, but does not a human being contain the entire range of animal and nonanimal possibilities? Angel—to wolf?

(JAMES begins leading the line of SERVANTS around the room, everyone holding on to the hips of the person in front.)

TONY: A true human being chooses between seven evolutionary plateaus.

JAMES: *(Giggling as he leads the line of SERVANTS)* To be able to make such a choice is, I think, something quite beyond human capability.

MARY: Then this piece of delicious cherry pie, baked with loving hands, is no longer yours.

JAMES: *(Dropping out of the line)* Hey—my hands seem covered with blood. Why do I see blood?

MARY: Didn't you forget something?

JAMES: I'm sure I have.

MARY: We're looking into each other's powerful eyes—just like before.

JAMES: *(Gazing toward the ceiling with his blind eyes, grinning broadly)* Possibly, possibly!

TONY: It's a piece of pie.

JAMES: I don't believe you.

TONY: Oh!? It's a piece of warm, delicious pie.

MARY: If you wash it down, maybe, with a glass of warm milk?

JAMES: Ohhhhh, no!

TONY: C'mon, it's a kind of drug.

JAMES: Here's an idea, help me to my feet.

TONY: Totally unnecessary.

JAMES: *(Laughing and stumbling to the floor)* Please. Postulate somebody who needs help.

TONY: I can't imagine such a category. After all, you fall down, you get up.

JAMES: *(Sprawled happily on the carpet)* This time it's radically different.

TONY: Why?

JAMES: This is different.

TONY: What's different about it?

JAMES: Let's say I've decided to stop expending all this unnecessary energy.

TONY: I don't believe you.

JAMES: *(Rising)*—But it's okay.

TONY: See? You've struggled to your feet . . .

JAMES: Of course, it's an involuntary biological manifestation.

TONY: I don't see anything biological.

MARY: It's like having heart problems.

JAMES: No, it's involuntary.

TONY: Nobody's convinced.

JAMES: Don't ask to be convinced, just humor me.

TONY: No.

JAMES: It's the best medicine. Humor me. When I say "three," we all start to revolve, which produces a certain revelatory dizziness.

MARY: All of us revolve?

JAMES: Oh, yes.

MARY: Ah, like the major planets of this and other more desirable solar systems?

JAMES: Maybe, though the names don't come immediately to mind, so I was focusing more on personal experiences.

MARY: That could be problematic.

JAMES: Ready for a surprise? One!

MARY: Okay. Two!

TONY: Okay. Three.

(TONY and MARY spin, but quickly get dizzy and have to support themselves on walls or furniture.)

Hey, I'm beginning to see where this is leading us—but you didn't say anything about stopping.

JAMES: *(Laughing, because while they were spinning, he has taken a piece of pie from the little doll-man, and he now holds the slice of pie in his hand.)* Hey, I got sticky, gooey, smelly pie juice on my hand. *(He laughs some more, puts the pie on the table, then sits on the table, but blind as he is, he ends up sitting on the piece of pie.)* Uh-oh, you're not gonna believe this, but I just sat in a piece of warm, delicious pie.

(There is a loud crash. JAMES laughs, but TONY and MARY hold their ears and try to escape by sending themselves into a spin.)

TONY: One—

MARY: Two—

TONY: Three!

(They spin as another loud crash is heard, and as they stagger to a stop, a deep VOICE is heard filling the room.)

VOICE: Space, calling . . . Empty space is calling James. Do you hear empty space calling James?

JAMES: Who the hell is trying to communicate with me?

VOICE: This is empty space calling James.

JAMES: How is this possible?

VOICE: Empty space calling James.

JAMES: Wait a minute—James thinks about this and James realizes he doesn't think empty space can talk. James thinks only individualized human personalities have access to language!

VOICE: Do you hear empty space calling James?

JAMES: *(Totally frightened)* Shit, shit, shit! *(Throws his piece of pie against the wall.)* Okay, for the moment, I will entertain a belief I do not believe. What is empty space trying to communicate that I don't know already?

VOICE: Empty space calling.
Empty space calling James.
Be in contact, please.
Continue—
continue to be in contact, please.

JAMES: *(Hugging TONY)* What do you think I should do about this?

TONY: *(Backing away)* Please. This isn't my problem.

JAMES: *(Angrily)* Of course it's your problem! Approximately ten minutes after it's my problem—

(The SERVANTS have run into the room, each carrying a silver tray with a glass of milk.)

Hey, what is this? Is somebody suggesting that all my problems—PROBLEMS—PROBLEMS!—get dissolved into the flux-fluxity-flux-flux—the minute I swallow my not so totally self-evident pride by washing it down with a glass of warm milk?

(He grabs some milk and runs around the room as the SERVANTS follow and end up, somehow, upside down on the long table.)

TONY: *(Shouting above the confusion, waving his saw)* Look, nobody's asking you to drink milk. Nobody's asking you to poke out your eyeballs with a pair of scissors that don't even cut good. And nobody's asking you to be on good behavior whenever the roof falls in. Because whenever the roof falls in nobody expects anything but just another catastrophe.

(This quiets JAMES, who takes a sip of milk.)

JAMES: Hey, this is really good stuff. I mean really good stuff. I mean—this is really good stuff. But is it good for me? Or is it bad for me?

(He turns to offer some to TONY.)

TONY: *(Holding up his hands)* Later.

(JAMES turns and offers some to MARY.)

MARY: *(Holding up her hands)* Later.

TONY: *(Threateningly to JAMES)* You drink it.

JAMES: No problem, I like it.

TONY: Then drink it.

JAMES: Why wouldn't I drink it? I like it.

TONY: Okay, then drink it.

JAMES: I like it, no problem. So why wouldn't I drink it?

(He looks at it. Takes another sip—then, after a moment has passed, winces and holds his stomach.)

Oh . . . shit!

(The lights fade to darkness.)

THE END

PERMANENT
BRAIN DAMAGE

Permanent Brain Damage. Produced by the Ontological-Hysteric Theater at the Ontological Theater at St. Mark's Church, New York City. November 1995–March 1996. Written, directed, and designed by Richard Foreman.

THE BALD MAN: D. J. Mendel
THE MAN IN THE BELLBOY HAT: Robert Cucuzza
THE MAN IN THE SKULLCAP: Stephen Jordan
THE LADY WITH THE FEATHER: Jennifer Krasinski
THE SCHOOLGIRL: Claude Wampler
THE YOUNG MAN IN A SKIRT: Cradeaux Alexander

A NOTE TO *PERMANENT BRAIN DAMAGE*

Because so much of this particular play is in the stage directions (in my production, there were only a few lines of dialogue and the vast majority of the text was recorded—by me, in fact—and then played over the loudspeakers during performance)—I felt it might be interesting and useful to follow the text with a second version, which is the original text I took into rehearsal.

It is a much longer text. We began staging the play to that text, but midway through rehearsals I began to (1) get sick of the sound of my own voice and (2) realize that the density of action I was inventing rendered much of the text excessive.

But I can well imagine a director staging the original text in a different way—with less action perhaps—and giving much more of the text to the actors who might speak it onstage—and so using more, or different, sections of that original text.

Usually I would not want directors to cut my texts (though they should feel free to reassign lines and imagine different settings and stagings if they like). But because of the unusual nature of this one play, I would not object to a future production (based on the original uncut text rather than the one I finally produced) utilizing all or parts of that uncut text.

A paneled room. The walls are lined with pictures—twenty to thirty large, framed black-and-white prints of a Rouault etching: an old king in profile, a leering smile as he peers from the corner of his eye. Bookcases surround the room, shelves filled with decorated yet identical storage boxes. Flowers, lamps, and candles are on top of the bookcases, also half a dozen small, framed eye charts, as well as some small windmills. A large windmill—its base integrated into the room so it looks like a large cabinet—sprouts arms large enough to brush the ceiling when they revolve. Also sitting on the rear bookcase is a tall, thin obelisk on a pedestal. A large oak table dominates much of the room, and crumpled papers are scattered over the carpet. A glass wall is set between the stage and the audience. Letters and fragments of words festoon the walls onstage and the glass wall.

Throughout the play there is music. Often this music is two or three female voices, singing in tight dissonant harmony, like a melancholy Middle European folk tune. But there are occasional eruptions of more circus-like music or thirties jazz, all looped to form brief repetitive patterns. And very often the music is replaced by a cacophony of voices babbling in three or four indecipherable languages at the same time. Throughout the play the action is accompanied by appropriate crashes, pings, gongs, and thuds.

The play begins as a babble of voices rises, thuds sound, and a gong rings,. A completely bald, heavily bearded

man in a white suit, a white bib around his neck, a
monocle in his eye, and a cigar stuck in his mouth,
races onstage carrying a blanket which trails behind
him on the floor. A young man in dark glasses with a
female wig and a large beret, wearing a skirt and in
heavy feminine makeup, hurries in after him, grabs the
end of the blanket and pulls it away, sending The Bald
man tumbling to the floor.

As he enters, four others have come onstage. Among
them a man in a suit, wearing a bib and a bellboy hat;
another in a dark suit, wearing a red skullcap. Two
women also appear, one a more mature lady in a black
cocktail dress, wearing pearls and a headband with a
black peacock feather; the other a perverse young
schoolgirl in a short jumper and leather gloves. All of
them except for The Bald Man wear over their shoulders bright red ceremonial sashes that tie at the waist.

All through the play, whenever any one of the characters leaves the stage, he or she will immediately
reenter to sit and watch, with insolent smiles, whatever
is happening to The Bald Man.

As the babble continues, The Schoolgirl helps The
Bald Man to a chair, as two men fight over a blanket in
the rear. She kisses his bald head and strokes it.

Almost the entire text of the play is heard over loudspeakers, spoken by a deep, ominous male voice.

VOICE: **Nothing to be afraid of, really. Is there ever anything
to be afraid of?**

(The Bald Man rises and looks back to see others
preparing to put a blanket over his shoulders. He hesitates, then runs from the room. Several follow and
immediately reappear at another entrance. The Bald
Man returns to his chair. The others close in again—one
holds a frying pan over his head, another cracks an egg
into the frying pan, and The Bald Man holds the top of
his head as if splattered by the egg.)

VOICE: **Well, maybe there are things to be afraid of after all.**

(The Bald Man rises as The Schoolgirl takes a pillow, and lays it on the large table. He considers lying down on the table with his head on the pillow, then thinks better of it, and runs from the room—as she chases him. They immediately reappear at another door. He, slowly now, goes and lies down on the table. She sits on the edge of the table, next to his head, and lifts a small round mirror that she holds behind her head like a halo, as the female voices are heard singing for the first time. She grins, revolving the halo behind her head as the two men in suits slowly approach. They also hold mirrors behind their heads. The Bald Man gets off the table and suspiciously examines the tableau. Then the others with mirrors approach him and frame him in mirrors. He pushes away from them and goes to take an eye chart from one of the bookcases.

The Young Man in a Skirt comes in slowly, pushing a stick of wood with a bicycle wheel on one end that he rolls across the floor, approaching The Bald Man. All the others line up behind The Young Man in a Skirt, and The Bald Man holds the eye chart under his chin and rolls his eyes up towards the ceiling ecstatically.)

VOICE: (As the line dissolves and all except The Bald Man slowly exit.) **He says, "I can't imagine being anyplace different from the place where I am right now." And then the other one says, "You should be ashamed of such a lack of imagination." And then he says, "What you see is what you get." And then the other one says, "Going back in time disproves any such belief system." And then he says, "What I believe certainly is nothing what I call believable because, I'm ravished by all contradictory possibilities."**

(The others run back onstage, rattling spoons inside water glasses. They stop, slowly lick their spoons, and turn their backs on The Bald Man. Then they suddenly hit the bottom of their glasses with their spoons, and whirl to face him. There is a pause, then they all quietly but in unison say, "Boo." And The Bald Man falls to the floor.)

VOICE: (As The Bald Man slowly rises and the others back away) **He says, "Nothing that ever frightened me ever turned into more than a passing fancy." And the other says, "If time passes you can call that an emotional calculation." And then he says, "My mistakes are very productive and so I'll ignore any warning signs and signals of disaster, thank you very much."**

(The Schoolgirl has become dizzy, and falls to the floor. The Young Man in a Skirt reenters, holding an egg. He sits on the edge of the table and whirls it over a silver tray as the singing rises; The Schoolgirl recovers and decides to spin in imitation of the egg, which makes her so dizzy that she again falls to the floor. The Man in the Red Skullcap runs in and jumps on the table, holding an egg, which he positions just over The Bald Man's head. The others all have eggs now, and they kneel, displaying them. But The Man in the Bellboy Hat faints, and the others come to examine him.)

VOICE: **Afraid? Not afraid? Who knows the best way to accurately chart all those distinctions. Sometimes when you're afraid you have good reason after all, and sometimes when you're not afraid you really should be, even if you don't know why.**

(The Schoolgirl has reentered carrying a very large, bejeweled egg which she places on the table in front of The Bald Man, who seems transfixed. The others place their small eggs at significant points on The Bald Man's body, and he lifts up, in pain or ecstasy. The babbling continues. Then The Schoolgirl reveals a small stuffed duck. She proceeds to stuff a series of eggs into the

duck's rear end, announcing proudly, "Right into its little asshole." When she has finished, a gold ribbon is
pulled from the duck's mouth that stretches halfway
across the stage. The Bald Man immediately pushes the
girl and her helpers out of the room. The babbling is very
loud. The Bald Man finds a sack on the floor, steps into
it, and starts pulling it up over his body as they others
regather in the room. The Young Man in a Skirt macks
two pieces of wood together, and the babbling stops.)

VOICE: (As The Bald Man gets the sack up over his head)
**Question please, how does one penetrate the space inside
this very room? Ladies and gentlemen—one exits. Then:
One turns back toward the door, opens it, and enters.**

(The Lady with the Feather has moved to a microphone
that stands by the big table. She giggles, then covers her
eyes and speaks into the microphone: "But suppose—
just suppose—one is already inside this room.")

VOICE: **Then, ladies and gentlemen, one re-enters.**

(Several of them move as if to leave, but have a collision with an imaginary wall, cry out in pain, and hold
their noses, and The Schoolgirl laments, "Oh shit, they
bopped their noses.")

VOICE: (As the men tie a rope around the top of the sack, making escape impossible) **But here is a man who asks
himself—suppose that one is already inside of this
very room. Then one cannot ENTER this room, perhaps—except—BUT therefore—how does one GET
INSIDE, indeed—this very room?**

(The Schoolgirl finds a zipper on the side of the sack,
unzips it, and as the babble rises, The Bald Man steps
carefully out of the sack. The others mass in front of
him, and then he pushes his way through to leave the

room. But he immediately re-appears from another entrance, pushing past The Young Man in a Skirt, who is grinning stupidly behind his dark glasses and holding in front of his chest one of the eye charts.

The Bald Man slowly turns to confront the eye chart, and is about to start reading out loud the letters when there is a flash of lights, and everyone screams in pain and holds their eyes. After recovering, The Bald Man tests his eyes by counting the number of people in front of him. "Four." Then he decides to identify himself in contrast, and calls out, "One." The singing returns, and he reiterates by pointing to his bald head and whispering, "One."

The Schoolgirl is at the microphone and says, "Okay, we arrive at the second plateau." The singing gets louder, and The Bald Man holds his ears in agony at the noise, at which the others applaud politely, cooing to the music at the same time.

The Bald Man goes to one of the boxes in the bookcases and extracts a small gold hammer. He comes to The Man in the Skullcap, who is sitting on the edge of the large table, and uses the hammer to test the reflexes of his knee. The music stops. The man's knee has not responded, so The Lady with the Feather comes and makes his lower leg swing slightly as he grins at The Bald Man, who then runs from the room. The others laugh and make a circle around the table, holding hands as the music returns, and all the windmill arms start revolving. The Bald Man runs in through another door, and without being seen, picks up a chair and lifts it as if ready to attack The Man in the Skullcap, but they suddenly whirl and stop him with accusatory fingers exclaiming "Ah-ah-ah!"—and at the next moment, with a crash, a large grotesque golden head with ribbons and popping eyes and protruding spikes hurtles down through the ceiling and hovers over the table.

The group looks at the head, then looks to see The Bald Man's reaction, and then, as if blaming him, point to the head and warn him, "Oh-oh-oh!"

And the head slowly lifts out of sight again.

The Schoolgirl is at the microphone and says, "We arrive at the second plateau." The Bald Man staggers to a chair, and they all laugh at him as the music and the windmills stop, and the two men take two small golden hammers and come to test his knee reflexes. First they shake hands with him, then tap his knees. Nothing happens, and one of the men mutters, amazed, "Jeez." Then The Bald Man slowly rises, comes towards the footlights, and whispers, "Here's a better idea."

He goes to a rear bookcase. He looks to see who's watching, and of course everyone is watching. He takes a bottle, fills a glass, and drinks. Then he crosses to the microphone and growls into it, "I'm imagining a powerful medicine named 'O-X, O-X, O-X!'—What does that spell? I take it once a day with the following effect. Once each day something happens in my perception, nothing terribly unusual, but that ordinary thing is, in fact—"

A gong interrupts and sends him spinning away from the microphone. But he recovers and returns, to speak over loud music—"Jesus Christ, Jesus Christ! This man or woman who takes this medicine. He or she is effectively persuaded that otherwise unexceptional moment—Here it is! Here it is!"

All the others by now have reappeared, wearing silk red robes. They swirl to the music, showing off their robes, vamping across the stage for one another. As one of the men poses, The Bald Man strips off his robe and puts it on himself, then starts to perform his own dance, but is immediately dizzy and falls to the floor.)

VOICE: (As The Bald Man struggles slowly back to his feet) **Here is a man, questioning whether the wearing of this robe lends himself and others surrounding him the consciousness of the real that is greater, denser, deeper—oh much deeper.**

(The others are whirling about the room, and The

Schoolgirl gushes over the music—"Oh, I really like this. Oh, I really like this a lot!")

VOICE: (As The Bald Man finds a hand mirror and studies himself) **Hummm. On the subject of finding oneself beautiful—is that true vanity? Or a necessary psychological pre-requisite? Because beauty, after all, is quite relative. So one can manipulate as one chooses. The only risk being: the source of one's positive feelings is the same as the source of one's negative feelings. So— if one feeling is evoked, the opposite feeling is evoked automatically. Which is okay, of course, because anything automatic, puts one in touch, somehow, with the truth, certainly, behind it all.**

(One of the men has appeared, displaying a gold hammer. He waits for The Bald Man to position himself, and then hits The Bald Man's head. Another gives The Bald Man an ice pack, and upon seeing this, the man with the hammer hits himself in the head.

The Lady with the Feather offers a new red robe to The Bald Man, but he is distracted by The Schoolgirl and the jeweled egg. He grabs the egg, studies it, but then decides the robe is more important, so he gets rid of the egg, takes off the robe he is wearing, drops it to the floor, seizes the new robe, and crosses the stage to stuff it into one of the boxes in the bookcase. The others have all regathered and sit watching him. A ticking clock is heard. The Lady with the Feather has retrieved the robe he had thrown to the floor and holds it up, offering it to him. He hesitates, then grabs the robe and, indeed, goes and stuffs it in another box, at the rear of the room. But, seeing many of the others leaving the room in disgust, he decides on another hiding place, and takes the robe to stuff it into a box far downstage.

As this is happening, the two men and The Young Man in a Skirt enter, each carrying a large white disk, which they crouch behind, resting their chins on the top edges.

The Bald Man studies the disks, then as he reaches out to touch one of them, the lights flash, and he staggers backwards. The men whisper, "Bye-bye, piglet," and hurry off, carrying their disks. Then The Bald Man, recovering, turns to see The Schoolgirl entering, using her hands to balance on top of her head a small cabinet that is open in the back and has two small double doors on the front.)

VOICE: (As the babble returns) **The room of radios. The room of radios.**

(The Young Man in a Skirt has returned with a hammer. Holding it in his fist, he smashes it from the rear of the cabinet, out through its double doors, and The Bald Man reacts as if he had been hit in the head.)

VOICE: **Ladies and gentlemen, how does one enter this room?** (The Bald Man falls to the floor.) **Put in such a way, the question may seem unanswerable, because one— whoever that one may be—that "one" has indeed entered already, repeating the very words "How does one enter this room?"**

(The Bald Man grabs a hammer from someone else, goes and kneels in front of the cabinet which has now been placed on the table, and smashes the hammer through.)

VOICE: **—and that's just it, apparently—"How? How DOES one enter this room."**

(The Schoolgirl has taken the hammer, circles around, and hits The Bald Man on the head.)

VOICE: **Ladies and gentlemen—here is a man who makes discoveries by repeating himself as follows—**

(The Bald Man takes a robe from one of the boxes, and also finds a small gift box which he tosses to the floor,

then takes the robe and some wrapping paper to wrap
the robe inside the gift box as a present.)

VOICE: **How—does one enter this room—and the response
to that question is—"How does one enter this room?
How?—does one enter this room?"**

(The Schoolgirl has repositioned the box and thrusts her
empty hand through, which startles The Bald Man into
paying attention—but he is immediately distracted to
see two others going down on the floor as if praying to
him, facedown on the carpet, their arms outstretched.
The babble is very loud now, and The Bald Man puts
away the box and comes to study them. He arranges a
hand on the floor, whereupon a loud gong rings, and The
Bald Man steps with his full weight on the hand lying on
the floor—which belongs to The Lady with the Feather.
As the vocal music rises to ear-splitting intensity, he
grinds his foot on The Lady's hand, and she screams and
writhes in agony on the floor. All the others shriek in
horror to see what is happening.

After a while, The Bald Man stops, and the music
lowers. He hands his hammer to The Schoolgirl, bending his head in expectation of deserved punishment,
but she simply lifts the little cabinet and goes to the
side of the room as The Bald Man feels his head, wondering why no blow was forthcoming.

Then The Bald Man holds the sides of his face in
anguish and regret as The Schoolgirl repositions herself
with the cabinet slid down over her head, her face
emerging through the double doors, her tongue sticking
out the side of her mouth and her eyes crossed as she
massages her crotch with her hammer.)

VOICE: **Here is a man, totally disgusted now with claims to
understand him not, but this man is even more disgusted
with his own guilt at believing that such a professed lack
of understanding is due to some ethical failure on his part.**

(One of the men places a crown on The Schoolgirl's head, and The Bald Man collapses to the floor.)

VOICE: **Because this man really believes that he has made available what should be easily understandable by all those in full possession of his or her own—"aliveness."**

(As The Bald Man struggles to his feet, The Lady with the Feather rushes in and holds his head between her hands.)

VOICE: **—though he well understands, this same man—**

(She releases her hands, and again he falls, as she rushes to the side and, from one of the walls, pulls a string taut to make contact with his bald head as he struggles to his feet.)

VOICE: **—that not one of us is, in fact, in full possession of that life ruled and shaped by forces one can never identify or understand completely.**

(A thud, and The Bald Man falls again. The Lady removes the string as the two men run on with a large white disk four feet in diameter with a hole in the center. The man kneels and puts his head through the hole. The windmills start to turn, and the disk placed upright on the table. The Bald Man runs after it and again thrusts his head into the hole so that it sticks out through the disk.)

VOICE: **And yet—and yet—this same man believes that the only moral position possible is the position from which he DOES INDEED speak—**
(The Bald Man is hit on the head by two small gold hammers.)

VOICE: **—to those, only those, in full possession of such a life of one's own, which is never possible, in fact.**

(The men have removed the disk and rolled it behind a chair on the other side of the stage. The Bald Man hesitates, then goes and sits in the chair, whereupon the disk is carefully lifted and lowered over him, so his head sticks up through the hole and the disk acts as a large white collar. The disk suddenly seems to burn the hands of the two men holding it, and they remove their hands, leaving it balanced on The Bald Man's shoulders.

The Young Man in a Skirt has entered, with a rolling pin and a small rolling board on which there sits a lump of dough. The Bald Man watches as The Young Man starts working the dough.)

VOICE: **So those—to whom this man does speak, those so postulated do understand him, rest assured—even if they are not in fact those who do in fact exist.**

(The Young Man in a Skirt looks up at the audience and displays his work, asking "Nice, ya?" And as the singing rises, he produces a rather shaky tone, and then starts singing in bad falsetto as he rolls his dough—"I am very good at this, good at this, good at this. Oh! I am very good at this, tra-la-la-la-la!"

The others giggle and applaud him daintily. He finishes and holds up a flat pancake of dough and exclaims, "So?" Then he takes the pancake and carefully slaps it on the top of The Bald Man's shiny head. The others gather around the white disk, then reach out slowly to touch the pancake, bringing their fingers back to lick, verbalizing with an "Ummm!" which can hardly be heard over the music.

Then they lift the disk off The Bald Man, and The Schoolgirl comes to take another taste of the pancake on his head. But as the sweet taste sends her into an ecstatic spin, two others come and start repeatedly hitting the pancake with hammers. The Bald Man cringes under the blows, as The Young Man in a Skirt dances

in with a floral wreath which he places on The Bald
Man's head.

The music fades, and the babble is heard quietly as
The Young Man slowly bends down over the seated
Bald Man to give him a kiss on top of his bald head.

The Bald Man reacts, and rises, as a baritone voice
sings a phrase over and over, far away. The Man in the
Bellboy Hat holds a mirror up for The Bald Man, who
studies himself in his floral wreath.)

VOICE: **He says, "If the world offers little in the way of
desirable experience, I'll just look elsewhere for my
unhappiness."**

(The Schoolgirl comes slowly, takes the wreath and
places it on her own head, and starts to slowly dance,
all by herself.)

VOICE: **And the other one says, "Do close your eyes for a
more ultimate bedtime story."**

(Helped by The Man in the Skullcap, The Bald Man
climbs into his sack and is sealed up tight as it's tied at
the top.)

VOICE: **And he says, "Thank you, but I'm already sound
asleep."**

(The singing fades, and The Schoolgirl keeps dancing
in the silence. Then, task finished, The Man in the
Skullcap goes to leave the room, but is tripped by The
Man in the Bellboy Hat, who sits near the exit. He falls
to the floor. Then he rises, and returns to smack the
sack, as if blaming The Bald Man for his fall. He waits
for a response, then smacks a second time. Then he
takes a seat as The Schoolgirl dances into the shadows
at the rear.

The Young Man in a Skirt unzips the sack, and The

Bald Man emerges, looks about, and runs out of the room. The others have gathered in the rear, and as he runs out, they come down to where he has exited to see what he might be doing in the next room. The Lady with the Feather is holding over her head a large framed picture—an exact replica of the Rouault paintings that cover the walls.

After a glance offstage, they cover their eyes and spin three times [including The Lady with the Feather who spins with the picture up over her head]. Then they stop—each of them has a prize ribbon—and they all go to pin a ribbon on the picture on the wall (all are identical) that they individually deem worthy of first prize.

As they do so, The Bald Man sneaks back into the room. He is wearing a crown made of pencils and a false nose, both of which cause him to strangely resemble the Rouault etching. The Lady with the Feather creeps up behind him, and as he turns—sensing her presence—she crashes the etching over his head; when he emerges through the picture frame, a gong starts the music. The others half chatter, half giggle, and revolve their hands mockingly at The Bald Man, who lifts the etching to look at it—only to have The Man in the Bellboy Hat grab it and again crash it over his head, causing him to fall to the floor.

He creeps down to the front of the stage, and The Schoolgirl holds a white cardboard square—attached at the end of a stick—directly in front of his face and warns, "Oh no you don't.")

VOICE: (As The Bald Man struggles to his feet and The Schoolgirl keeps the white square hiding his face) **Get the understanding of this man who testifies that—when no specific words want to pour forth from inside himself— yet nevertheless this man wants to be in speaking—**

(The Bald Man starts doing a single exercise, hands on

hips—squat, straighten up—hands over head—squat, straighten up—repeated over and over.)

VOICE: **—as if he might say to us in the agreed-upon language, "I want to be in China" or "I want to be in the beautiful countryside, or high on a mountain overlooking the sea, in China."**

(A bell rings, and music accompanies his exercising, and now all the others join in doing the same exercise.)

VOICE: **So. This man wants to be in speaking, even if this man has nothing specific to say to us. And rest assured, idle conversation does never satisfy this man. Oh no—Oh no.**
     And he does indeed understand the advantages of silence, when one indeed has nothing to say, really—

(The Bald Man stops exercising and turns to watch all the others continuing.)

VOICE: **Except—except, what is it now that gives one the power of having something to say?**

(The Schoolgirl has run out and come back with a white disk, which she gives to The Bald Man, who holds it in front of his face.)

VOICE: **Because if indeed one has nothing to say, does that "nothing" in itself, just possibly become—HAVING, inside that "nothing"—something to say?**

(A clock is heard ticking. The Schoolgirl returns, carrying a white sphere with a question mark on it. She gives it to The Man in the Skullcap, and The Bald Man reappears from behind his disk to study the sphere. Then he disappears again behind his disk, and The Schoolgirl tears a page from a book she is carrying, takes the book,

and places the open book against the ass of The Man in
the Skullcap. In that position, the two of them hurry
out of the room.

The Man in the Bellboy Hat grabs the white disk
from The Bald Man, who, as a result, collapses to the
floor again. Then he recovers and creeps across the floor
to where The Young Man in a Skirt is trying one of the
red bathrobes. He touches the hem of the bathrobe, and
The Young Man pulls away in fear and retrieves his
rolling pin, which he uses to try and keep The Bald
Man on the floor, pressing down on his shoulders. But
The Bald Man growls, grabs the rolling pin, and The
Young Man runs and cowers in the corner.

The Bald Man slowly approaches him and taps him
lightly on the shoulder with the rolling pin. The Young
Man turns, and The Bald Man bends down his head and
indicates his pencil crown. The Young Man reaches out
and nervously takes the crown, placing it on his own
head. The music rises and, feeling quite glamorous in
his robe and crown, The Young Man parades slowly
across the stage.

The Man in the Bellboy Hat comes to confront The
Bald Man, who cocks his head at him and then takes off
his false nose and places it over the nose of The Man in
the Bellboy Hat. Then he runs to the other side of the
table to see what The Man in the Bellboy Hat will do
with his new nose.)

VOICE: **This man knows that to be inside such a feeling,
well—that's what it feels like. But: It always changes.
And what changes is always a surprise.**

FALSETTO VOICES: **A surprise, a surprise is coming, a surprise.**
(The others have gathered at the table with pads of
paper on which to take notes on The Bald Man's behavior. A telephone rings, and they crumple up pieces of
paper and throw them at The Bald Man. He growls at
them and crosses to the other side of the room.)

VOICE: (As they keep throwing paper at him) **Here is a man, not quite sure what's been happening to him. Except he does know he has been speaking—having a conversation of sorts. Except the rules of the game, for this man and others—well—there are no rules.**

(A loud thud, and as the windmills start revolving, the giant head again falls throw the ceiling, frightening the people at the table. They chase The Bald Man from the room, and then turn to shake their fists at the big head, which slowly rises to disappear again. Then they notice that one of their number, The Schoolgirl, has collapsed on the floor. They come to examine her, but a flash of bright light sends them scurrying to the walls with an "Ow!" and covering their eyes.)

VOICE: **So one person alone can play this game. But bear in mind, please—here is a man whose brain has been damaged by life.**

(There is another flash, and they whirl to see where it might have come from. The babbling is heard, and then, very faintly, a voice singing an off-key, quavering rendition of "Sunny Side of the Street." They all seem transfixed by this singing as it becomes louder and louder. Then strident piano music—not matching tune or tempo with the singing—is also heard, and they all become dizzy and fall to the floor. They struggle back to their feet, stagger back and forth, and then, suddenly, all launch into a loud choral version of "Sunny Side of the Street." They sing their hearts out, even though they are obviously still unsteady on their feet. This goes on for quite some time as the windmills turn rapidly to the warring, dissonant music. Then the phone rings, and all stop singing and regroup as The Bald Man runs into the room.)

FALSETTO VOICES: **A surprise. A surprise is coming.**

(The Bald Man studies the others and slowly goes to sit in a chair.)

VOICE: **Here is a man before us—of whom it can truly be said he was doing some excellent thinking.**

(Just as he sits, The Man in the Bellboy Hat pulls the chair out from under him, and he falls on the floor.)

VOICE: **But then this man turned against his thinking. Why did he turn against his thinking? Because his thinking imprisoned him.**

(The Man in the Skullcap and The Young Man in a Skirt, both wearing white dunce caps, have come on slowly with a large white beam of wood, which they slowly position so that one end rests on the chest of The Bald Man as he lies on the carpet.)

VOICE: **Hard to believe, but his thinking imprisoned him—**

(The Bald Man takes control of the beam, keeping one end tucked under his arm, rising from the floor as the two others leave, slowly swinging the beam, which has become for him a kind of weapon. The large head again falls into the room. He rests his stick against the table and goes to examine the head as it hangs over the table. A high electronic tone is heard.)

VOICE: **But now this man has escaped by turning against his thinking—**

(The Bald Man again seizes the beam and points it accusatorially at the head, which slowly rises through the ceiling.)

VOICE: **—and by turning against his thinking, vast new realms seem available to this man who, though very**

powerful, is, in fact, inside a prison. So he has turned against his own thinking.

(As The Bald Man comes forward to look up into the ceiling where the head has disappeared, the others are shuffling silently into the room behind him. They are bunched in a group, and they wear amazingly realistic head masks that make them all look like elderly wise men with long white hair and white beards, sunken eyes and wrinkled skin—acquiring the aspect of ancients gods—but each topped with a black bowler hat. The Bald Man doesn't see them at first.)

VOICE: **He turned against his ability to manipulate the English language. He turned against his sense of balance—look, look, look—**

(He senses something behind his back, turns, and upon seeing them, drops the beam and runs to the side of the room. The Gods slowly advance, shuffling forward and slowly bending down to laboriously pick up the beam, then holding it as a horizontal barrier in from of themselves.)

VOICE: **He turned against his ability to orient himself in space using his eyes. He turned against muscular coordination, using his limbs mostly. He turned against sensory gratification. He turned against an available sense of his body, bouncing against things in space—and there was no space in his own private world. There was no space. There was no space.**

(He sees them holding the beam and shuffles forward slowly. He confronts them. Puts his hands forward on the beam and slowly applies pressure, as if trying to force the Gods backwards out of the room. This happens in silence and slow motion, as the electronic tone recommences.)

But the deliberate struggle simply forces the beam higher into the air, slowly lifting over the Gods' heads as they gently take control, allowing it to rise over and behind their own heads, then dropping it with a loud crash to the floor. Then several of them advance toward The Bald Man, place their hands gently on his shoulders and back, and force him slowly to the floor. Other Gods release metronomes that start ticking on top of the bookcases. And the smallest God slowly advances to strings that cross the stage horizontally on either side of the glass wall. Some of the strings have a few small metal balls along their length, and the small God reaches up to touch one of the tiny balls—which causes a loud "ping," and faraway calliope music is heard.

The Gods are slowly shuffling about like feeble old men as The Bald Man rises, and one of them places a small cabinet over The Bald Man's head. Then turning him around, the cabinet resting on his shoulders—his head inside it—we can see the front hides his face behind a padlocked door. One of the Gods slowly unlocks and opens the door to see if The Bald Man's head is still inside, while another God brings the original small cabinet onstage, and still another God slowly and feebly thrusts a gold hammer through the back of that cabinet and with a feeble, trembling hand forces it through the double doors.)

VOICE: (Whispering) **This is the truth speaking. This is really the truth.**

(The God's infirmity is such that the hammer falls from his hand and falls onto a silver tray held shakily by another God. At the same time, the door is being reclosed and locked to re-imprison The Bald Man's head. Another God hits with a golden hammer the side of the cabinet enclosing The Bald Man's head. Then as the Gods slowly shuffle about, carrying their objects to appropriate shelves, one of them comes to again unlock and peek into the cabinet containing The Bald Man's head.)

VOICE: (Whispering) **Is this the truth speaking? Is this really the truth speaking?**

(As two other Gods measure the box's size with giant calipers, the God peeking inside slowly thrusts an extended finger into the box and seems to be poking it into The Bald Man's eye. Another God comes and clumsily pushes the feeble aggressive God away, relocks the box, and lifts it off The Bald Man's head, while The Bald Man slowly sits in a chair that a God is placing under him as he lowers himself toward it.

The calliope music is softer now, and the windmills are spinning, and the metronomes tick—each in a different rhythm. But The Bald Man decides not to sit after all, seeing that a God has placed a silver tray on the table, and on that tray, one large heart-shaped cookie. He picks up the cookie, holds it up to the light, and finally decides to take a bite—but in doing so he obviously hurts a tooth, moaning in pain as the Gods fall to the floor, and he staggers to the chair but falls on his knees just as he reaches it.

One of the Gods has apparently been out of the room, and now slowly shuffles forward carrying a silver tray with two glasses, a small milk container, and a small whiskey bottle. He finally reaches the table and sets down the tray. He pours milk into the glass. Nothing but metronomes are now heard. Joined by the sound of birds singing in the distance. The Gods on the floor rise, brush themselves off. Some of them take off their masks and look incredulously at those still masked. One without a mask pushes one still masked with his finger, and the God falls to the floor. The others become frightened and run from the room.

The remaining God and The Bald Man slowly struggle to their feet as the babbling is heard. As the God crawls out of the room on his hands and knees, The Bald Man holds his head and spins dizzily behind the table, trying to orient himself.

He supports himself on the table, examining the tray. After some consideration, he moves the milk glass and carton to the side, and seizes the whiskey bottle and empty glass. As the others—now returned to their very un-Godlike selves—slowly refill the room, he pours himself a glass of whiskey. He smoothes a patch of table clean with his hand, then reverently places the whisky glass on the table. Then—to quiet things down before taking the desired drink—he starts turning off the metronomes, but after most are silenced, he turns, startled, back to the table as if out of the corner of his eye he had seen the whiskey glass moving. He stares at it— then jumps back as if it suddenly did move, then gets a hold of himself, comes forward, replaces the glass a few inches to the side and waves a finger at it as if telling it not to move again.

He runs to silence the remaining metronomes, then starts slowly back to the glass.)

VOICE: **Now, try naming those parts of this man's body that feel most vulnerable, most stupid, most deceitful, most lustful, most incompetent, most vulgar, most alone, most in pain, most deformed, most defiled, most defenseless, most defenseless.**

(During this, The Bald Man has taken the glass, then consumed its contents and wiped his mouth with his bib.)

FALSETTO VOICES: **Where's YOUR table manners?**

(This startles him, and as a telephone starts ringing and piano music pounds out, he runs from the room carrying the glass and whiskey bottle. The minute he turns his back on them, the others start running about— searching for something that seems to be missing.

Looking into the boxes that line the shelves, looking under the table, etc. The windmills are spinning again, and the singing of "Sunny Side of the Street" returns. Then, convinced that what they are looking for is not in the room, they all run off, as The Bald Man reappears at another entrance.

He sits in the chair, and as he is pouring himself a drink, the others reenter slowly. He downs the drink, and snorts and trembles and contorts himself in reaction to the strong whiskey. The two men come and lift him up under the arms and start walking him around the room as if to wake him up from a fit of drunkenness.)

FALSETTO VOICES: **Where's YOUR table manners?**

(The babble is very loud, and the two men are counting out the steps. They stop in front of The Schoolgirl, who takes the empty whiskey glass The Bald Man still holds, smells it, and reacts with an "ugh" of disgust, then gives him back the glass as they reseat him.)

VOICE: **Well, isn't it visible in his eyes? Isn't it visible in the way he lifts his head? Isn't it visible in the way he gesticulates with his two hands? Isn't it visible even in the way he doubles over his entire body to receive multiple blows from his own powerful forehead?**

(The Bald Man has poured himself another drink. Downs it and reacts with another extended vocal growl and physical contortions, which lead into a fit of coughing and choking he seems to have difficulty controlling.

In the meantime, the others are slowly passing out rolled-up newspapers to one another. His coughing calms down, and The Lady with the Feather puts a blanket over his shoulders as the others fondle their rolled-up newspapers and The Schoolgirl comes forward with a white pillow. She suddenly slams the pillow over his face, and as a telephone bell rings, The

Lady with the Feather helps to hold it firmly in place as The Bald Man's legs start stretching and quivering as if he were being suffocated.)

VOICE: **Here is a man in front of us at long last, ready to answer to that question he asks himself again and again and again, which is—question number one. Finally—**

(They take the pillow from his face, and he recovers.)

What gives this man that kick, that emotional kick? Because we know already that very little remains that enables this man to receive a genuine emotional kick. Indeed—if anything remains.

(The Man in the Skullcap has been bent over the table, and now The Schoolgirl takes the pillow and whacks him hard on the behind.

The windmills begin spinning, and The Bald Man comes and bends over the table. The others now take their rolled-up newspapers, slowly approach him, and spank him with them, faster and faster. Then a gong rings and they reposition, and are busy spanking one another as the ladies pull up their dresses to facilitate the spanking. They change positions again, many different combinations are explored, and as THE VOICE then speaks again, they become exhausted and sad, and turn to watch The Bald Man as he stares up into a bright light, and then bends over the table again and starts laughing.)

VOICE: **But perhaps—a certain quality of light. At best, yes. And that's all that remains. I'm afraid that's all that remains, he says. A certain quality of light.**

(The Bald Man goes and slowly looks at each of the others, and one by one, they pull sadly away from him.)

VOICE: **And this man reflects upon this light and understands his sadness seems to be sadness not to himself, really, but only sadness to others surrounding him, who never receive that particular emotional kick. But rather receive their own, private emotional kicks from other things—equally sad from his perspective, such as experience with other people.**

(He comes to The Schoolgirl, who rests wistfully, leaning on the table, and he pushes her face away from him and goes back to his position bent over the table, exposing his rear end for more spanking.)

VOICE: **Such as—sexual, yes. Or emotional, yes. Or other kinds of experiences, yes.**

(The Man in the Bellboy Hat has come back into the room carrying a big sack just like the one in which The Bald Man had previously hidden himself. But this one is stuffed with feathers, and The Man with the Bellboy Hat shakes it excitedly, then uses this sack, like a human-sized stuffed sausage, to repeatedly spank The Bald Man. The music of the singing women is very loud now, and The Man in the Bellboy Hat gets so excited that he throws the sausage sack on the floor and leaps on it in gleeful embrace. He does this several times, until The Bald Man sees this happening, rises and deliberately lifts off The Man in the Bellboy Hat by the seat of his pants, and throws the big stuffed sack out of the room. Then he staggers drunkenly back, watching the others as the music becomes very soft, and the windmills stop spinning.

On the other side of the room, The Schoolgirl has lifted a black cloth off an object on a small table that has been covered all evening, and she slowly shimmies the cloth down to reveal the object, which is a large roly-poly doll with small arms and legs, and a big round belly, a tiny pink penis, and a round, pink bald head with a big beard that bears a striking resemblance to The Bald Man.

She lowers the cloth completely and turns to grin seductively at The Bald Man as she lifts the doll off the table and advances toward him with the doll in her arms. Commenting on the resemblance, she croons, "Heyyyyyyy." Then she sits the doll on the edge of the table. The doll can also be seen to sport argyle socks, and a black and gold halo rising behind its head.

The Bald Man circles around to look at the resemblance, and The Schoolgirl slowly points to the doll's bald head, comes and points to The Bald Man's head, then comes to the front of the stage and touches one of the little silver balls on the taut string. As she touches it there is a ping, then a flash of light that causes all the others to scream and hold their eyes in pain. The electronic tone is now heard over the singing as The Bald Man staggers to the far side of the room and the others circle the doll to examine it. They touch it gently, they begin to caress and kiss it.

Then they see The Bald Man looking back at them. The two men slowly take off their hats and kneel, and the two women kiss them on the tops of their heads. Seeing this, The Bald Man picks up the cloth that had been covering the doll for most of the evening and covers himself with it.

The tone becomes louder, and they all turn; four of them slowly approach The Bald Man, hidden under his cloth. Each seizes a corner of the black cloth, and they stretch it out, slowly lowering it to the floor, forcing The Bald Man down onto the floor under the cloth. This is done reverently, as if it were a religious ceremony that returns The Bald Man to the earth. They end up each kneeling at a corner of the cloth, foreheads pressed to the carpet.

Then a ping sounds, and The Lady with the Feather whirls into the room carrying a tiny fringed magic cloth and a gold hammer, and wearing an amazingly tall cylinder hat with tassels and a domelike top. She puts the cloth up just below her eyes and vamps across the room to lively organ music. When she reaches the far side of the room, she lifts the cloth to cover her face completely, then pops it down to exclaim softly, "Boo!" She giggles at her own silly hat and behavior, participating in what resembles a magic ceremony, replete with antique props.

She hides behind the tiny cloth again, travels up to The Bald Man under the black cloth, and spreads her small magic cloth over the lump that apparently indicates the location of The Bald Man's head. Then she giggles, and hits The Bald Man's invisible head with her golden hammer ten times, as a little bell rings to register each hit.)

VOICE: **Paradise, paradise.**

(Then she whips off both cloths at the same time. The others are sitting back on their haunches and laughing quietly as The Bald Man slowly gets to his feet.)

VOICE: **Is this why the magic of the world no longer exists for this man? And what is this man left with, then, when magic is taken away from him?**

(The others make their palms meet over their heads and form a line.)

VOICE: **And what is this man left with, then, when magic is taken away from him? This man is left with—well: the world itself, of course. Magic?**

(The others shift as the organ music continues and exit in line, doing an imitation crawl-swimming stroke with their arms.)

VOICE: **No magic in that. Okay—magic! NO MAGIC!**

(The Bald Man touches one of the silver balls on the taut string, causing a flash that blinds him and also blinds the two men who have circled back into the room. Then, to the music, he punches them each in the chin.)

VOICE: **That's the magic! No magic! No magic! No magic. That's the magic—no magic!**

(The Bald Man is now doing his squatting exercises to the music as The Lady with the Feather—her magic hat having been disposed of—runs forward, holding out a red robe. He stops and considers the robe as a gong brings the music to a halt.)

VOICE: **There is no longer any real "kick" for this man. This man knows that he is upset, but he cannot discover— not just the reason for this upset—but even the very feeling itself.**

(The Bald Man has allowed The Lady to help him into the robe. Then, as the music returns, she and The Man in the Bellboy Hat start ballroom dancing. The others applaud the dancing, and she breaks away to come down as if to dance with The Bald Man, but instead, she slaps his face. He staggers back, then she spits in his face, then turns and starts to dance by herself.)

VOICE: **Oh—he is upset—he knows this—but without being able to really FEEL that upset inside himself as a feeling inside himself. Or inside the people around him.**

(The Lady, dancing by herself, suddenly breaks down into tears. A telephone is ringing. Then, as the music fades, one of the Gods returns, shuffling slowly towards The Bald Man as the lights dim in the room.)

VOICE: **It is as if that feeling—which somehow he knows to be his true feeling—is, in fact, hiding from him.**

(The Bald Man turns away from the God, who then slowly brings up his hand and soothingly holds The Bald Man's head between his hands.)

VOICE: **Can this man be blamed, can this man be responsible, for confusions caused by a special—well, if this man is surrounded by a special—well—aura?**

(The God releases his hands, and The Bald Man turns to look at him.)

VOICE: **—but postulated nevertheless, as a provocation?**

(The Man in the Bellboy Hat rushes into the room carrying a telephone, but he trips and falls, and as the telephone crashes to the carpet, the God hurries from the room. The Bald Man reaches out after him.)

VOICE: **In spite of his anguished feeling that no one is provoked, in fact. Unless one thinks of this—as a possible—self-provocation?**

(The Bald Man has run to the entrance in the hope of catching a last glimpse of the disappearing God. But, disappointed, he leans against a bookcase. The phone has been recovered and placed on a table. Then it starts to ring. No one answers. The Bald Man slowly approaches the phone, picks up the receiver, and speaks. "Hello? Hello?" There is no answer. He looks at the receiver, then hangs it up.

The women's singing has returned, and the others all hold their heads in dizziness. The Bald Man checks them out, then bellows in anger—"What the hell is YOUR problem?")

VOICE: **Ah. You've broken the connection, my friend.**

(The Bald Man looks about worriedly for the source of the voice. He picks up the receiver again and angrily asks, "Hello? Hello?" He slams the receiver back down.)

VOICE: **It's too late, my friend, much too late. Much too late.**

(The Bald Man staggers over to lean on the table as the others collapse to the floor. All but The Lady with the Feather, who, at first befuddled, then goes to take the little bald dollman—which earlier someone had placed on one of the bookcases—and set it on the table next to The Bald Man. The others revive as The Bald Man circles around to look at the doll. Then he senses them trying to peek over his shoulder. He turns to confront them. There is a pause, and then The Young Man in a Skirt steals the doll and carries it to the side of the stage. Here someone hands him an eye chart with which he covers the doll's face. The Bald Man comes up to the eye chart and starts reading the letters out loud, though it sounds more like grunting: "E—F—P—" But The Man in the Bellboy Hat growls "Wrong!" into the microphone.

The Bald Man, frustrated, runs around the table and collapses on it, rolling his upper body faceup as the two men place a small model of a house over his head, opening double doors in the model that allow his head to pop through. The Bald Man's head is immediately covered with a serving tray, on top of which is a roasted pig's head with an apple in its mouth. The others pull strings from the tray which, held to the corners of the room, make the pig's head the center of a string starburst pattern, and The Schoolgirl, who is holding the tray steady on top of The Bald Man's head, screams out, "Pig for dinner!"

The strings collapse, the tray disappears, and The Bald Man crawls under the table to surface in front, reaching up from the floor to open the doors to the model house and peek inside. As he does this the two men point at him and shout in unison, "Wash those hands, Mister!"

The Bald Man scurries back under the table. The Lady with the Feather reappears with a plate loaded with food and slips it to him, under the table, as the others gather round. The Bald Man shoves the plate of food out so it slides along the carpet to the middle of the room. He starts crawling after it as the others go down on their hands and knees, crawling after the food. The Schoolgirl hitches up her skirt and jumps on The Bald Man's back, throwing her arms up in the air and screaming out, "Pig for dinner!"

The babbling is very loud as all the others laugh. She falls off The Bald Man's back. He staggers up as the others all run and hide their faces behind eye charts as everyone starts singing an eccentric version of "Sunny Side of the Street," which seems chanted with a nasal twang on just one note, following the lead of The Voice over the loudspeaker, intoning—

"Get your coat
Grab your hat
Find the sun
Never come back.
Tie yourself inside a sack
Never come back—"

As they all sing behind the eye charts, bouncing them up and down in rhythm, The Bald Man tries to lift the little house off the table, but repeatedly falls down, then tries again. Next he shifts into his squatting exercises, all performed in rhythm to the music.

A gong rings—the music stops—and the others lift the eye charts over their heads and shout goofily at The Bald Man, "Hello again!" The Bald Man whirls, and as a rock-and-roll voice starts singing "I'm lookin' for trouble. I'm lookin' for trouble,"—The Bald Man takes a bridal wreath from one of the boxes, plops it on his head, and starts pirouetting balletically to the inappropriate music.

The others begin to cry, somehow affected by his efforts to be graceful. Then there is a sudden flash, all scream, and the windmills begin revolving. The Bald Man whips off his wreath and runs to once more stick his head out through the double doors in the little house.

Another flash, and the others again scream, momentarily blinded—but they immediately recover and grabbing knives and forks, run towards the small house, rubbing their silverware together as if sharpening it for the kill.

The Bald Man, frightened by this, gets out of the house and cowers behind it as the others start to bang their silverware on the table like a pack of hungry children.

The Bald Man runs from the room, and the others stop banging but give forth with a wail of disappointment—"Awwwww!!"

But The Bald Man immediately runs back into the room, rolling the large white disk with a hole in the middle. The other two men lift the disk and once more set it on his shoulders, with his head peeking through the hole. All the others immediately crouch down and huddle in under the disk, as if hiding under a giant mushroom. The Bald Man, his head still bobbing about in the hole, rolls his eyes up to the ceiling, and the others gathered below seem to feel secure and happy: all go, "Ooooooo!" with delight.

Nothing more happens for a while; their faces slowly droop with sadness, and they utter a soft "Awwwwww . . ." of disappointment.

They come out from under the white disk and stare at The Bald Man's head, sitting in the center hole. The soft singing of the women is heard, and as The Bald Man slowly goes to his knees, still supporting the disk on his shoulders, the others move to the bookcases.

The Bald Man lowers his head sadly, and the disk moves so that it stands upright on the floor, with his head through the center opening as if in a guillotine.

As very soft, sad singing is heard, the others slowly begin to clear the bookshelves of all the boxes that fill them. As they are removed, behind each box on the back wall of the bookcase, a white question mark is painted. This takes quite a while—no one hurries, and there are perhaps thirty or forty boxes to be removed and taken out of the room, two at a time, leaving empty bookcases, marked with thirty or forty white question marks.

But the music soon fades, and as the task of clearing the shelves continues, The Voice is heard speaking sadly and softly.)

VOICE: **But here is a man who can testify that for himself,**
finally, for the last six months—less than that? More
than that? No matter—
The evocative perfume of atmosphere,
Alas, has evaporated.
All magic places, all images of time and atmosphere,
These no longer ravish this exhausted human being.
Because perhaps
From dwelling upon them in excess,
This man has drained them—
Or eaten them away, as one says,
Without even knowing
How to prepare oneself for a proper farewell.
Leaving
Empty husks of memory
Toward which this man gazes
With empty,
Sad eyes.
But notice, but notice, please—
In the center of that sadness
No final lurch forward
To grasp what,
If saved—
Might just perhaps, rekindle—
Inside this man
Inside of whom beauty falls to pieces—

(Having cleared the room, they come and look at the
top of The Bald Man's head, which is still thrust
through the hole in the white disk. Then The Schoolgirl
points to his head, and the entrance rear is filled with
a ceiling-high white screen, upon which are several
small black question marks. They all line up on one
side of the stage, at the very front, and as a soft voice
sings "Smile . . . smile . . . smile . . . " repeatedly, they
lift their open palms towards the audience, and making
slowly circles with their hands, they slowly drift offstage in line, trying indeed to smile.

The stage is empty but for the man with his head through the disk. A small bell rings once.)

VOICE: **Well, somebody said it very clearly that when all seems lost, only then the weather changes and the sun starts shining with a brilliance nobody else could ever imagine. Incoherent in its brightness, perhaps, but nevertheless—here it comes. Here it comes.**

(The Young Man in a Skirt and The Man in the Skullcap have reappeared with brooms, and are quietly sweeping the crumpled newspapers on the floor.

The Lady with the Feather appears, balancing a tall wicker basket on her head. Following her is The Schoolgirl, dragging a waist-high empty tub. the Lady slowly positions herself, then proceeds to dump the contents of her basket—crumpled newspapers, skulls, and a few pieces of raw meat—right onto the head of The Bald Man, which still pokes through the large disk. He slowly pulls out of the disk and comes up behind it to look over it and survey the garbage on the floor.

Faint, faraway organ music plays a happy tune. The Bald Man crosses and very deliberately thrusts himself headfirst, upside down, into the big tub, with his legs sticking up in the air.

The Man in the Skullcap gathers some newspapers from the floor and drops them so they float down over the upside-down man in the tub.

Then the man in the tub reemerges as the others are moving across the room, and The Bald Man puts his head back through the hole in the large disk. The Young Man in a Skirt has placed another large disk on the big table—this one with a black spiral etched on its surface, and The Lady with the Feather pulls a long string taut from the center of that disk till it reaches The Bald Man's head. She holds it there until The Man in the Skullcap crosses and plucks the string—which makes a "ping"—and they all try to suppress a giggle.

Then The Young Man in a Skirt plucks the string by reaching around the disk. It also makes a ping, and again they all giggle.

Then The Schoolgirl comes down to the strings across the front of the stage, reaches up, and touches one of the small silver balls: there is another ping—but no flash this time—and they all laugh more openly as The Lady returns the string to the spiral disk, and all but The Man in the Skullcap exit. The Bald Man lifts up, standing now with the disk on his shoulders forming a large collar, through which his head is visible.

The Man in the Skullcap has been holding his head and spinning, and now he reaches to the floor, picks up two pieces of raw meat, and studies them carefully. He slowly balances one piece of meat on The Bald Man's head. Then he takes the other piece of meat, places it on his own head, removes his hands, and balances it there.)

VOICE: **Ahhhh—this very minute—secretly—must—must— reinvest in some unexplored corner of mental life. — HIS mental life, of course!**

(A church bell has been ringing in the distance. Now a doorbell rings insistently, and the others enter, carrying large bundles wrapped in brown paper, which they place on the white disk that rides on The Bald Man's shoulders.

As they do so, he growls and starts spinning, and the bundles fly off his disk to distant parts of the room. Someone lifts off the disk and he is handed one of the packages, which he looks at for a moment, then discards into the large tub.

As the others leave the room, he lifts the tub and turns it upside down so the package and a few remaining bits of garbage fall to the floor. He carries the tub across the room and places it upside down on the big table. Then he goes and grabs a piece of *meat from the floor, then balances it on his head.*)

VOICE: **—And this man's entire body seems reinvested as a thinking machine he knows not, yet, how to use.**

(A gong rings. The Bald Man starts for the rear bookcase, but the meat falls off, so he retrieves it and tries anchoring it on his head with one of the forks that was discarded in a previous scene. He now continues to the rear bookcase, and as the meat falls off again, he lifts—with great effort—the obelisk and staggers with it, just making it to the table and managing to set it on top of the upside-down tub. The organ music and the babble are quite loud now, joined by an electronic tone, and as the doorbell rings again, the others run into the room carrying the large stuffed sausage. The Bald Man tries to take it away from them, but they quickly succeed in placing it on the table, where they stand it up and start vibrating it and uttering guttural syllables as if performing a magic rite.

Then, as The Bald Man grabs his sack and starts slipping it down over his head so it will cover his whole body, leaving only his feet free, the others all run to the sides of the room, hiding their eyes, as the sausage tumbles down. The Voice is heard singing two clashing versions of "Sunny Side of the Street" simultaneously: the classical version, and the nasal, aggressive version—

> "Get your coat
> Grab your hat
> Find the sun
> Never come back.
> Tie yourself inside a sack
> Never come back—
> Fall down dead,
> Drink the sun
> From your head."

As the aggressive version becomes dominant, The Bald Man starts lurching about in agony inside his sack. And in time with the blaring mélange of music, the others lift their arms to the sky, shaking them, then making magic passes towards The Bald Man, who has fallen and is now rolling on the floor inside his sack.)

VOICE: (Singing)
"Get your coat
Grab your hat
Find the sun
Never come back . . ."

(The music is quiet now, and The Voice stops singing. The others fall silent and stare at the sack, inside of which The Bald Man now rests motionless.)

VOICE: (Very quietly) **Now, somebody is going to sing somebody else's favorite song.**

(The Bald Man slowly rises to a sitting position inside the sack, and The Voice begins to sing, very softly, with a cracking voice. The others hide behind eye charts.)

"Get your coat and get your hat
Leave your worries on the doorstep.
Life can be so sweet
On the sunny side of the street."

(The Bald Man struggles to his feet, still inside the sack, and, very faintly at first, The Voice is heard singing a second version of the classical tune and lyrics—this one in a rasping rendition that gets louder and louder until it finally drowns out the more wistful rendering.

The others start sobbing and leave the stage in tears. The windmills are turning. The Bald Man stands without moving, all alone inside his sack. Eight rapid, loud thuds are heard—which stops the singing.

There is silence as the lights brighten a bit, then fade to black.)

THE END

(UNCUT ORIGINAL TEXT)

Here is a man, here is a man who indeed inhabits this very room. Here is the very floor, or tables, or the comfortable chair upon which he rests a physical body which deteriorates from that very comfort provided.

(This is true, this is the truth speaking)

Yet here is a man who chooses not to be re-energized but rather to sink deeper, deeper into that very self which he well understands echoes the slow erasing of that very self. But nothing in his life, now, wins his allegiance. And so it continues. That nothing. That nothing.

And this slow withdrawal from life is, perhaps, the very adventure—that something—adventure—which renames this man. So name it. Name the adventure. But can it be said, finally, to be adventure which bestows one's true name?

(Is this the truth? Is this the truth speaking?)

Or is it something other than adventure—a configuration of forces, that names one. The planets that name one? The dust of submolecular particles? The light reflected off windows through which no sunlight penetrates to illuminate a particular room—which also may or may not be a room that is already a named room?

What is this room named? Come on now—what is this room named?

(We do not know, we do not know)

Is this room, so dominated by the sound of a human voice—is this room named "The room of radios"? The room of radios?

(This is true, this is the truth speaking)

What was this room named, however—before having been named the room of radios?

(Pause.)

The room of nonanticipation. The room of nonanticipation. And this is strange, of course, because here is a group of people assembled inside this very room, with the majority of the people so assembled, in fact, full of anticipation. So one should not have said "radios," perhaps, but more accurately pronounced the words—"holes in air." Holes in air.

(What are holes in air? What are holes in air?)

Here is a man who can give no definition of the term "holes in air," because this is a man who has never really seen holes in air. Because air is invisible to this man. So at least this man does not lose his balance.

(Holes in air, holes in air.)

Here is a man who has tried and tried and tried, but does not lose his balance. Here is a man trying to reascertain that which enters his head without vanishing immediately, because it IS true, that what continues is the self-evident fact that this room of radios is, by self-definition—the room of radios—yes. The room of radios. With no real radios, however, because what this man feels in his entire body is the desire to express what is absent when the muscles of his limbs do ache, which he imagines may be relieved by movements the specifics of which he does not imagine. Which means how, in fact, does this man manifest himself in this very room where such invisible-to-himself movements, are indeed taking place, nevertheless, below or above the threshold of this man's consciousness?

Ah! The room of radios, indeed. The room of radios. The room of radios, indeed!

*   *

How, please, how does one penetrate this very room?
    (Pause)
Ladies and gentlemen—one exits. Then. One turns back towards the door, ladies and gentlemen—opens it and enters.

But suppose one is already inside this room?

One, ladies and gentlemen, reenters.

But here is a man who asks himself: Just suppose that one is already inside this very room. Then one needn't ENTER this room, perhaps—except—which is to say—BUT—how does one GET INSIDE this very room?

Here is a man who does not know the answer to this question. But no one follows him into this question, I think, because—partially—it is true. Here is a man—who is certainly HERE! Here! Here!
    (We're here! We're here! We're here!)

How does one enter this room?

Ah! This is not really the land of the LIVING—is it now? Which is not to name it, ladies and gentlemen, the land of the dead. Oh no, not dead exactly.

Here—inside this perfumed—vestibule, quite different from what can be defined by the terms alive, dead, etc. Oh no—the *postulated*, ladies and gentlemen—which, by being *postulated*, comes into existence, but never an existence that is identical with living, exactly: not, with the future that does go on, perhaps—except here is a man quite ready to TWIST every perhaps of his own imagining into the absolute of a very private YES YES YES!

And IS this twist into "YES"—is this the one remaining adventure, ladies and gentlemen? Here it is—in the palm of one's hand—or should one say—here one has this very man—because stupidity is discovered to hold great promise, ladies and gentlemen. And here is a man whose room is redecorated into an even deeper ugliness which enables his whole world to come full circle in order never to be forgotten.

And a blackboard is erased—is that somebody's memory? But that blackboard thinks—"I redefine myself," never realizing it's somebody else who rubs it clean. And a book thinks—"I turn my own pages"—but does it now? Well, this confusion is normal because nobody else is really needed here in this particular room—but—is this also? Normal? Normal?

    (This is the truth, this is the truth being spoken)

Rest assured, ladies and gentlemen. Here is a man, located in some other place than the place that is right here now—. And this said man possesses so much more reality in that other place than in this place—here.

    (Holes in air, holes in air, holes in air)

Here is a man, giving himself a gift.
    (This is true, this is truth speaking)

The gift is a robe he wears. Here is a robe, and here is a man deciding to wear this robe, asking himself at the same moment—Why do I wear this robe?
    (All wear robes)

Why do I wear this robe? Why wear this robe?
> *(Pause)*

Here is a man, questioning whether the wearing of this robe gives to himself and others surrounding him the consciousness of greater reality, denser reality, deeper reality.

But here is this same man concluding that he and he alone of all those co-present with him in this room—he alone should be the judge of that reality which is his own reality. So this man passes judgment—this man rules that his sense of reality is indeed inside himself, but—what does this mean to this man—who wears this robe on the outside of his body—
> *(Robe on him)*

Who repeats to himself again and again and again that much greater reality belongs to him in some other place that is not this place, this room, in which he does indeed find himself now.

But, ah, none of this works for this man. In fact, wearing such a robe affords him perhaps less reality, less "sense of reality." Because more sense of reality did exist before this robe was covering his body. Yes, yes, but how to apply such realization that—okay, okay, now—one has been wearing, in the widest sense of the term—wearing a particular suit of reality that drains all sense of reality. Okay. Okay. How to strip oneself of such offending disguises is in no way easy to determine because—does one begin by returning such a robe?—the very gift itself?
> *(Gathers the robe about his body)*

Oh no! Never never never the return of the gift itself!
> *(Pause)*

How strange—here is a man who has become deeply attached to his robe—one possibility. Or perhaps, possibility number two, the robe itself is valued for its ability to provoke a particularly powerful lucidity concerning one's true condition.

But how does this lucidity profit such a man?

Such a man concludes—ah—another level of reality is available to me, and he asks himself—Where am I? And he answers himself—I am in no place, which means I no longer need what seemed so necessary to me.

(*Robes off, into drawer*)

But of course, the robe is still available if needed.

But right now—here is a man who needs nothing. Nothing. Nothing.

(This is the truth, this is the truth speaking)

How does one enter this room?

(*One enters*)

How does one enter this room? Here is a man who would like to believe that the answer to this question is obvious; because his answer is no longer phrased as a question. Because, this man says—"Because an arrival is always something—nonverbal." Is it not? Is it not?

And the proof this man offers—? Such arrival still would have taken place whether or not there was someone speaking about it, which is to say—here is a man who thinks it would have happened—somehow.

And he calls attention most of all to his own hesitation. Ah, he does hesitate—hesitates—this hesitation so that something else can happen in the very small space cleared by that hesitation and, indeed, it does happen. It does happen.

Ladies and gentlemen, how does one enter this room? Put in such a way, the question may seem unanswerable because one—whoever that one may be—that "one" has indeed entered already, repeating the very words "How does one enter this room?" And that's just it, apparently—"How DOES one enter this room?"

Ladies and gentlemen—here is a man who makes discoveries by repeating himself as follows: "How does one enter this room—." And the response to that question is "How does one enter this room."

(This is the truth, this is the truth speaking)

Here is a man totally disgusted with claims to understand him not, but this man is even more disgusted with his own guilt at believing that such a professed lack of understanding is due to some ethical failure on his own behalf.

Because this man really believes that he has made available what should be easily understandable by all those in full possession of his or her own aliveness (though he well understands, this same man, that not one of us is, in fact, in full possession of that life ruled and shaped by forces one can never identify or understand completely). And yet—and yet—this same man believes that the only moral position possible is the position from which he DOES INDEED speak to those, only those, in full possession of such a life of one's own, which is never possible, in fact.

So those to whom this man does speak, those so postulated, do understand him, rest assured—if they are not those who do, in fact, exist. So each one of you, ladies and gentlemen, to whom this man is now apparently speaking, may indeed be those who fail to understand him. But here is a man who says, "Damn your lack of understanding, and damn myself also," he says, "for being myself victimized by your refusal to understand me. So that if we are both thereby damned, ladies and gentlemen, should we both not, then, well understand each other? Must it not be, then that we well understand each other?"

(Yes, yes, yes, yes to this question. Yes yes yes)

Here is a man who asks time itself to stop, never realizing that time itself has stopped again and again and again in the hopes that human beings might imagine paradise itself—the arrival at such a desirable destination.

But this man hesitates, believing his imagination will never live up to such a reality—by which he means his own paradise, that lack of reality—Paradise.

And is it possible? Is it possible, really possible, that thought goes roaming through these active yet recalcitrant people, within whom such activity does persist, pursuing directives—oh so independent of those very thoughts that do roam between such people, coagulating into tiny shapes tumbling between those very people—such as—this thrust of a hand, slightly, slightly—that gesture—lifting toward the forehead where nothing emerges from any real source, except a kind of . . . Say it again! Say it again! Say it again! Invoking for the hundredth time an idea one can never possess, of course—rubbing up against that same idea that one can never possess with a voice already wounded.

Oh voice! Oh voice, already in such pain!

> (Ah, this music, I am ravished indeed, by such music, such music.)

> (I've had it, my friend. I've really had it. I've really had it.)

Here is a voice we dare not allow to speak directly, because the madness of this voice is infectious, and all one would need do is to hear this voice speaking directly for itself and one would be intoxicated by that speaking, and one would immediately leap from windows or plunge directly into rivers from the power of whose turbulence no escape was possible.

But rest assured, rest assured—this voice is not the voice you are listening to, because it is not here in this room. While you, listening, are here in this room, this table is here also, but this voice, this voice is not here in this room, but is, in fact, only a hole carved deep inside everything else here made manifest, including this man, who assumes physical impenetrability—an object inside a second object—and this man who does not speak—risks everything—who notices that life—his life, of course—which is no more than the occasion for life to present itself—indeed, life—this man notices each perfect example—life, life, life!

Here is a man who notices that Life is full of lunges that go nowhere. Lunges towards ideas that dissipate, towards actions that are abandoned, towards possibilities dropped. And it is true that occasionally, he notices exceptions arise, and one thrust into idea or action or possibility does in fact fulfill itself, which does then—this is what this man notices—the evocation of a response from the world outside one's private preoccupations.

And the world outside responding, every once in a while, with an appropriate grimace of recognition, does seem to change things for one's life.

But contrary to belief, such a response, such sudden interaction with life's seeming flow—this is never what gives the heaviness of truth to one's life.

Here is a lamp, for instance, being turned on—but this response, this pale yellow light offered in response to one's impulse, fulfilled—this is, in fact, deceptive seduction—this illumination of sorts, executed with precision by that ruthless illusion calling itself life on this earth. Oh hollow and fallen thing which this is—though difficult for those listening to this truth to accept as truth indeed.

But here is a man who tells us this false and fallen thing blinds us. This life which promises adventures fulfilled does, in fact, blind us to the truth we seek, because that truth is that very blindness itself—that impasse that SHOULD be celebrated—because only those impulses never fulfilled do pour forth blinding truth. Oh yes—always! Blinding truth, which to be true is blinding. And tragedy does know this impasse to perfection. And comedy knows this impasse also. Divine stumbling, divine short circuit, this alone holding the key to that unopenable door whose very impenetrableness bounces one back from the illusion of this life in this fallen universe—which is indeed fallen.

And here is a lamp that testifies to this fallen state. And here is great wisdom that testifies to this fallen state. And here is air, filling this room—breathable to no end but an end in error—and here is a man who sees for himself, God is no key, for that key leads him back to God himself—just one more level of this same universe. Death itself—that is no key, for that death leads him back into the very same universe, as he is transformed into a definable nothing that is also nothing but one more level of this same nothing universe.

But one thing only, only, only, which is continual impasse, continual frustration, the meaningless gesture that never comes to fruition—this alone—his true connection to the particular meaningfulness that is a human being's real possibility, as opposed to all other things—this lamp, that chair, this air, this sound of the voice talking—all of which decorate this prison, this universal prison, and this man knows this knowledge, which is the bitter medicine that must be swallowed. The bitter medicine that cures. Cures. Cures!—of his attachment to that universe so precisely postulated by his consciousness which is itself renamed—error! The revealing of which—this error renamed consciousness—!

This room of radios, built solid from echoes—do you hear what this man hears?

Here is a man who simply cannot opt out of his own self-destructive motives. This is a man who can only listen to himself. Don't pity this man, however. Don't pity this radiant human being whose intense self-listening burns him from the inside until real silence—speaks to him like thunder.

(Hotel Radio, Hotel Radio. How many radios are listening inside Hotel Radio, Hotel Radio, Hotel Radio, Hotel Radio?)

Get this. Get this, please. Get this man—get the understanding of this man.
(I've had it, I've really had it, I mean I've really had it!)

Get the understanding of this man who testifies that when no specific words want to pour forth from inside himself—yet nevertheless, he wants to be in speaking—as if he might say to us in the agreed-upon language, I want to be in China, or I want to be in the beautiful countryside, or high on a mountain overlooking the sea in China.

So. This man wants to be in speaking, even if this man has nothing specific to say.

And rest assured, idle conversation does not satisfy this man. Oh no—oh no—this is understood. And if someone were to suggest that perhaps if this man were to read something from a book—this man would explain—if he were able to speak—that it would be very very hard for him to find something fulfilling in a book.

Yes, yes, yes, he insists—because there are too many books, after all. Just as in a similar sense, there are too many people. Too many people. Which this man understands—the notion of too many people—this is an upsetting reality to ponder. But he realizes that to justify his opinion—? Well—that done, then he's tricked into conversation. But okay, he says—unable to silence himself—okay. There are too many people because, if there were just one person, that one person would be unique—i.e. God. I.e.—the totality, in himself. Is this man thinking about himself? An unthinkable subject. But since there are so many, many people, which means a splintering of the potential great radiant one into the actual million many-many—means that each millionth part holds only a millionth part of the whole; and a millionth part is— well, that's not very much, that's nothing very significant. Which is why there are too many people therefore, as well as too many books, and too many ideas.

(*Pause*)

Instead of the complete book, or the complete person or idea. Just a million splinters.

(*Pause*)

But forgive this man, for these words didn't really want to come forth from this man in particular. They were tricked out of him, in fact. Though it is true that he did say he did want to be in speaking, like being in China, or being in the countryside.

Yes, yes, yes. And he does indeed understand the advantages of silence when one indeed has nothing to say. Except— except—what is it exactly that gives one the power of having something to say?

Because, if one has nothing to say, does that, in itself, just possibly, become—HAVING something to say?

Possibly. Possibly. Even though it's brief. Because having nothing to say could be brief indeed.

But—this man asks himself—How would brief have to reconstitute itself until brief slides imperceptibly from brief, into nothing at all—nothing to say? But this man cannot answer this for himself—here is a man who never stops asking himself questions, and the next question is— Is this where I will remain for a very long time? But he does not mean this physical location, of course, but rather this—"place" of having nothing to say. As a location.

(*Pause*)

But, in fact, it will not last. Even if, right now, he has the feeling it will last. Because he knows that when you are inside such a feeling, that's what it feels like. Then it changes. And what changes it is always a surprise.

(A surprise, a surprise is coming, a surprise)

Not something this man has planned, oh no. But a surprise. Count on the surprise. A contradiction in terms, which sounds like taking the easy way out, perhaps.

But! But! But! Here is a man who chooses never to take the easy way out. Which is not a moral position this man selects, but simply a matter of preference. Which is certainly that preference for never taking the easy way out—that in itself is certainly having something to say—if someone such as this man has a preference with which, in fact, he does surprise himself. Not on purpose—which was the point. Not on purpose! But a surprise!

(*Pause*)

Which means, here is a man with something to say to himself after all, which he knew was true, which means, he knew what it was he had to say to himself, and to others—

(Surprise, this is a surprise, surprise!)

—even if parts of himself didn't know about this same surprise.

Because here is a man, not at all sure what's been happening to him. Except—he does know he has been speaking—he has been having a conversation of sorts. But he is no longer certain that a conversation is quite what he means when he refers to having something to say. In fact, he is reasonably sure a conversation isn't.

(*Others exit.*)

Well, two can play this game.

(*He exits.*)
Except the rules of the game, for this man and others—there
are no rules.
(*He returns.*)
So one person alone can play this game. Only bear in mind
please, here is a man whose brain has been damaged by his
life. That's why this man is not a good conversationalist.

What do you mean, your brain has been damaged, sir?

Well—life has twisted it out of shape, of course.

But you don't seem, well—stupid, sir.

Oh, Please, please! Give me that much credit, please, please.

There is so much you could teach me, sir. If you tried.

Ah, this is not the moment for teaching, I'm afraid.

What am I to do, sir?
(A surprise, a surprise is coming, a surprise)

Here is a man—here is a man making a specific suggestion.
Which is to allow oneself to be transformed, as he suggests,
by his own personal example. Which is, of course, to let the
mysteriousness in oneself be there. Because then, as this is
carefully allowed to happen—this man will then try very
hard, he promises, to perceive that mysteriousness, in order
to make it something done together, ensemble. And just
think of it—then he and those others surrounding him in this
room will be transformed into something he does hope will
happen—because this man is sharing his most intimate
problems, which are really very painful problems, he tries to
assure all those listening to him.

When such a person finds himself or herself underutilized,
as he does find himself, of course; and when such a man asks

himself—What is this "me" like, really inside my deepest and most genuine feelings—and he does remember— "Paradise, paradise." Inside this very room—located within this very particular city—both of which shall remain unnamed, of course. But you may guess the name of this city even if you do not guess the name of this room, or the singular adventure defined therein.

And then again, none of your guesses may be correct. But it's evening, after all, and here is a man who dares to remember labyrinthine routes to those large—are they still there?— once-upon-a-time cavernous restaurants? Close to the deserted train station at the edge of the river. Are they still crowded with men and women of mysterious beauty and accomplishment, all held in the embrace of this particular city in which the complexity, the density, the sheer fascination—much like one is fascinated by the vast territory of one's half-remembered childhood?

So. This city—inside of which, hidden—this man decides to do—nothing at all. Because everything desirable seems to him a false thing—the immediate reversal of what is promised as the desirable object.

Indeed—everything do-able seems to melt less into its opposite, and more into its antiself. "Discover! Discover!," he berates himself. Is this why the magic of the world no longer exists for this man?

And what is this man left with when magic is taken away from him? This man is left with—the world itself, of course. Just the world. This man is left with NOTHING—but the entire world. THE ENTIRE WORLD!

Which, however—the entire world—because it is the ENTIRE world—includes, of course, that left-out magic of the world, which this man still hungrily postulates. So isn't that which he postulates—a part of the world also? Except—

if it's something postulated—then is it still magic? Is it still magic? Or mere infantile desire, which does mean, never-theless—even if it's no longer magic—ah!—it's still part of the world, isn't it? It's the world—and here is a man in front of us, certainly. In the world, certainly, who takes the justifi-able position that the world as postulated of course includes magic—even if that magic is postulated only as a memory, or a hunger, or a childishness.

(*Pause*)

Here is the opinion of this one foolish man, of course.

But this man's opinion does exist—a part of the world equal, perhaps, to all other parts of the world. Magic? No magic in that, right? Magic! NO MAGIC! That's the magic! No magic! No magic! No magic, no magic! No magic!

Here is a man before us—of whom it can truly be said he was doing some excellent thinking. Then this man turned against his thinking. Why did he turn against his thinking? Because his thinking imprisoned him.

Hard to believe, but his thinking imprisoned him. That was his thinking about his thinking. Except it was something other than his mere thinking about it, so perhaps it was his feeling about it. Yes, he was, and indeed in a certain sense, still IS a person trapped by powerful feelings and powerful thinking.

But now this man has escaped by turning against his think-ing—and by turning against his thinking, vast new realms seem available to this man who, though very powerful, is, in fact, inside a prison. So he has turned against his own think-ing. He turned against his ability to manipulate the English language. He turned against his sense of balance—look, look, look! He turned against his ability to orient himself in space using his eyes. He turned against muscular coordination, using his limbs, mostly. He turned against sensory gratifica-tion. He turned against an available sense of his body bounc-

ing against things in space, and there was no space in his
own private world. There was no space. There was no space.
  (This is the truth, this is the truth speaking, this is
  the truth)

This is what this man does with his powerful mind, which is
no longer used in thinking, but used instead to slice up those
many experiences of a lifetime into smaller and smaller
pieces of those same experiences.

Because if this man makes these pieces, each piece, small
enough—very tiny—then each piece of his experience
becomes brilliant, perhaps—if it's small enough—so that
each piece of his life glitters like one of many small dia-
monds hovering in front of his eyes—slipping through his
fingers like particles of glass—as he briefly holds and then
releases the tiny moments of a life, each signed with a tiny
face centered with two tiny eyes that sparkle.

But this man is not sure this is truly happening.

He asks himself what tiny piece of the world, so small it
sparkles—which of these jewels that tumble from my memory are still genuinely interesting to me?
  (Surprise, this is a surprise, surprise surprise.)

Here is a man who contradicts himself. Who dares to
announce, no piece of the world is genuinely interesting
to this man. Only—the whole world at once. Only when
everything is included in one single experience named
"Everything at once"—only then is the world interesting to
this man. And this is experienced as a contradiction because
nothing IN the world is interesting to this man—only the
whole world at once.

Which raises the obvious question—How?—How?—How?
—can one experience every experience in only one experience?

This is not yet knowable, even to this man. But here is a man who really doesn't know this. But this is the only thing, after all is said and done, that is interesting to this man.

> (This is the truth. This is—this is the truth being spoken—the truth!)

How does this man know this to be true? Except—even without being able to formally conceptualize this idea—this is what he knows. But how does this man know this total thing? Because he can't explain how he knows this total thing. He can just say, "I know this. I know this." Without believing that he himself will be believed, of course. And he is not necessarily being believed, which in and of itself—this "not being believed"—this is, in itself, very interesting to him.

> (*Music stops.*)

But ah—this "not being believed" is but one item within those items that make up a world, and not the entire world —which means with this newfound "not being believed"—? This man has found one single thing that, while not the entire world, is nevertheless interesting to him. So when he says there is no longer even a piece of the world that is interesting to him, he is no longer telling the truth, it seems, and this is interesting. Interesting.

Understand this—understand this now. If the world becomes totally unrepresentable, is that just this one particular man falling outside the picture? Here is a man who thinks not, because if this man falls outside the picture, this man thinks this means—that picture—wherever that picture resolves itself—that picture could not hold inside itself—this man. And the fault is, therefore, more a fault of the picture than a fault of this man, who is still here! —And here he is, ladies and gentlemen!

Inside a picture defined by four walls and bright light, which renders the space inside four walls visible. And this picture is, in fact, a picture of a entire world, ladies and gentlemen.

But where, exactly, is this man locatable inside this picture towards which he is now directing himself and others?

Because is something inevitably wrong, ladies and gentlemen? The question is—in what part of the not-quite-yet visible body does a man such as this man feel most vulnerable?

Here is a man who feels vulnerable in all parts of his body, but which part most vulnerable?

The most vulnerable part of the body being that part which is outside the "me," or the "myself" or the "my own," entirely, which is to say—in the world outside his body is the part of this man's body that feels most vulnerable, most stupid, most deceitful.

   ("This is true, this is the truth speaking, this is true.") Most lustful. Most incompetent. Most vulgar. Most alone. Most in pain. Most deformed. Most defiled. Most defenseless.

   (*Masks on.*)

Ah, this is no mere experiment, ladies and gentlemen. Rest assured. What this is, is—something to reinvigorate oneself, and it does reinvigorate the man who is here, now.

Something that must be done, in the sense that, if not done, this man experiences a frustration he is not able to identify as such, but it goes to work inside him, and something is unfulfilled. Do believe this. Do believe this.

Because I am walking a thin line between, well—did I make the mistake of referring to myself directly? Well, do believe this, nonetheless. Do believe this?

   (Hey, is what's happening catching up with what's being said? Or is what's said too hard, much too hard—)

Enter a room where amazing people gather, realizing that

one is never fully visible to oneself in one's own experiences. This is the cross one must bear.

And launching oneself into a certain language of rigor and ambiguity, one immediately realizes the inappropriateness of such a choice or of any choice, really. So, careful, careful, be very careful.

Here is a man whose brain—like your own perhaps—has been damaged by life. Which is why this man is not good at conversation. Because his brain has been damaged.

     (This is the truth, this is the truth speaking, this is
     the truth.)

Because his life has twisted his brain out of its true shape. And neither he, nor those in attendance who wait for him to speak, seem on the surface of things—stupid, in fact—as a fact.

But oh, do believe, do believe in that deep level of stupidity. Do believe in that now. So that one is able to say—as a kind of ultimatum, of course—that one's arrogance is always misplaced. And one is never the person one thinks oneself to be.

Let's just say that here is a man who decides to see the darkness, where other people see light. But what can this possibly mean? Let's just say—here is a man who refuses to allow his own angst to be reinterpreted as the more ordinary angst of his fellow human beings when confronted with a dilemma only half-recognizable as such.

So this man is banished to some nether region where the best he can do is just—suppose, just suppose that this man assumes the royal mantle of one who understands very well the rules of this particular game which is the attempt at serious confusion.

Because one who succeeds in confusing himself does find

that, when all is lost, then immediately the weather improves and one does notice—an internal sun is shining after all.

And since here is a man who speaks directly to those who, like himself, never really liked this life—what this man has figured out, using his brain against himself, is a way to just ease from this life into another. Though nobody else notices this happening, or that it has already happened.

Because this man has been preempted, not by some archetypal who-so-ever. No—but by the sound of his own voice, really, which does indeed lead one, really, oneself really, into the promised land which is here, in fact.

In a place where, finally, this man can allow himself to give way to the exhaustion he has always desired, because when he sinks exhausted into this "thing," then he is at his best. Because his mind is racing, and he demands of the world surrounding him—"What do you understand of me?" And the answer is—"Well, since you can't enter my mind, what you understand of me is NOTHING. Because my words do not, let me assure you, express my mind."

"Therefore—no matter what I do, I am never understood. Because my words, certainly, are the reverse of what's going on in my mind—not a mirror-image reversal, of course. But let's put it this way, shall we? My mind . . . is alive—at least that part of my mind that can never be calculated, while my words, on the other hand, are dead things, certainly, because just look how I shove them around! Which is the proof, ultimately, because I somehow"—this man says—"still hover in front of your eyes. And though, still hovering in front of your eyes, at that very same moment my word flow stops." And indeed, his word flow stops. Which is not to say that words are necessary, when this man presents us, instead, with an empty life, surrounded only by beauty.

Oh no—spiritual self-laceration is not to his taste, you understand. So what this man does with his life is—finally— nothing. Nothing at all is what this man does with his life.

And if one were to say to this man that the world is thereby deprived of nourishment, through the fruits of his talents, this man would answer, "How immoral—even to consider the world outside oneself when one is doing one's private considerations." Though this is a man who well understands that most would maintain, with some violence, the exact opposite.

But the fact of the matter is, here is a man who believes that the less he participates in the world's business, the more, well . . . spiritualized the world itself becomes. Because then, and only then, does the beacon nature of this man shine, and the world is thereafter bright. This man does not mean to credit himself, you understand. He simply allows the face of the world to burnish itself through his own inaction. And then the world shines, all by itself. Thank you very much. Thank you very much.
    (*Pause*)

Ah, there are amongst us those who do not approve the broadcasting of such sentiments, certainly. But believe, do believe that here is a man who, when he sits back, leaning away from the world, that gesture of renunciation polishes the world's surface—which does cause this man to believe that were everyone in the entire world to perform that same act of renunciation—he is well assured that then the world itself would whirl totally in some gloss of total beauty. Revolution upon revolution around the axis of its divine center. Unslowed by the wobble of misdirected human effort. And—pure bliss—ladies and gentlemen in fortunate attendance—though some amongst you may chalk up such visions to this man's self-indulgence. Here is a man who asks—through not asking.

"Ah, do you really believe that MY purpose here on earth and your purpose here on earth and your sister's purpose here on earth and your uncle's purpose here on earth and your best friend's, etc. etc. etc.—? Is the purpose of all this, ladies and gentlemen—you really believe the purpose of all this is simply to produce—something OTHER? IN ADDITION?—more and more and more of whatever it is that is here now, surrounding us here on this earth?"

Here is a man who offers to tell a secret. And the secret is— we ourselves aren't here, really. This is not really where this collection of individual me-myselves is, in fact, located.

This is the secret. Though of course—no one explains real secrets, ever—the proof being that . . . within the hour, everything this man has said will be dismissed and forgotten one hundred percent. Even though this is a man who hopes that what he says or what is behind what he says that can never be said—this will not really be forgotten, he hopes. Because this man, too, is capable of self-delusion, sinking deep into his chair, swallowing strong liquors, actualizing that fusion he is able to intuit as the bright blinding light of his incoherence—
    (*All drink.*)

Ah, because ah—utter incoherence? This is something that shines at the end of a tunnel, ladies and gentlemen—that light towards which this man strives with tremendous effort. Such tremendous effort.
    (*Drinks again.*)

But why, why, why, why this tremendous effort? Here is a man who refuses to explain this, and so the question might be asked—if explanation is withheld, then why bother to identify the OBJECT of this inexplicable pursuit? And this man smiles. Here is a man who uses a smile to imply that he wishes to identify that bright thing—that incoherence which is bright—for no other reason than because—he wants to do so. He wants to sing that non-idea. He wants to sing that non-idea which takes the shape of a beautiful word—"Incoherence. Incoherence." And is it not true that to pursue and sing whatever it is that one truly wants in each moment as it passes—this is to pursue such—incoherence. That much is known already, and this is the normal state of things. So know that also. Perfectly normal.

Oh, perfectly normal, perfectly normal.

Carpets cover the floor. This is normal.
    (This is normal.)
Feet suggest the idea of direction. This is normal.
    (This is normal.)
Heads spin, writing dizziness into history by accident.
    (This is true, this is the truth speaking—)
Roads less traveled become colorful. This is normal.
    (This is normal.)
Rooms. Rooms are redecorated, and the world around us comes full circle, in order to be not forgotten. And a blackboard is erased, and thereby thinks it redefines itself, not realizing somebody else is rubbing out its impenetrable message.
    (I know this, I know this.)
And a book turns its own pages. But this is normal. This is perfectly normal.
    (This is normal. This is normal.)
Normal people surrounding this man who is anything BUT normal, in and of himself, suddenly acquiring the ability to define themselves in the most bizarre terms imaginable even to themselves.

    (Yes, yes, yes, yes, yes, yes.)

Here is a man who says, "This is no longer myself I am talking about, but you, you, you I am talking about. You, banqueting off my banquets and claiming moderation, but far exceeding me in excess. You, who look into the distance and see only explosions behind your own eyes traveling backwards into an empty dimension called visionary—and exhausting all potential by naming you, the fulcrum of each dream that tries lifting a whole world someplace else. You certainly—garnishing nonsense as a lifelong assignment. You, certainly—following imaginary Satan like the disease of life itself which is hungry for change because change is only predictable enough to put the entire world to sleep—just like you, liar, you—miscreant, you—boil of trouble! You! Who in mirrors—turning into my own face itself—being my—you—thank you—face—which is everybody's double face with no model, because, reproduction copies its own contours only, which you isolated and named finally—you—you—you of an incoherent—you—you—you you you you you!

(Yes, yes, yes, yes, yes!)

Oh, face it, do face it, ladies and gentlemen. Here is a man in front of us at long last, ready to answer to that question he asks himself again and again and again, which is—question number one, finally—What gives this man that kick, that emotional kick? Because we know already, very little remains that enables this man to receive a genuine emotional kick. Indeed—if anything remains, it will be something hard to identify, of course—but perhaps—a certain quality of light. At best, yes.

And that's all that remains. I'm afraid that's all that remains, he says. A certain quality of light.

Here is a man who might well testify with sadness in his voice that a certain quality of light is the one thing left on this earth that gives this man that emotional kick. And this is not a sad reduction of possibilities, however, because for this man, this is a fact, just a fact, devoid of emotion—among other facts, emotional or otherwise.

But he tries, just once more, to capture something very elu-

sive in the realm of sensation. Here is a man, sad after all—
that a certain quality of light is the one thing left on earth
that gives him indeed that emotional kick—and this man
reflects upon this light and understands his sadness seems to
be sadness not to himself really, but only sadness to others
who never receive that particular emotional kick, but rather
receive their own, private emotional kicks from other
things—equally sad from his perspective—such as experience with other people.

Such as—sexual, yes—or emotional, yes—or other kinds of
experiences, yes. But as a matter of fact, for this man here,
focused on like a quivering cloud of brightness, covering his
own eyes because even that last remaining source of emotional caress, even that does exhaust itself for this man.

And there is no longer any real "'kick" for this man, which
is not upsetting for this man, rest assured, even though he
understands that something about his visionary qualities
generally upsets the people surrounding him.

And he turns towards them and smiles to himself only and
wonders—"Why be upset?"—when all he ever tries for himself, and for other people even more than for himself, is to
try and try and try and try thinking his way out of this major
dilemma of his own life, which is the fact, the dilemma, ultimately, that he cannot locate the real dilemma, which is hidden—and this is very important. This man knows that he is
upset, but he cannot discover—not just the reason for this
upset—but even the very feeling itself.

Oh—he is upset—this he knows—but without being able to
really FEEL that upset inside himself as a feeling inside himself or inside the people around him. It is as if that feeling,
which somehow he knows to be his true feeling, is, in fact,
hiding from him.

And this is a very peculiar sensation for this man, who concludes that the only way this can be dealt with is by trying to cast himself into life, in such a way that this hidden upset will more clearly reveal its location to his so-called consciousness.

Invoking, somehow, that hidden upset to surface within his life like an island in the midst of some endless ocean—some clear image, developed by the exotic chemicals of some very specific "throw of oneself" into life—that he does push himself into—like seizing himself by the scruff of his own neck to thrust forward his own, unprotected self amidst the rest of us, ladies and gentlemen, into a confusion of his own making, of course.

But why would this man want to spin himself into such confusion?

No one else can answer such a question in his place. All one can say is that this man—pick him from a crowd of many, please—this man is seized by some necessity which, because of its necessity, this man welcomes.

Why does this man welcome such a thing? Because it offers the promise of a certain intensity. Which this man may live to regret, of course, just as you and I and others much like ourselves, ladies and gentlemen, do regret so many of the adventures into which we are launched by the promise of a certain sweetness.

But can this man be blamed, can this man be responsible, for confusions caused by a special—well, if this man is surrounded by a special—aura?

Yes, this aura—this is what this man has been told. Indeed, here is a man who has been told again and again and again, by one of these special people who claim to register such subtle yet powerful fields of energy, things—even though no such person can be reliably identified in this room at this

precise moment—yet—"These people"—one of these people
who pick up on such things—and one uses the word "these"
whether or not such a one is actually present in the flesh,
because one wants to feel close to that possible network—
that network of possibility, above all else.

And the possibility is that here is a man who places his consciousness at some distance from himself, in the vain hope
of seeing such an aura surrounding his own distanced per-
sona. But the convincing representation of that aura—ah—
this rests in limbo. Which means unverifiable, even though
intuited.

So why does this man believe that each of you, individual
ladies and gentlemen, gives assent to the notion that his own
person is amazing to you?

Unless this is a man, in fact, less than one hundred percent
sincere in the postulations of his own amazingness—
but postulated, nevertheless, as a provocation to begin with.
In spite of his anguished feeling that no one is provoked,
in fact. So do think of this, perhaps, as a possible—self-
provocation?

How does this work?

Ahhh. Here is the center of this man's secret. A kind of . . .
aura—indeed. And exposing oneself to the powerful aura of
his self-provocation—
          (*Phone rings.*)

          (Hello? . . . Hello?)
                    (*Hangs up, other almost collapses.*)
          (What's wrong?)

Ah. You've broken the connection, my friend
          (Hello? Hello?)

It's too late, my friend, much too late. Here amongst us is a man who is very, very sorry about what's happened, which is, of course, something that hasn't happened.

> (I've had it, I've really had it now.)
> (*Music, drinks.*)

Ah, you understand now? Now you understand?
(This is the truth, this is the truth speaking)
Right in front of our very eyes, ladies and gentlemen—one or two brief moments, enough to contain a whole lifetime of experience. A wise spiritual teacher, disguised as a common day laborer, ripping off the very last layer of his disguise, until—there it is, naked and resplendent—I won't name it, but—what a wonderful disguise, allowing everything to continue as before.

In other words, ladies and gentlemen, an amazing end to an amazing adventure. But don't cry, please, don't cry real tears in public, ladies and gentlemen—just because you've joined with this man in stripping off such final layers of wisdom and sensitivity with which you did hope to transform life into something—well—minimally endurable?

Here. Still. Forever. Testifying to what can no longer be believed, is a man offering us powerful assurance that things amazing and similar have happened within his own endured existence. Because for many years what was most potent and poignant inside this man was the memory often evoked in certain images, certain vistas glimpsed on turning a corner, or upon lifting the edge of a curtain—of a certain . . . sensory perfume. The memory of the light, the atmosphere in which certain privileged perspectives of someplace imagined or experienced were, literally, drenched. Yes, to a certain street corner at a certain hour of a certain day, layered by a certain atmosphere. Perhaps even hundreds of these potent memory traces. Who can say how many, flashing upon one unexpectedly, their poignancy holding a secret, doubled in power through one's very inability to grasp what that secret, deeper than evocativeness itself, really was?

Ah, but here is a man who can testify that for himself, finally, that for the last six months—less than that? More than that? No matter. The evocative perfume of atmosphere, has alas, evaporated. All magic places, all images of time and atmosphere, these no longer ravish this exhausted human being. Because perhaps from dwelling upon them in excess, this man has drained them, or eaten them away, as one says, without even knowing how to prepare oneself for a proper farewell.

All this man does know finally, is that these most potent, unopenable treasures no longer provide nourishment, but now seem to him empty husks of memory, towards which he gazes with empty, sad eyes.

So imagine, please, the sorrow linked to that emptiness. That emptiness installing itself at the center of that heretofore beautiful, and therefore almost always invisible. . . .

Ah, this man, this man, this man—staring deep into the painful emptiness of all love disappearing. But notice, notice, no final lurch forward to grasp what, if saved, might just perhaps, rekindle—inside this man—inside of whom beauty disintegrates—?

Not exactly. Here is a man who truly believes that when beauty vanishes, then—mind, new wounded mind does tumble forward painfully in some other sense. Evolution of some volatile and dangerous energy, which energy—name it emotional, name it psychic—name it previously invested in oh such beautiful images from this man's treasured past, but this energy must, this man believes, this very minute— secretly—reinvest in some unexplored corner of mental life. HIS mental life, of course!

—But which door—which door opens upon this still

unnamed room towards which this man is traveling this very
minute—now? His necessary adventure, of course, rediscov-
ering that hidden room no longer in memory, somehow—

(The room of radios, the room of radios.)

Because this man has outgrown gentle, refined memory.
Uncovering what hides, now in some still-granular someplace else—not yet coagulated into image or object—that's
what this man believes. The only hint he has being that
when eyes close and no image arises in that blackness, but
only some field of black, seeded vortex particles of tiny
blackness—and this man's entire body seems re-invested as
a thinking machine he knows not yet how to use.

(Pause)

Well—. Here is a man who doesn't really—know what it is
that he intuits.

(This is the truth, this is the truth speaking.)

But if this man does have the URGE to say something—and
he does. Or the urge even, to babble only to himself—and he
does. Then this man DOES have a most desperate responsibility which is to let all things gush forward from the mouth.
And this man says, "I do think that I should do this thing! I
think that I should do this very thing! This very thing!"

　(All sing　　"Get your coat and get your hat
　　　　　　　　Leave your worries on the doorstep.
　　　　　　　　Life can be so sweet
　　　　　　　　On the sunny side of the street.

　　　　　　　　Can't you hear that pitter-pat
　　　　　　　　That happy tune is your step.
　　　　　　　　Stardust at my feet
　　　　　　　　On the sunny side of the street.")

THE END

**BENITA
CANOVA**

Benita Canova. Produced by the Ontological-Hysteric Theater at the Ontological Theater at St. Mark's Church, New York City. January–March 1998. Written, directed, and designed by Richard Foreman.

BENITA CANOVA: Joanna P. Adler
HER CHIEF RIVAL: Christina Campanella
BETTY: Susan Tierney
MADAME: David Greenspan

A bourgeois room in Paris, suggesting the nineteen forties, bedecked with Oriental rugs and brocade hangings. The walls are covered in striped wallpaper and pictures; Oriental fans and masks create a claustrophobic clutter. Several big, hooded lights hang in the room. At the front of the stage, a striped horizontal exercise bar, and along the back wall a low bench, covered with pillows. A few Hebrew letters also peek out from behind other decorative features. A glass wall separates the stage from the audience, though there are gaps in that wall.

Throughout the play, loops of music rise and fall continually, and various bells and thuds and crashes punctuate the action, or frame certain words of dialogue. In addition, the dialogue is often punctuated by the sound of a coin being tossed into a glass bowl, where it vibrates for a second or two, as if to suggest the figures on the stage are unreal porcelain figures—tap them to sound their hollowness.

As music rises (Josephine Baker singing "J'ai deux amours"), a deep voice is heard intoning "Benita Canova, Benita Canova" as many young girls enter slowly and assume provocative positions around the periphery of the room. One girl climbs on the bench and lifts her dress as another begins stitching a small appliqué rose on the seat of her underpants. All of the girls are wearing kneesocks and either soft red flannel jackets or vests. Some of them also wear little black French sailor hats with black pom-poms. Throughout the play, the girls continually fondle and play with one another in the background.

From one side of the stage, MADAME leads BENITA CANOVA into the room. MADAME is dressed in a severe black dress and cardigan sweater, with a small red pill-box hat on top of a mass of thick black hair. A lace handkerchief dangles from her hand throughout the play. Her face is taut with a hint of a threatening smile. She is, in fact, a man, quite well disguised. BENITA CANOVA wears a schoolgirl jumper over a white blouse and kneesocks. A red carnation is in her hair, which is cropped, and a yellow Jewish star is sewn on her dress. They come to a stop, and MADAME takes BENITA's arm. She speaks, in a heavy Middle European accent.

MADAME: Possibly, just possibly that feeling is mutual, my dear.

BENITA: What feeling?

MADAME: But unfortunately, animals—dead or alive—never conceptualize QUITE the way human beings conceptualize—

CHRISTINA: *(A tall girl with bows in her hair, who sucks a lollipop)* I can well imagine she must have been speaking about herself, Madame. And as far as animals are concerned, well, she doesn't consider herself either a dead gorilla or a live gorilla.

MADAME: Of course she was speaking about herself. But it would be very easy to imagine that even a dead gorilla imagines itself a mere—sleeping gorilla. And a sleeping gorilla imagines waking up perhaps, once upon a time, to do very bad things to little ladies, such that even little ladies may find it impossible to imagine.

(The music rises, and then a bright light flashes, and everyone except MADAME screams and cowers momentarily in pain.)

By which I do NOT mean to imply that such a sound-asleep gorilla is in this way CONCEPTUALIZING on the same level that a human being may possibly, possibly conceptualize!

BENITA: *(Whirls, then holds her head)* Her goddamned fucking brain is working against her, right in here.

CHRISTINA: Awesome.

BENITA: Microscopic rodents—eating away at her head muscles.

MADAME: Try riding the wave of such a wonderful catastrophe—little Israelite.

BETTY: *(A simpering blonde, wearing a little red pillbox hat like the MADAME's; she hisses quietly—)* "Benita Canova."

BENITA: Catastrophe: an easy word for a much more ambiguous situation.

CHRISTINA: *(As all the girls surround BENITA)* Oh—look at this, little Benita Canova's brain doing bad things to her facial expression.

BENITA: She can't find her facial expression at the moment.

MADAME: Immeasurable, my dear.

CHRISTINA: Oh yeah, a variety of shapes and sizes.

BENITA: *(Slowly walks away from the group)* She doesn't think her facial expression comes in different sizes, because her brain is telling her the size and shape of her facial expression is always indeterminate—and she goes back and forth inside her facial expressions like a hungry animal in deep trouble.

BETTY: *(Mockingly whispers)* "Help—"

CHRISTINA: *(Coming up behind* BENITA, *grabbing her hair, and twisting)* Oh, pleazie-weezie, just for me—start whispering "Help!"

BENITA: *(Breaking free)* Not yet. Try reading her facial expression.

CHRISTINA: *(Mockingly, as she licks her lollipop)* Wow, that really turns me on.

BENITA: Okay, stick around for dessert.

(She quickly pulls up CHRISTINA's *skirt.)*

CHRISTINA: Hands off, bitch!

BENITA: *(Turning away and holding her head again)* Brain— get back inside my head. Please. Please.

CHRISTINA: *(As the others leave)* Whenever I hear you saying "please," I can't seem to help myself.

BENITA: Oh, she didn't really want you to stick around, so that must have been her brain talking behind her back. Notice anything special?

CHRISTINA: Like what? What should she notice?

BENITA: The tip of her tongue, maybe? It comes to a sharp point just like a little knife.

(She sticks out her tongue and points to it, then she whirls to see the other girls in the doorway, pointing to their own tongues. She runs to push them out, but they hold up their hands and display little swastikas in their palms. She stops and turns away from them.)

BENITA: She was just showing you her tongue. She doesn't know WHAT she's saying to herself.

CHRISTINA: But that's so obvious—up till now—you haven't really been talking.

MADAME: *(Who has entered, carrying a bouquet of roses)* Let's be fair to Benita Canova. She HAS been talking. What's more, she's lured the rest of us out of our own silence.

(CHRISTINA lunges at her, making a cat's aggressive "meow!" But BENITA evades her claws.)

CHRISTINA: I don't think so, Madame. I think my own response is one hundred percent automatic.

BENITA: Obviously, that's the way you fulfill yourself.

CHRISTINA: Auto—*(Clicks her tongue)*—matically?

BENITA: Maybe—maybe auto—*(Clicks her tongue)*—matically!

(BETTY presents BENITA with a paper bag. BENITA looks in and pulls out a dead fish, and the other girls all meow! and kneel on the floor. MADAME has a long classroom pointer stick with which she indicates BENITA.)

MADAME: Without knowing how, my dear—you ask us to verify that which gives the ILLUSION—

(BENITA tosses the fish to the girls on the floor. They snarl like hungry cats.)

—of having no future. And so we shall indeed verify, that, which gives the illusion of having no future.

BENITA: Okay. You call it illusion—

(CHRISTINA sticks the fish up under BENITA's dress.)

BETTY: Skirts up.

BENITA: —So she says, inside every illusion, she's imagining vast activity.

(She lets the fish drop to the floor.)

CHRISTINA: Pathetic little asshole, how do you possibly imagine vast activity?

BENITA: *(As CHRISTINA dangles the fish in front of BENITA's face)* She lunges at it.

CHRISTINA: What do you lunge at?

BENITA: She lunges.

(BENITA grabs CHRISTINA's hair, and both scream and fight. BENITA gets CHRISTINA in a headlock as they strain against each other, but are immobile.)

She's a hole in something.

MADAME: *(Very calmly)* —Not necessarily my dear.

BENITA: *(Applying more pressure)* She's a hole in something!

MADAME: *(Deciding to lecture the group)* Depending upon what constitutes the medium in which this hole occurs, well—this hole is either a void hole—

(*MADAME holds a little silver flask from which she takes a sip as the two girls resume their struggle.*)

—or a solid hole. Does she understand me?

BETTY: The void part is always understandable, Madame.

MADAME: (*Speaking loudly, to be heard over their struggling*) This is the explanation for the solid part. If the medium in which one makes a hole is in fact a medium that is constituted by nothing real—

(*BENITA and CHRISTINA fall to the floor with a scream and roll, then separate, provocatively out of breath. MADAME is therefore able to continue quietly.*)

A VOID, in fact—then the hole in such a void must be—well, the opposite—a solid something. Because a scooped-out—void inside a void—well, the mind boggles, which is to say—its rhythms, boggled—coagulate.

BETTY: For such ideas, I think one should be put in jail, Madame.

MADAME: (*Turning to call on BENITA for an answer*) Why? Please tell me why, please?

BENITA: Because! She suddenly has the image of a mind so ravished, it goes bouncing back and forth inside her body like a tornado that makes her smash into everything in sight. Very beautiful in a sense!—but very destructive, hence jailable.

(*She starts to leave, but CHRISTINA grabs her hair. Though she escapes, BETTY throws her against the wall, and she bounces away and falls on the bench.*)

MADAME: You see how advantageous it would have been if the little Israelite had simply remained silent?

CHRISTINA: Too late for that.

(Some of the girls have returned, carrying what appears to be a small fluffy pink quilt with leather straps, and they proceed to imprison BENITA inside this homemade straitjacket.)

BENITA: No—stop doing this to me—no!

MADAME: Is that particular no in fact a yes?

CHRISTINA: I don't think she's in a position to answer complicated questions, Madame.

BETTY: She should try to say everything—

BENITA: However, she decides to say nothing. Actions instead of words.

(Held tight in her puffy straitjacket, she looks around the room, runs to an empty spot of carpet, and whirls until CHRISTINA catches her from behind and holds her still. A short bell tune is heard on a xylophone.)

Okay. She's in jail now. But she's still dangerous.

BETTY: That could be neutralized.

(BETTY is now being helped into her own straitjacket, as an electronic tone rises and falls.)

BENITA: Why do you do that on purpose?

BETTY: *(All wrapped up tight)* Am I more powerful now because I can't reach things? I do think I'm more powerful.

(Pause.) Don't you get it—?

BENITA: Okay. If she reaches for something, that makes something change immediately because she reaches for it, so she never gets what she reaches for.

BETTY: Do it anyway. Reach for it!

BENITA: Haven't you noticed? Her arms are missing!

CHRISTINA: *(Unwrapping BETTY)* I don't think so.

BENITA: *(Running into the wall in frustration)* Oww!

> *(The electronic tone rises, and BETTY stuffs her own straitjacket up between BENITA's legs.)*

She didn't get it, right? She failed.

MADAME: No—very successful, my dear.

BENITA: It's not working.

MADAME: Benita Canova hasn't realized, perhaps, that I, too, experience similar frustrations, my dear, on certain days of the week.

> *(CHRISTINA undoes the straps, and BENITA's straitjacket falls to the floor.)*

BENITA: Okay, she's going to lunge at something, but nobody believes her. *(Takes a step forward, then freezes)* Where was she a minute ago?

> *(Most of the others leave slowly, but CHRISTINA takes the straightjacket and holds it up. BENITA turns, looks at it, then walks up and presses her body against it as CHRISTINA wraps it around her and straps her in again.)*

You know, she feels somehow constricted.

MADAME: Then, by all means, take it off.

BENITA: Take off what?

MADAME: Do you believe you suffer from invisibility, my dear?

(Others have reentered, and drop playing cards over BENITA. CHRISTINA is helped into a straitjacket of her own.)

BENITA: Nothing surprises her.

(There is the sound of somebody breathing a deep breath. MADAME holds a stick with a little butterfly at the end. She flutters it around, then burns the butterfly over the flame of a little candelabra.)

But she doesn't know if it's herself turning invisible, or somebody else.

CHRISTINA: C'mon, little Jewish pancake, take my hand.

BENITA: How can she do that? —Plus, she won't.

CHRISTINA: Why not?

BENITA: Blame it on her so-called theoretical invisibility, please.

(Others take off BENITA's straitjacket as a breath is heard, then CHRISTINA begins singing in an operatic voice.)

CHRISTINA: *(Singing)* "Cipher, cipher, who's got the cipher?"

BENITA: What's a cipher?

CHRISTINA: Oh, she doesn't know—some kind of key, maybe?

(Others have carried in children's blocks with letters on them. They drop them on the floor, and somebody points at one with a stick.)

BENITA: You use that word like a fucking professional.

CHRISTINA: Well, fucking thank you. I was just trying to see if I could unlock something.

BENITA: *(Lifting one of the blocks)* Oh, you mean C-I-P-H-E-R? Thank God she doesn't know how to spell that alphabet kind of shit. *(Tosses the block back to the floor.)*

BETTY: *(Sniveling to herself)* I don't know what to do with my hands now that I'm not wearing that pink puffy stuff.

BENITA: Try putting them in your pockets.

CHRISTINA: Stupid, she's a girl, she doesn't have pockets.

BENITA: Try putting them under your dress—at least they'll be invisible or something.

BETTY: Once upon a time, knowing what to do with my hands was no problem.

MADAME: Sad to say, ladies, empty human hands no longer provide the self-indulgent rewards of such "long ago and far away," or such "never, never, never"—

(There is a thud, and MADAME whirls.)

Excuse me, please!

(She races to the bench where BENITA sits, as a deep voice over the tape repeats "Excuse me please, excuse me please," and the others run from the room. CHRISTINA sings and slowly crosses the stage to disappear as

MADAME brusquely grabs BENITA by the hair and forces her down, across her lap on her back, her legs spread slightly.)

CHRISTINA: *(Singing to romantic chords strummed on the piano)*

The girl who tried to kiss herself
Discovered when alone
Her lips had turned to razor blades
Her kisses turned to stone.

(As CHRISTINA drifts across stage singing, MADAME is lifting BENITA's dress and slowly advancing her hand up to BENITA's crotch.)

She sliced her body carefully
And nailed the stones inside.
She threw herself against a wall
To prove she hadn't died.

(As CHRISTINA disappears, BENITA rolls off MADAME's lap to the floor. There is the sound of a breath being taken, and BENITA is on her feet.)

MADAME: *(Rising slowly and coming forward as BENITA backs away to the wall)* Tell me, please—the name of this "thing" I reach toward—whenever it slips from my fingers, one last time—and I lose my balance one last time—though losing my balance has kept me heretofore alive—but—do I mean alive, really? I think not.

BENITA: What could you possibly mean, Madame, if you don't mean alive?

MADAME: Ah—! *(Uses her twisted handkerchief around BENITA's neck to pin her back against the wall)*—risky business!

BENITA: One last time?

MADAME: Yes. Did you in fact hear me say "one last time"?

(The other girls are peeking into the room.)

BENITA: Yes, she in fact heard you say "one last time."

MADAME: And I realize, in retrospect, it may not be, this time—one last time after all. *(Relaxes her hold and pats BENITA's face with the handkerchief.)* Risky business, my dear—

BENITA: Well, she knows that.

MADAME: *(As faraway a recording is heard of Josephine Baker singing "J'ai deux amours")* You know that?

BENITA: Of course she knows that.

(The girls have all started dancing with one another. BETTY dances with BENITA.)

MADAME: Risky business—clutching at the edge of something precarious—

BENITA: Letting it slip from her grasp on purpose?

MADAME: Not true. It never slips from our grasp, it simply eludes us.

BENITA: Is that built into your modus operandus, Madame?

MADAME: Wrong: I have no modus operandus. Find it, if you believe otherwise.

(She swoops out of the room, and the girls follow her, giggling. BENITA starts to follow, then thinks better of it and backs away against the wall. There is a thud, and as the music changes to the sound of a clarinet wailing a soft Yiddish folk tune, MADAME and the girls run back into the room aggressively. MADAME stops in front of

BENITA *and, very slowly, offers her a hand.* BENITA *hesitates, then comes forward to take* MADAME'*s hand. They link arms, staring into each other's eyes.)*

CHRISTINA: One person in this room evidently has a modus operandus.

(The girls join hands in a circle.)

Who is that so-called person?

MADAME: *(To* BENITA, *as the girls circle)* We simply use our imagination, my dear.

*(*MADAME *sweeps out of the room, and the girls break their circle to run after her, but the pressure inside* MADAME'*s head builds, and she falls to the carpet holding her head and shouting "Hey!" The girls turn back to her.)*

BENITA: *(Quiet now)* Are we leaving her alone with her modus operandus?

CHRISTINA: What makes the little asshole think she can change the subject whenever she wants?

BENITA: True, she notices in the immediate past, she changes the subject without realizing she's changing the subject—but she doesn't think that's a character flaw.

BETTY: You don't have enough character flaws to keep anybody interested for ten minutes even.

BENITA: Ah—that's because you get CONFUSED whenever she changes subjects.

CHRISTINA: Right, it's the moment of truth, sweetie.

BENITA: Changing the subject?

CHRISTINA: No. It's been the same subject for a long time now.

(The girls slowly group themselves in a clump, confronting BENITA.)

Guess what. We're about to divide ourselves into two equal teams—

BENITA: They won't be equal.

CHRISTINA: *(Putting a hand out)* Yes they will—with a handshake to seal the bargain.

BENITA: She's not interested in touching that clammy hand.

CHRISTINA: But you don't even know what happens next.

(BENITA is sitting, and CHRISTINA comes and crouches over her, straddling her legs.)

A rough-and-tumble game of field hockey. Oh, nobody gets hurt seriously. A few bruises—a scraped knee.

(MADAME sneaks into the room in the rear, listening.)

Maybe something bad happens to a nose. But nothing serious. Fun for both of us.

MADAME: Did I hear "both of us"?

BETTY: Both—everybody, I suppose?

CHRISTINA: We are on the verge, Madame—ready to explode with naughty words. Forgive us in advance.

MADAME: But there's nothing to forgive.

BENITA: Protected by her own private and personal god, she speaks.

(Three loud knocks are heard. The girls scream and run to the corners of the room in fear.)

CHRISTINA: *(Recovering, irritated)* Oh? Is your own personal GOD knocking down the door? I hope not—

BETTY: I don't think a God without even a face offers anybody much protection.

BENITA: Really. Isn't that an unusual opinion?

(She faces them and concentrates in a special way. Her face grows red, and the muscles of her neck strain, and suddenly BETTY falls to the floor and writhes in pain.)

CHRISTINA: *(Blaming BENITA)* Stop changing the subject, asshole! *(Turns to BETTY who is still moaning on the floor.)* Stop that! This is not part of my fucking reality.

(She storms out of the room, followed by the others.)

BENITA: Well, she knows that, asshole, so for that reason, start filling in the blanks!

(Pause. She is alone. She holds her head.)

Hey, there is a blank me someplace, and it digs into the middle of her brain like a hungry animal with an invisible face.

MADAME: Visible on the wall, striped like a prison, you are trying to penetrate, my dear?

BENITA: Suppose my reflection were invisible?

MADAME: Do you mean would I still fall down and worship it?

BENITA: Are you worshiping something, Madame?

MADAME: I don't know, but I'm certainly worshiping something now. Let me give you a kiss.

BENITA: You mean for sex, Madame?

MADAME: No, I don't think I mean that. A kiss of peace, perhaps.

BENITA: What the fuck is that?

MADAME: Find out, my dear.

BENITA: Am I destined to betray you?

MADAME: Please try.

BENITA: I don't know how.

MADAME: Then something's definitely lacking, my dear.

(The girls slowly reenter the room, all carrying field hockey sticks and wearing black sailor caps. They surround BENITA CANOVA threateningly.)

CHRISTINA: Just maybe, maybe you should pray for us, asshole.

BETTY: Maybe you should pray for me especially. Because my make-believe name is Betty and Betty's supposed to be the tough one.

BENITA: Tough and pretty. How many votes do I get?

CHRISTINA: Look in a mirror, sweetie.

BENITA: Too late, 'cause my mirror's got a big crack right down the middle.

(She lifts her skirt and sticks her behind out at them. The girls all shout "Hey!" and as Mexican music explodes, CHRISTINA sings loudly as the others go to support themselves on the wall as they aggressively wipe their feet on the carpet, in rhythm to the music.)

CHRISTINA: *(Sings)*
Bad girls, dirty girls!
Kiss yourself, beat yourself!
Sticks and stones, breaking bones!
Evil names, dirty words!

(BENITA is writing her name on the wall in white chalk.)

MADAME: Erase that—erase that! How dare you cover that wall with filth!

(The music stops.)

BENITA: Time passes, nobody'll notice—

MADAME: Erase that!

BENITA: It'll vanish by itself. *(She turns and starts out of the room.)*

MADAME: Do not turn your back on me, Benita Canova! She turns her back on me. Punishment is required, ladies, and this is what I propose . . . Two teams are chosen, then, following a pause for suitable preparations—a rough-and-tumble game of field hockey, my dear. Scratches and bruises, possible results—washed away by tears, possibly—

BENITA: *(Having returned with her own hockey stick)* It hurts now, thank you.

(There is a flash of light, and the girls scream and hide their eyes.)

CHRISTINA: All she ever thinks about is saying her prayers.

BENITA: There's nothing wrong in that.

MADAME: I see something wrong.

BENITA: Would it be wrong to try and protect myself— *(Brandishes her hockey stick.)*—with this dangerous piece of wood?

MADAME: Of course it would be wrong—but that must never stand in the way of someone named—Benita Canova!

CHRISTINA: *(Leaning sensually over BENITA)* Oh Benita Canova —if I, for instance, am not your friend, and I am certainly not your friend, this could also be a source of energy—get it?

(A bell rings several times, during which a voice is heard singing in German, music-hall-style, "Fräulein, my little Fräulein"—at first faint, and then louder, and louder until it is deafening. The girls close in on BENITA, and suddenly all the hockey sticks are in play, and they struggle in a tight knot against her, everybody screaming; until she finally breaks through the crowd and CHRISTINA charges to the other side of the room.)

CHRISTINA: *(Screaming over the music)* It's true, it's true! If I am not your friend, shithead—this could also be a source of great energy for both of us!

(The music stops.)

BENITA: Did Benita Canova do something that frightened somebody?

CHRISTINA: When Benita Canova says something, it's never as believable as this.

(They all run to the exercise bar. Holding on to it, they mock her by squealing, falsetto, "Ohhh-ohh—" and lowering themselves to the carpet in mock fear.)

MADAME: Dear Benita Canova, do you really think your ancient and venerable God is speaking to you from the inside of a world from which he himself has totally withdrawn? Oh—leaving hints in things, of course. But his withdrawal being, you understand, just another make-believe adventure—like your own make-believe adventure.

BENITA: *(As ravishing music rises and MADAME whirls ecstatically)* Okay, you really think it's God she's after?

(As the beautiful music rises, the girls come screaming and press BENITA into the wall, as MADAME continues her romantic whirling. Then BENITA escapes and runs to confront the dancing MADAME.)

Stop that, Madame!

(The music cuts, but MADAME still whirls, singing to herself.)

Stop that, Madame!

(MADAME waltzes to the bench, and she and BENITA sit next to each other.)

Okay. She's still trying to find out, of course, but she doesn't think it's GOD she's after.

MADAME: Please, don't let your wonderful illusions vanish, Benita Canova! Because without your illusions, you will be forced to see things both as they are and as they are not—totally without separation.

(Once again, MADAME suddenly pulls BENITA by her hair, and whips her down over her lap on her back, staring up at MADAME. The girls leave the room.)

And this may be too much for such as yourself to assimilate. Because the truth, after all, hides in very strange places. Do you agree?

BENITA: Well, let's just say—the world tries to be beautiful, but it fails.

MADAME: Again, please.

(Soft Yiddish music is heard.)

BENITA: Let's just say—the world's going in one direction, and she's going in another.

MADAME: Again, please!

(MADAME drops her dangling handkerchief, and her hand hovers between BENITA's thighs.)

BENITA: You dropped your handkerchief, Madame.

MADAME: Don't be concerned about other people's dirty handkerchiefs, Benita Canova. Concern yourself rather with things within my power. Know that I have the means to make you happy.

(Her hand plants itself firmly on BENITA's crotch.)

BENITA: What means do you have—to make her?

MADAME: Be silent! Happiness, as you should certainly know by now, is unachievable.

BENITA: She doesn't know that! *(Rolls off MADAME's lap onto the carpet)* She herself has had moments of happiness.

MADAME: *(Rising)* Are you absolutely certain?

BENITA: She considers them—moments of happiness.

MADAME: Do you know the difference between what is and what is not possible?

BENITA: If she throws herself into violent activity, will you profit, Madame?

MADAME: *(Bending over her)* Each of us will profit, my dear.

(She turns and hobbles from the room. BENITA rises and shouts after her.)

BENITA: Explain yourself, Madame!

(Loud harpsichord music erupts and MADAME runs back into the room, leading the girls, who run to strike poses against the walls. Again, one of them stitches the underpants of another who stands on the bench. MADAME takes BENITA by the hand and, leading her across the room, explains with eyes blazing—)

MADAME: Find girls! Attractive girls who enjoy . . . physically attacking each other! —Eh? Eh? This—dear Benita Canova—was the content of the note, passed to me by the disheveled man with the mysterious white hair, muttering under his breath as he passed close by me, on my way to the hotel for an important rendezvous! *(Lowers her voice and steps slowly forward, alone, muttering to herself)* But—following his instructions, of course, I went into the room where the women were struggling with one another, and I could see limbs and faces discolored by scrapes and bruises. And at this— tremendous moment, I ran into the street, staring up into the total bowl of the empty sky, which was blank, and pure, like a field of white snow.

(There is a loud thud, and the girls all scream and cower as a deep voice intones, "Excuse me, please! Excuse me, please!)

CHRISTINA: Oh, I'm sorry, Madame, but the minute Benita Canova enters my fucking life—

BENITA: She never entered your life for even one minute.

(CHRISTINA slaps, scaring BENITA—and all the girls add an aggressive "Meow!")

MADAME: *(Chuckling to herself)* Little pussycats.

CHRISTINA: *(Bearing down on BENITA)* Multiple collisions between us, an unavoidable next step.

(All the girls, including BENITA, are lined up against the wall, and as CHRISTINA starts singing to ecstatic music, they all start masturbating themselves and rubbing their backs against the wall.)

So I decided, and she decided when I decided . . .

(As the music builds, they moan ecstatically and slide to the floor. Then they rise slowly and repeat the same thing. The lights are very dim, and MADAME now holds a leather dog leash. BENITA comes forward, offering herself, and MADAME clips the leash onto a black velvet ribbon that BENITA wears around her neck. As the girls slide to the floor again, MADAME whirls BENITA around the room.)

MADAME: The young woman I was dreaming about entered my field of vision, of course, and I whispered, "Oh, you are never really my friend, my dear." *(Hauls off and slaps* BENITA *across the face.)* Bitch!

*(*BENITA *spits directly in* MADAME*'s face.* MADAME *touches her wet face ecstatically.)*

And this was a source of great energy for me! Can she believe this, believe this? Believe this! Because, to further confound my expectations in the most provocative way possible, she presented me with a terrible gift.

BENITA: What a wonderful idea.

MADAME: And as I reached for those goodies with trembling hands, her very smile sliced into my heart because in accepting that gift, I, in turn, confounded the expectations of her entire degenerate race. Because that's the kind of person I was—an enigma!

(A human-sized gorilla has crept slowly into the room behind BENITA*'s back. She turns now and sees the gorilla, who wears a golden crown and carries a small gold medallion dangling from its fist.* BENITA *runs from the room as the other girls creep across to surround the gorilla.)*

And the gift, so innocent, was an implied threat, of course. A small gold disk with all the forbidden letters of the alphabet embossed on one side. And I whispered hoarsely to myself—Is my own name discoverable amongst these grotesque letters?

(The gorilla lowers the medallion to the carpet and slowly leaves the room as the girls go down on the carpet to study it.)

And I looked at the other side of the disk, which was completely empty. "This side is even more pregnant," I said to myself. And I held the blank side of the disk up to the mirror, and its nothingness was reversed in the mirror. And I was tumbled by a wave of intellectual emotion—*(Slowly falls to the carpet.)*—as I realized that nothingness reversed—induced in me a range of possibilities—I had not the means to articulate to myself.

BETTY: Does this mean—we're losing touch with reality, Madame?

MADAME: Of course we are losing touch with reality. That's our one point of contact with reality—stupid girl.

(**BENITA** *comes slowly into the room, carrying a small box wrapped as a gift. She now, also, has long dark hair and is wearing a red pillbox hat, much like* **MADAME**.)

MADAME: *(Looking up from the floor, languorously, as the xylophone tune is heard)* What does the little whore want from us this time?

BETTY: Are you in love with someone, Madame?

MADAME: Not at all—!

CHRISTINA: Not even me, Madame?

MADAME: *(Stops and thinks, then shrugs)* Well—why not? And through you, of course—the whole WORLD, possibly!

BETTY: Wait a minute, are we still out of touch with reality?

MADAME: I hope not.

BETTY: *(As all the girls jump to their feet)* That means you've been lying to us!

MADAME: *(Struggling awkwardly to her feet)* I stand corrected, of course!

(She straightens out her back as the xylophone tune plays again, and Yiddish music is heard.)

I do hope—we are indeed out of touch with reality, because—were we in TOUCH with something so tremendous . . .

(The girls are looking up into the light and slowly collapse.)

—Well—possibly we would die from such contact. And would we not be, then—dead indeed?

(MADAME slowly adjust her focus and sees BENITA holding out her wrapped gift.)

BENITA: It's a surprise.

MADAME: *(Taking the box)* The little Israelite always surprises us. Do you betray us my dear?

BENITA: Not yet.

MADAME: What does the little whore want from us this time?

BENITA: What does she want? A knife, Madame?

MADAME: The better to slice you, my dear.

BENITA: A pair of dark eyeglasses?

MADAME: The better not to see you.

BENITA: *(Lifting one of the girl's skirts to check on her underwear)* Sewing equipment?

MADAME: *(Lifting BENITA's skirt and putting a hand on her behind)* My hands are unsteady, of course—

BENITA: *(Whirling, taking MADAME's withdrawn hand)* Of course, hands tremble slightly. But could she trouble you . . . for a drum?

MADAME: A drum? My God—a DRUM?

BENITA: A drum, please. She'd like to make some unpleasant noises.

MADAME: And for such purposes—I'm asked to provide the little Israelite with a drum?

(One of the girls rolls a big bass drum into the room.)

CHRISTINA: Where did that fucking drum come from?

BETTY: It's big for a drum.

MADAME: She holds to her principles, ladies.

(BENITA takes a drumstick and whacks the drum once.)

This is why she suffers. Her sex, ladies—a recognizable part of her personality.

CHRISTINA: Her sex, Madame? She hides her sex in OTHER things, Madame.

BENITA: Let us count the many ways.

(BENITA starts hitting the drum in rhythm to the Yiddish music that rises. Most of the other girls get in line behind her and they all march out of the room. CHRISTINA remains, reaches under the bench, and pulls out something wrapped in a cloth. She holds it out to the audience, through a gap in the glass wall, whispering, "Try some, try some." The sound of the drum is still heard

offstage—and then it stops, and BENITA *runs in carrying a very small version of the same drum; she no longer has the long hair and pillbox hat.)*

CHRISTINA: *(Turning to* BENITA, *unwrapping the cloth, revealing a black wad)* It's the moment of truth, sweetie. Have a taste of this black, sticky stuff, please!

(Girls circle BENITA *with a big red cloth, which they drape over her.)*

BENITA: No way.

CHRISTINA: Take a bite, please.

BENITA: *(As another girl reveals a second wad, and others point to them with sticks)* What is totally forbidden is that we swallow forbidden substances that turn us into unclean things that give us pleasure instead of delivering us from a relatively unsatisfactory universe—like this universe—here, now, forever.

CHRISTINA: Oh? She wouldn't be the first of her persuasion to have tried something a little bit painful, you know.

MADAME: I don't think she understands, my dear.

BENITA: What doesn't she understand—?

(The xylophone tune is heard, and MADAME *is holding something under a white cloth. She whips the cloth away, revealing a well-polished meat cleaver.)*

MADAME: Watch carefully, please!

(Music rises as BENITA *spins, using the red cloth as a cape, and* MADAME *crosses up to a table where the girls have gathered, grabs* CHRISTINA's *hand, and chops it off*

with the meat cleaver. There are screams of horror and pain as CHRISTINA sinks to the floor, showing her forearm wrapped in a bloody cloth.)

What's just happened, my dear?

(The cloth is removed, and CHRISTINA's hand seems normal.)

Do explain with a suitably Hebraic complexification.

BENITA: It was a trick.

MADAME: Dig deeper, please.

BENITA: It was a momentarily effective illusion.

MADAME: Which you momentarily accepted, of course.

BENITA: She momentarily accepted it, yes.

MADAME: *(Holding one of the wads out to BENITA)* Dig deeper, please. On behalf of everyone else in this room I will ask you once again. But now understand that I am asking you for the very first time—to swallow a convincing portion of this cold, black sticky material!

(The music has risen and a voice is heard shouting out numbers in guttural French.)

BENITA: She won't swallow that stuff!

MADAME: *(Screaming)* But now I must really insist! Bite into it! Bite, bite!

ALL: BITE! BITE! BITE!

(She takes a bite of the wad and gags. Then others

bite and gag, and stumble about the room until they collapse to the floor. The music has stopped, and CHRISTINA *is holding her stomach and muttering, "Oh shit—." Then the deep voice is heard exclaiming, "Excuse me, please, excuse me!"* BENITA *and the girls look up for the source of the voice. A telephone rings a few times.)*

VOICE: Ah, Benita Canova, it seems, is open to new experiences of every possible variety. Is this, then, the heroic aspect of little Benita Canova? An aspect that so many of us—alas—might secretly desire, secretly to emulate, inside our own less-than-adventurous lives of routine and responsibility?

(The girls all giggle.)

Well, nobody should laugh, of course, at what they only partially understand.

(The girls object, whining—"Hey?"—feeling insulted by the voice.)

But then again, even laughter of the most self-indulgent, self-satisfied variety—even such laughter, pitiful as it may be, does provide one with a hint, inside its own self-confessed stupidity—

(Even more insulted, they rise with a loud "Hey—!")

—a hint of some much GREATER intensity of laughter.

(Organ music rises as all but BENITA *leave the room.)*

Which—though still intimately entwined with unavoidable human blindness—that promise of intensity—ah, hard to resist. Very hard to resist.

BENITA: *(Staring up at the source of the voice)* What intensities are we talking about?

MADAME: *(Entering with a large bouquet of roses)* Please don't think there's something special about this particular intensity, ladies.

(The others are returning, with CHRISTINA leading the gorilla back into the room.)

It's like all other intensities.

BENITA: What intensities are we talking about? *(Turns and sees the gorilla squatting on the carpet.)*

CHRISTINA: You can't figure it out, huh? Well, you just better open your eyes wide, Benita Canova, because here it is, right in front of our very eyes. The magic animal . . .

(BENITA gets as far away as she can from the gorilla, cowering on the floor so that she and the gorilla are taking very similar poses. But one of the girls comes and slowly lifts BENITA's legs in the air, while BENITA rolls on her back, offering her sex to the gorilla.)

BETTY: But like all magic animals—a little confused, maybe because not everybody in this room has the same kind of great-, great-, great-, great-grandmother.

CHRISTINA: *(As the gorilla slowly crosses to BENITA and begins to penetrate her sexually, while the others gather to watch)* No matter what happens, keep smiling, Benita Canova, you're having a very important experience, trust us for once.

BENITA: *(Beneath the gorilla)* Sure she trusts you—and what happens after she's trusted you.

CHRISTINA: It doesn't change things, asshole, you just "feel" better because you trusted somebody, even if you get screwed big time for trusting them, because on a certain level—you really want to get screwed—doesn't she?

(BENITA is moaning in sexual ecstasy. CHRISTINA has seated herself on the bench next to MADAME and bends backwards across MADAME's lap as MADAME firmly places her hand over her crotch.)

Doesn't she? Doesn't she?

(There is a thud as CHRISTINA rolls off MADAME's lap to the floor, and the other girls swoon to the floor, moaning; the gorilla rolls off BENITA, and the voice says, "Excuse me, please!" BENITA rises and runs downstage, supporting herself on the exercise bar.)

MADAME: Eyes fail—at the most crucial moments, of course.

BENITA: Not her problem, of course. Because she offers no resistance, she just stuffs herself with experience after experience after experience after experience.

MADAME: Yes—and you profit in this arena—amazing Benita Canova.

(MADAME slowly sinks to the floor, lying amidst the girls on the carpet as the gorilla rises and watches.)

BENITA: You mean she who profits is she who loses one tiny secret thing?

MADAME: We discover how CLOSE is our resemblance to one another—in all but the most trivial of details—

BENITA: You make distinctions that should not be made in public.

MADAME: "Benita Canova."

BENITA: *(Turns and looks at the gorilla)* Her real name? I don't think so.

MADAME: Oh please—doesn't she tell the truth about everyone in this room including myself? My real name is—Benita Canova, and I—I have lost it completely!

BENITA: Lost what completely? *(Slowly turns away from them and whispers to herself)* Lost what completely?

MADAME: *(Rising slowly from the floor)* Benita Canova, Benita Canova—

ALL: *(Joining in with MADAME and rising)* Benita Canova, Benita Canova, Benita Canova, Benita Canova—!

(There is a thud and a flash of light, all shield their eyes and scream, and the voice says, "Excuse me, please!")

MADAME: Forgive me, little Jewish Liebchen, I do remember having a name of my own—though now I do remember only having lost the name—"Benita Canova!"

BENITA: *(Runs up and pulls a rope that rings a loud bell)* I am Benita Canova.

MADAME: *(Whirling ecstatically)* I am Benita Canova, and I have lost it completely—! *(Races out of the room, but immediately reenters and squeaks in a falsetto voice)* "Benita Canova, Benita Canova, Benita Canova!"

CHRISTINA: *(Taunting BENITA as MADAME exits)*—"Benita Canova!"

BETTY: "Benita Canova!"

(All the girls laugh and run from the room. BENITA whirls and holds her head, then comes to a stop and whispers to herself.)

BENITA: Then we are all, in fact—named Benita Canova. And we have all, in fact—lost it completely—

(All the girls race back into the room, arms linked, one girl carrying a candelabra, while at the end of the line is CHRISTINA, in a bridal veil and sporting a big false nose.)

CHRISTINA: *(Waving her hands in the air and singing in a grotesque nasal voice)* "Benita Canova! Benita—"

MADAME: *(Racing into the room, carrying a large silver tray piled high with brownies. Everybody stops and looks at her. She grins crookedly, enjoying the surprise.)* I've baked brownies, ladies. Containing powerful drugs.

CHRISTINA: She no longer believes you, Madame.

MADAME: No, believe me. I'm totally FASCINATED by drugs, ladies—as long as they're sufficiently powerful. *(Offering the tray to BENITA)* Does that come as a surprise to you?

BENITA: She still believes in surprises.

(All look at (BENITA incredulously.)

She does, she is innocence itself—

MADAME: Of course, a most powerful drug, my dear.

BENITA: *(As the girls start to advance on her threateningly)* Everybody—stay away from me!

BETTY: *(Screaming from offstage)* Madame help, help, Madame. Look what I found hiding in the toilet, Madame. Look, look—!

(She runs onstage, lugging the gorilla, now dead [a stuffed replica, of course]. But she trips, and the gorilla falls on top of her, and she screams hysterically as the xylophone tune is heard and the others scream and run about, until BETTY crawls free and runs to the far wall, trying to catch her breath. BENITA picks up the candelabra and slowly advances to get a better look at the gorilla.)

BETTY: Careful, Benita Canova—that magic animal could easily tear all of us to pieces.

BENITA: *(Putting the candelabra at the gorilla's head)* This magic animal is acting like a dead gorilla.

(She flops the gorilla on its back, and some of the others pull back in fear. But CHRISTINA comes forward and puts a pillow under the gorilla's head, then strokes its forehead.)

CHRISTINA: Careful, Benita Canova, being temporarily asleep isn't the same thing as being dead.

BENITA: You mean it's just pretending?

CHRISTINA: Such a complicated question.

BENITA: Maybe.

BETTY: You better hope it's asleep.

CHRISTINA: As long as it stays asleep, your situation is much less precarious, Benita Canova.

BENITA: You mean it won't do all the bad things to me I'm imagining?

BETTY: Oh, you are so innocent.

MADAME: *(Entering with a tray upon which sits a large loaf of bread with a knife stuck into it)* Wrong, my dear.

(She advances to organ music and leans down towards the girls and the gorilla as BENITA stretches out on the floor, resting alongside the sleeping—or dead—gorilla.)

Innocence is a disguise that never lasts forever.

BENITA: Not so innocent, really. She knows one thing that lasts forever and forever and forever . . .

(Josephine Baker is heard singing "J'ai deux amours," and the organ music rises and obliterates that as BENITA slowly reaches out, seizes the pillow under the gorilla's head, and suddenly starts smothering the gorilla with the pillow. The girls rise and run out of the room in horror—coughing as if they were being choked—and BENITA reaches out to grab the bread knife. As the music builds, she begins violently stabbing the gorilla again and again and again. The girls run back into the room, screaming in horror, whirling dizzily and falling to the floor—still holding their ears and screaming—as MADAME whirls in ecstasy.)

BENITA: Oh my God! Oh my God—*(Throwing her knife away.)* Fuck, fuck, fuck, fuck! Thank God I killed that fucking thing. Thank God, thank God.

MADAME: *(Overlaps)* I too, thank God—thank God for the real Benita Canova!

BENITA: *(Leaning against the wall, as all is silent now)* Oh Madame, I am really CLEAR now, Madame, in spite of all previous naiveté and confusion—

(Josephine Baker sings softly in the background, and

CHRISTINA *crawls over and tries to revive the gorilla by feeding it bits of bread. The others carry candles and a ceremonial sword and kneel around the gorilla.)*

I am now experiencing a considerable and gratifying distinction between my own self—and this terrible beast against whom I have so amazingly avenged myself—

MADAME: But of course, Benita Canova! *(Runs to* BENITA*'s side.)* There is certainly a considerable difference between the two of you.

BENITA: You say a considerable difference—but from the tone of your voice, I suspect—

MADAME: —No such thing.

(Violin music rises, and at its height, BENITA *runs and flops down to lie stretched out, directly on top of the gorilla, as the girls pull back and gasp in shock.)*

BENITA: *(As the music stops)* Your words contradict your deepest feelings.

MADAME: Contradictions abound, Benita Canova. Do I make a hole in your understanding?

BENITA: Forgive me, but I am forced to demand of you—how such contradictions finally resolve themselves.

MADAME: At the end of history, my dear. Do I make a hole in your understanding?

BENITA: I'm a hole in something.

(There is a flash of light, making the girls scream, and BENITA *lifts up from the gorilla.)*

That's the reason of history coming to an end, I suppose.

MADAME: Yes, that's the reason, Benita Canova. Do I make a HOLE in your understanding?

BENITA: I am a HOLE in something.

MADAME: *(Defiantly)* I too. I am a hole in something!

BENITA: My name is Benita Canova and I have a HOLE in my understanding—

MADAME: My name is Benita Canova! And I make for myself a hole in my understanding, because—hesitating—as I am hesitating—ready to pass through wide open doors into a second life—

(There is a crash of thunder, frightening the girls, some of whom run from the room as the music rises and MADAME rants deliriously, and a shaft of bright light from a room offstage highlights her body.)

—because this life, here and now, so terribly important to Benita Canova—this life of pain given and pain received—tedium and occasional exhilaration—

(Girls have run back in with whips, and some start whipping themselves or others as MADAME sinks to the bench and thrills to receiving such blows from one of the girls.)

—but a SECOND life—hides in a certain second room—

(Another crash of thunder, and screams now accompany each whiplash.)

—if it can be called a second room—because this second room is certainly in direct communication with this first room!

VOICE: *(Overlapping the screams and music)* A child is being beaten. A child is being beaten.

(The music stops, and the girls run from the room. MADAME dashes to the wall and leans against it in silence. Then she poses her body languorously and speaks, suddenly quiet and composed.)

MADAME: And the contents of that second room, though unrecognizable as content, can be scanned only, like a rhythm into which one is afraid to cast oneself completely—

(Agitated music begins softly and builds as she becomes more excited again.)

Because—what kind of madness—my God!—to give way to such rhythms—whenever one vividly imagines . . . such amazing rewards—!

(BENITA has been affected by the rising music and dares to run across the room to slap CHRISTINA across the face.)

CHRISTINA: *(Falling to the floor in shock)* That hurt me!

BENITA: My name is Benita Canova! *(Grabs the discarded sword from the floor and waves it in the air.)* —And I am a VOID in something—and it is my deepest blind desire to discover a certain relevant situation—

MADAME: Amazing!

BENITA: —and to throw myself into that relevant situation—!

MADAME: —Amazing!

BENITA: —again, and again, and again!

MADAME: *(Overlapping)* Embrace me, little Jew, embrace me, little Jew, embrace me right now please—please— please—please!

BENITA: I do it—but I don't do it! I do it—I don't do it. I do it— I don't do it. *(Throws away the sword.)*

MADAME: Does Benita Canova have, in fact, two different bodies that are both, in fact, Benita Canova?

BENITA: Not true!

MADAME: Which one of us is more likely to know the truth, my dear? The one most beautiful—*(Picks the up sword off the floor and points it at BENITA.)*—or the one most in pain.

BENITA: We are both being punished, Madame.

MADAME: *(Advancing towards BENITA)* I am being punished!

BENITA: We are both being punished. *(Scrambles up, sitting on a table to get away from MADAME.)*

MADAME: Yes, but is it Benita Canova who imagines her arms and legs—

(She smacks her sword on the table, provocatively between BENITA's thighs as BENITA yelps in fear.)

—going in totally unimaginable directions?

BENITA: Stop now, please!

(She jumps off the table and manipulates it so it is between them.)

We're going to use this table as a barrier between us—

(MADAME chases her around the table.)

You stay on your side of this fucking table!

(As the music builds, MADAME climbs over the table to get at BENITA, who crawls under it to escape, but as MADAME comes across, she falls down on the other side, losing her wig in the process, revealing a bald head.)

MADAME: Oh, help me! Help me! Please help me to my feet! Help, help, help—!

(All stare in shock at the bald MADAME.)

CHRISTINA: Somebody needs help, Benita Canova—

(She slaps her, and BENITA staggers as the other girls laugh.)

You don't get turned on when somebody just like you, in fact, needs a special kind of help?

(MADAME is crawling across the carpet, and BENITA poses against the wall seductively.)

BENITA: Okay. Okay. She can crawl towards me on the floor, if she likes—! C'mon, c'mon . . .

(One of the girls rips off MADAME's skirt to the others' laughter.)

And when she gets very close, right here between my delicate white thighs. Ah, ah, ah!—these are her instructions. She places her hands on my dirty feet.

(MADAME has crossed so she is on her hands and knees in

front of BENITA. *Someone gives her a towel and a bowl with water, and she goes to use the wet towel on* BENITA*'s ankles.)*

No, don't wash a Jew's dirty feet!

*(*MADAME *cringes back, and* BENITA *starts rubbing her own body sensually.)*

She places her hands on my dirty feet—then she follows her hands her hands, groping up to my knees—

(The girls help MADAME *up, pressing her against* BENITA*'s body.)*

—and she starts pulling herself straight up my slippery body, which wobbles a little—yes! Because my little body, it may or may not be strong enough to keep standing if someone keeps HANGING ON to me like she's hanging on to me!

*(*MADAME *moans and falls back to the carpet, revealing a tiny male penis which had been hidden all night under her/his skirt.* BENITA *slowly moves over* MADAME*— who lies face up on the floor—and, as organ music rises, lowers herself onto the penis.)*

So we both, theoretically at least, tumble back to the floor on top of each other.

*(*BENITA *crawls off of* MADAME*, who gets to her feet and poses heroically as the girls give her a towel which she elegantly holds as a temporary skirt to conceal her penis for the rest of the evening.)*

MADAME: Thank you, my dear, but I expect no reward.

(She backs up and gracefully sits on the bench.)

I expect no happiness.

(Girls take off MADAME's *shoes and start washing her feet.)*

I expect no pathetic sexual favors, prettied up in ribbons and wrapping paper.

(The girls carry in a large tray, piled high with a huge collection of wrapped gifts, which they place on the table. All the girls now wear party hats, and some carry toy party horns.)

I expect no self-deluded emotional fulfillment what-so-ever.

(There is a pause. Then BENITA *goes and grabs one gift. The girls start blowing on their horns as* CHRISTINA *sings mockingly, "Beni-ta! Cano-va!" They giggle as* BENITA *freezes, holding the package, afraid now to open it.)*

Careful, my dear—resist opening such tempting packages without first coming to the understanding that such gifts—if they are indeed gifts—may change our relationship completely.   .

BENITA: *(Thinking to herself)* Before going any further—

MADAME: Oh, do go further, much further.

*(*BENITA *puts back the gift. Then she feels her face, which seems to her incomplete. She rubs her mouth as organ music rises, then goes to a shelf where she picks up a lipstick, and she slowly applies an excessive amount of lipstick to her mouth until she looks like a little girl who's just been into a jar of strawberry jam. She turns slowly, to display her new face to the girls, and as they see her face, they blow their toy horns while* CHRISTINA *sings, "Beni-ta! Cano-va!" As they giggle,* BENITA *turns*

*back to the glass wall between the stage and the audi-
ence and kisses the glass, slowly moving her mouth
across the surface so it leaves a big smear of lipstick.
Then she takes the lipstick and starts to write her name
in large red letters across the glass—but before she finishes, there is a flash of light, and the girls scream and
hide their eyes as* **BENITA** *runs from the room.)*

MADAME: *(Rising from the bench, her voice ringing in con-
demnation)* As I anticipated, my dear! But why bother
scratching such filth onto my beautiful walls, since I
myself have already REVEALED much more terrible
secrets.

BENITA: *(Dashing back into the room)* She wasn't aware you
revealed any genuine secrets to her.

*(**CHRISTINA** starts to sing—"Beni-ta"—but stops midway
as* **MADAME** *glares at her.)*

MADAME: *(Turning back to* **BENITA***)* Of course not! Because I
would only reveal the important ones—"invisibly"!

BENITA: Not good enough. Write them down with a tiny pin-
prick of blood—

(The girls gasp and look at their fingers.)

In your private notebooks, of course.

(She turns and runs from the room.)

MADAME: *(Howling in anguish)* Missed opportunity! All this
time—she should have been looking deep into my eyes—
do that now, please! Deep meaningful glances! And then
decide—should she return such, oh—so desirable gifts?

*(**BENITA** has run back into the room, crossing the stage*

and seizing a package which she tosses into the air and catches as the girls give a scream of surprise.)

BENITA: *(Quietly)* It doesn't matter what I decide. *(Tosses the gift to the floor.)* Because Benita Canova . . . always profits from her mistakes.

MADAME: *(Disgusted)* You see? See, ladies? SUCH people never MAKE mistakes!

BENITA: How do you know such people never make mistakes?

MADAME: Powerful eye contact, my dear! *(Runs to the side of the room, hoping to avoid such eye contact.)* Every one of my guesses turns out one hundred percent correct!

BENITA: *(Stepping forward courageously)* Then she's glad we've met, finally.

MADAME: *(Flabbergasted)* Glad? Why, of all things, glad?

BENITA: Because compared to you, she's the opposite, and opposites always attract.

(She runs forward and gives MADAME a sudden kiss on the lips.)

MADAME: *(Stunned)* Not really.

(She wipes off BENITA's kiss with the back of her hand.)

Not this time at least.

(She elegantly walks out of the room, still holding the towel as a protective skirt. One of the girls is standing in the shadows where MADAME exited, holding a large stuffed dummy in evening dress, with an oversized skull for a head. BENITA turns away from everyone.)

BENITA: *(To herself)* Okay. Maybe on this special occasion . . .
I did say one wrong thing, after all.

*(She starts to giggle hysterically, then slaps herself hard
across the face to stop the giggling. Then she feels the
pain and lifts her hand to her cheek and quietly says,
"Ow." The girls giggle at this. A high-pitched tone is
heard, and BENITA slowly looks over to the pile of gifts
on the table.)*

Oh well, there are still all those . . . unopened packages.
I wonder what's inside. *(She hesitates, nervously.)*
Well—maybe she'll just—save them for later. I suppose?

*(The tone gets louder and louder as BENITA fights her
desire to go and open the gifts. Finally she can control
herself no longer. She rushes to the table and starts to
unwrap the largest one—but the voice interrupts, and
she turns away guiltily.)*

VOICE: Oh Benita Canova . . . never, never, never. Never open
such dangerous gifts.

*(She runs to leave the wall, but where there had been
an exit, there is now a solid white panel, and she
smashes into it with a thud, cries out in pain, and falls
back onto the bench, holding her bruised head. Faint
music is heard, the German music-hall singer chanting
merrily—"Fräulein, my little Fräulein." BENITA slowly
looks up and brings her hands down slowly until they
rest at her side. Very slowly, as the singing gets louder,
the lights fade to black.)*

THE END

PEARLS
FOR PIGS

Pearls for Pigs. Produced by the Hartford Stage and International Production Associates, Inc., at the Hartford Stage, Hartford, CT, April 1997, and at the Tribeca Performing Arts Center, New York City, December 1997. Written, directed, and designed by Richard Foreman.

MAESTRO: David Patrick Kelly
PIERROT: Peter Jacobs
COLOMBINE: Jan Leslie Harding (Hartford);
    Stephenie Cannon (NYC)
DOCTOR: Tom Nelis
LARGE MALE DWARFS: Scott Blumenthal, David Callaghan,
    David Cote, Yehuda Deunyas, John Oglevee

A NOTE TO *PEARLS FOR PIGS*

As I have explained at the beginning of this volume, I am quite open to variant stagings of these texts. I was, for instance, happy to attend a production of *Pearls for Pigs* that was staged in Paris by the French director Bernard Sobel. He staged the play in a large theater with no scenery to speak of. There were some rolling walls, covered with brown wrapping paper, which, during the course of the action, was torn away to reveal sections of the play's text written underneath. The actors were in normal street dress. The play opened as a small door collapsed and all the actors tumbled out in a heap, as if they'd been stuffed inside, and then continued being tangled in that heap as they spoke the first few pages of dialogue.

Towards the end of the play, the rear wall of the stage lifted, revealing a second auditorium—with a steep bank of empty seats facing the existing audience in Sobel's theater. The Maestro delivered his long monologue at the end of the play, moving about amongst these faraway empty seats. It was an excellent production, very far in style from my own (which toured to the same theater in Paris later in the year, making for a wonderful occasion to compare styles), and I would hope that other strong directors would do as Sobel did, and not be excessively influenced by the way I stage my own plays.

A large paneled room, frescos high on the walls, massive dark pillars to the rear and sides. There are many small tables lined up down the center, cutting the stage in two. In the center of the rear wall, a small decorated proscenium, with a faded red curtain behind a small forestage just a bit higher off the ground than the tables. Many large hooded lights hang above. Large pictures of indistinct faces hang at angles from the walls, almost obscuring the frescos. The room vaguely evokes the turn of the century—a café theater with the stage at the rear. But this is only evoked by the appearance of the room— it is a room that remains mysterious and ambiguous as to time and place, even when the lights are very bright.

Scattered through the room, in addition to the tables and a few bookcases, are several posts that rise from the floor, with hand cranks on top which can be spun in circles are parallel to the floor. To one side of the tables, a large black coffin rests on the floor. There are also several tall poles with bright lights on top.

Throughout the entire play, various repetitive music loops are playing—sometimes soft and ominous, sometimes cresting into dissonant vaudevillelike climaxes. The action and dialogue are continually punctuated with cymbal crashes, drum thuds, and the ping of a small bell. The lights function in a similar fashion—sudden flashes and changes framing sections of text in unexpected ways.

As the play begins, the stage is very dark. From the rear corner, the MAESTRO suddenly appears, then whirls *and stops, confronting four* **LARGE MALE DWARFS** *who hurry after him, one of them carrying a large mirror.*

The **MAESTRO** *is dressed in a leather jacket with a white scarf. The* **LARGE DWARFS** *resemble hermaphrodites, with dirty aprons, bare legs covered with mesh stockings, and very large buttocks visible from the rear. They are beard-ed, and wear strange cone-shaped hats that vaguely resemble black beehives, and large ruff collars framing their heads.*

The **MAESTRO** *sees himself in the mirror they hold, then turns and advances towards the audience as* **PIERROT** *and* **COLOMBINE** *enter at the side.* **PIERROT** *is in his classical loose white costume, with a white face, while* **COLOMBINE** *is in a sexy contemporary black pantsuit with a ruff collar and a small party hat. The* **MAESTRO** *surveys them all, then speaks to the audience.*

MAESTRO: I hate the actors who appear in this play.

PIERROT: Oh no, no! I rather like the actors who appear in this play, even you, Maestro. What I hate is the play.

MAESTRO: Oh no, no, no, I like the play very much, but I hate the actors.

PIERROT: I have an idea. Let's reverse roles. *(Runs to look at himself in the mirror.)*

MAESTRO: Ah, what an unsettling idea.

(The **DWARFS** *grab back the mirror from* **PIERROT** *and immediately start hitting him with meat cleavers. All scream.)*

PIERROT: I'm bleeding. I'm bleeding.

COLOMBINE: Oh my God!

MAESTRO: Do any of us really believe what we're saying?

COLOMBINE: Oh, I hope not.

MAESTRO: Of course we do, we believe it totally.

COLOMBINE: C'mon now, we've well memorized our parts, Maestro.

MAESTRO: *(Giving COLOMBINE a kiss)* Now. Let's escape.

(Pause, he looks about.)

Impossible? We could begin improvising.

PIERROT: But the audience would have no idea if we were improvising, or if it was all planned in advance.

MAESTRO: There must be some subtle way we could clue them in.

(He maneuvers COLOMBINE onto the coffin and climbs on top of her, ready to make love.)

PIERROT: I don't think so.

MAESTRO: For instance. Tonight, the play's canceled!

(The others react in shock.)

This is my genuine intention, ladies and gentlemen.

(He starts to penetrate COLOMBINE as they begin love-making.)
Yet here we are. Waiting to turn this into a play.

(They both come to an obvious climax. Then MAESTRO looks up—totally detached—)

Seen enough? How can we be stopped from doing that?

(He jumps onto the table.)

PIERROT: I don't know.

MAESTRO: Music, please?

(He runs to touch the curtain in the little proscenium up center as the DWARFS run on holding two tall poles, each with a curtain descending from a crossbar at the top of each pole. As they revolve, behind each curtain two DWARFS are seen embracing—but, realizing they are visible, they run off, embarrassed.)

What's behind this curtain?

COLOMBINE: Just one more goddamn curtain.

MAESTRO: Ah . . . real empty space.

COLOMBINE: Right.

MAESTRO: Death.

COLOMBINE: Right.

MAESTRO: You say "right" so casually.

COLOMBINE: Right.

MAESTRO: I'm glad to see you smile.

COLOMBINE: *(A DWARF runs on to hand COLOMBINE a knife)* You needn't take my smile so seriously, Maestro.

MAESTRO: The truth is:
We never, never see into the abyss
that desires us—totally.

COLOMBINE: How much pleasure—*(Kisses him quickly, they both revolve.)*—is there in that desire? *(Flamboyantly slits her throat and collapses.)*

MAESTRO: *(Running to the other side of the tables)*
Well, a twist
could be called pleasure
during one or two
of its many twistings.

(PIERROT stabs him from behind, and the MAESTRO collapses with a theatrical moan.)

PIERROT: You see what my touch is capable of, Maestro?

MAESTRO: *(Recovering)* All this is a calculated effect, of course. I'm into magic.

COLOMBINE: Prove it.

MAESTRO: It might hurt.

COLOMBINE: Prove it.

MAESTRO: *(Turns away to receive a saw and a small box from one of the DWARFS)* I no longer saw people in half.

COLOMBINE: One half of me believes it, one half doesn't.

MAESTRO: The issue at hand seems relevant to the following consideration. Is it I who pour forth words, and having done so, am I as empty as this magic box is empty?

COLOMBINE: *(As the DWARFS try to sexually molest her)* Everybody get away from me!

(She runs and grabs the box from the MAESTRO. She looks into it.)

Is a box always empty?

MAESTRO: If it were always empty, would it be magic?

(They both run to the coffin and open its double doors.)

COLOMBINE: I misunderstood one of his words.

MAESTRO: All of them.

COLOMBINE: M-A-G-I-and-a-surprising-K—that word.

MAESTRO: Can you handle this, my dear?

(He is forcing her into the coffin.)

COLOMBINE: It seems totally empty.

MAESTRO: From your point of view, accurate.

COLOMBINE: *(Lying down in the coffin)* But from yours, Maestro?

MAESTRO: Perhaps you misinterpret one of my words.

*(**COLOMBINE**, lying in the coffin, calls, "HELP!" as the **MAESTRO** slams the two doors shut and jumps on the coffin. Exciting music rises.)*

MAESTRO: Ladies and gentlemen, in order to sum up approximately thirty years of theatrical adventurism, I will proceed to amaze men, women, and children by telling time mentally.

*(**DWARFS** ring gongs.)*

I'll write the time on this piece of paper. Now I'll seal this paper in this envelope. Now with this hammer I'll nail the envelope to the naked floor.

(He hammers it to the floor as a white disk is bounced rear. The remaining DWARFS hammer down on COLOMBINE as she tries to rise from the coffin, then collapses back inside.)

Next, an available witness to my worst crimes will appear and take the original piece of paper from a now bloody envelope.

PIERROT: Who witnesses such crimes, Maestro?

MAESTRO: You, of course.

PIERROT: How did you know I was a witness?

MAESTRO: From your tone of voice, my friend.

PIERROT: But I'm careful to control my emotions.

MAESTRO: Then it must be my ability to read minds.

PIERROT: *(Opens envelope and compares it to a visible clock)* This says eight-thirty-four, which doesn't agree with the clock.

MAESTRO: *(Whirling the hands of the clock)* Ah—maybe the clock is wrong, at least some of the time.

COLOMBINE: *(Rising from the coffin)* Ah, a human clock?
MAESTRO: Not likely. If it were human, it would be wrong ALL of the time.

PIERROT: I have an idea. *(Writes on the MAESTRO's slip of paper.)*

MAESTRO: I know exactly what you're doing.

PIERROT: *(Looks up)* Then it's as good as if you were doing it yourself.

MAESTRO: Right. You're correcting what I wrote and writing— *(Glances at clock.)* Eight-forty-five.

PIERROT: That's what I wrote.

MAESTRO: All we do now—is wait till eight-forty-five, and what's written on this paper will agree completely with what shows on the dial. Next comes the hard part—*(Tearing up the paper.)*—translate that into general rules of behavior.

(Clock strikes.)

Too late. Some more accurate clock somewhere strikes—but it's an irrelevant number of hours, because here in the palm of my hand, all hours are etched painfully into my very life.

COLOMBINE: Let me see your hand.

MAESTRO: Never.

PIERROT: Help! I hear a clock ticking.

MAESTRO: So do I. But whereas ordinarily I might put my hands over my ears, upon this occasion, such an alternative is denied me, and instead of calling it time passing, I call it something else. —What do I call it? Obviously the name is avoided.

COLOMBINE: *(Grabbing for his hand)* Let me see your hand—

MAESTRO: *(Pulling away)* Did you hear what I said?

PIERROT: Tick-tock. Am I an important clock?

MAESTRO: What makes one clock more important than another clock, since the time told is always the same time?

(He runs out of the room.)

COLOMBINE: Somehow, you make this tiny wristwatch of mine seem important. Now let's find something else important in this room.

PIERROT: *(Looking about frantically)* This table is important. Oh my goodness—am I a table? I can imagine people eating off of me.

MAESTRO: *(Entering from another door)* Stand up! Bend over!

PIERROT: Oh no, please, not that.

MAESTRO: Hands on the floor, please. Arch your back, and everybody pull up chairs on either side—we're about to place dinner on your backside, sir.

PIERROT: I could hold out my hands and food could be there instead. Or balanced on my knees if I sat down.

MAESTRO: If it was an adhesive food.

PIERROT: *(As a DWARF brings a large tray of food to PIERROT)* Not even. I could do it. See! See! *(Holds the food to his knees and waddles about.)*

MAESTRO: *(Turning away from the others)* This makes me realize I could be a fantastic table.

PIERROT: *(Stops, anguished)* No, I was the table!

MAESTRO: I could be a table. I could be a chair—

PIERROT: Ohh . . . !

COLOMBINE: *(Leafing through a large book as the DWARFS start caressing her)* Oh, so many possibilities, Maestro. Somebody should leaf through your pages—

MAESTRO: That sounds less like a chair than a book.
(He is isolated in a spotlight and speaks to the audience as the others freeze momentarily.)

Believe me—all these revelatory experiences mean something, ladies and gentlemen. They pile up for later reference, so that leafing through them is like leafing through the pages of a book.

PIERROT: *(Pointing at COLOMBINE and the DWARFS)* Look at all of the bad things that are happening to a book.

MAESTRO: The entire book can be destroyed.

COLOMBINE: Much worse, if a single page gets ripped loose—

(She rips out a page.)

MAESTRO: You took the words right out of my mouth, my dear little Columbine.

PIERROT: Nobody wants to risk the falsification of an entire life.

MAESTRO: My life? In particular, of course. *(Grabs the book.)* Here—these are some of my favorite pages. *(Shakes the book so all its pages flutter to the floor.)*

COLOMBINE: Can they be reassembled, Maestro?

MAESTRO: Try picking up just one.

PIERROT: *(Picks up a page)* I can't make heads or tails of this.

MAESTRO: Read it to me.

PIERROT: Read it out loud?

MAESTRO: If I hear it spoken by a human voice, I might comprehend it better than just reading it.

PIERROT: All of the letters are run together so it's just letter after letter ad infinitum. I don't know how to pronounce that.

MAESTRO: Can you read it to yourself, however?

PIERROT: Well—if I simply project my own meaning onto it.

MAESTRO: Ah, you've been keeping that a secret.

PIERROT: What?

MAESTRO: Your own simpleminded meanings.

PIERROT: I don't think so. It's just that my poor, poor brain has been damaged by life, Maestro. That's why I'm not a good conversationalist.

MAESTRO: *(Slowly spinning one of the floor cranks)* What do you mean, your brain has been damaged, my little dressed-in-white dream boy!

PIERROT: *(Slowly collapsing to the floor)* Life has twisted it out of shape, so of course I'm not a good conversationalist.

MAESTRO: Wait a minute—are you an actor, sir?

PIERROT: Why do you say that, sir?

MAESTRO: I recognize dark lines, penciled in around the eyes. I recognize certain grimaces, pulling the face towards inexplicable emotions—am I indeed trapped?

(Others retreat a step, smiling guiltily.)

Perhaps if I hold out my hand toward an audience I can only imagine—but then I am shaken by the appearance of a face at the rear of the darkened auditorium. And I see in those deep eyes half-recognition only. And I calm myself by repeating again and again that I am safe inside the walls of my private kingdom.

(He gazes into the audience, then whirls and runs off-stage. The others are aghast at his exit, but he suddenly reappears from a second door and runs in, jumping onto a chair as DWARFS hurry forward to strap him in a white chiffon skirt and a large white feather headdress.)

But as usual—this does not work and my heart pounds in my chest until the noise of that pounding dominates the stage. The curtain falls. No one dares to tell me what effect my performance produces. But outside on the streets again, it's as if nothing had happened. I buy a newspaper. Nothing. No pictures. No words of praise for my accomplishments. *(Hitting his chest.)* Thump thump thump.

PIERROT: Ah, we behave as we behave, Maestro.

MAESTRO: Yes. We thump as we thump.

COLOMBINE: We take you very seriously, Maestro. Though your image is comical.

MAESTRO: I accept that. I accept that!

COLOMBINE: Comical by choice?

MAESTRO: That's the question, isn't it?

PIERROT: No! No! No! You put us all in a position where we possess nothing but questions, Maestro.

MAESTRO: Since I bestow such riches, I am therefore poverty-stricken.

COLOMBINE: Poverty? Dressed so, with a capital "M"— Magnificently?

MAESTRO: I didn't dress myself. This was the way in which I was, by someone—or somebody—dressed.

COLOMBINE: By who?

MAESTRO: I don't know.

COLOMBINE: Make a guess.

MAESTRO: No.

COLOMBINE: Why not?

MAESTRO: *(Howling)* IT WOULD ONLY BE A GUESS! *(Jumps off his chair and races around the stage.)*

PIERROT: Why do you erupt at the slightest provocation?

MAESTRO: A certain performer throws his arms in the air, and opens his mouth wide. His facial expression is inexplicable.

PIERROT: Does someone quiz this performer?

MAESTRO: Yes.

PIERROT: Is he able to explain himself?

MAESTRO: Well . . .

COLOMBINE: Are you dressed like a god, Maestro?

MAESTRO: Certainly not.

COLOMBINE: I always thought that would be the way a god dressed, and you were therefore trying to be impressive.

(As she speaks, the others bow down before him and end up stretched out on the floor at his feet. There is a loud trumpet fanfare, as if for a king's entrance. The MAESTRO whirls in surprise and runs out of the room, and all of the others chase him, falling over one another in the confusion. As the door is slammed behind the last of them, another door opens and the DOCTOR rushes into the room, ridiculously dressed in a frogman suit with flippers and oxygen tanks strapped to his back. He looks about for the MAESTRO—who then pops in from another door, still in his skirt and feather headdress.)

DOCTOR: *(Speaking with an accent)* Why you are dressed like a chicken, Maestro?

MAESTRO: Okay! Why are you dressed like a frog, Doctor?

DOCTOR: Begging your pardon. The aqua therapy from this morning was taking longer than to be expected.

MAESTRO: Your aqua therapy's not my problem, Doctor.

DOCTOR: So he's not angry with the aqua therapy. So then, what he's angry?

MAESTRO: I'm angry for another reason, Doctor—

(He smashes his body against a padded panel held by the DWARFS. Other DWARFS are rolling large blackboards onstage.)

DOCTOR: See if I guess this.

MAESTRO: What do you mean by "guess"?

DOCTOR: Using my deductive ability, what else?

MAESTRO: Is that guessing?

DOCTOR: Guessing, guessing, the moment I should commit myself.

MAESTRO: That's it.

DOCTOR: What?

MAESTRO: That ability of yours to take mental pratfalls on my behalf.

DOCTOR: This is my job.

MAESTRO: —or, I should say, your DETERMINATION to take mental pratfalls on my behalf—that's what angers me about you, really makes me angry. I'm so angry.

(The music rises, and the MAESTRO makes a run around the entire room, building up speed to smash again against the padded panel. He bounces away and falls into the DOCTOR's arms. Briefly, they dance.)

DOCTOR: Now I know, now I know, now I know.

MAESTRO: *(Overlapping)* Now I know, now I know, now I know. *(Backs away from the DOCTOR)* If you think I'm too forthcoming for a doctor/patient relationship—?

DOCTOR: With you, Maestro, no guessing necessary.

MAESTRO: I don't like guesses!

COLOMBINE: I know what the Maestro likes.

DOCTOR: I do the guessing. You are dressed like this because another somebody intended or makes the request.

MAESTRO: I don't know.

DOCTOR: Make a guess.

MAESTRO: Why wouldn't I just say "I don't know," turn away from you, and continue my life as normal?

DOCTOR: In the Maestro's case, no such thing as normal— something else is driving the Maestro.

MAESTRO: I refuse to be victimized. Tell me, Doctor—*(Noticing that the DWARFS are again bowed down to him.)* Why is my mere appearance so overwhelming to people?

DOCTOR: Oh, I don't think this is so overwhelming.

(The DWARFS roll onto their backs and laugh.)

MAESTRO: Then I'm sorry. I'm truly ignorant of the effect I produce.

DOCTOR: Okay, my itsy-bitsy stuffed peacock, have a seat—

MAESTRO: No thank you.

DOCTOR: Why not?
MAESTRO: No thank you!

DOCTOR: Does he know how to take a seat?

(The DWARFS are busily offering chairs.)

MAESTRO: Of course I do.

DOCTOR: Then he's not ignorant in regard to taking a seat.

MAESTRO: I am deeply ignorant.

DOCTOR: *(Laughs as **MAESTRO** wipes a chair seat clean with his skirt)* There's no arguing with the Maestro.

MAESTRO: Of course not.

(They play a game of starting to sit, then straightening up as the other starts to sit—back and forth—who will believe the other has committed himself to being seated and so sit himself? After a few tries, they are both frozen in indecision.)

DOCTOR: So try the famous imaginary seat?

(Both start to sit, but miss their chairs and fall on the floor.)

MAESTRO: My God!—I have no control of this situation, Doctor.

*(Both are rising, with chairs lifted, ready for battle against each other. **DWARFS** rush in and rip the chairs from their hands.)*

DOCTOR: Quite the contrary.

MAESTRO: Now look! I come to you demonstrating I'm in trouble. I expect help.

DOCTOR: Of course expecting help, sir. This is exactly why I'm of a contrary disposition.

MAESTRO: Careful, Doctor—! I have no control over myself.

DOCTOR: This I doubt.

MAESTRO: Oh really? Watch this!

(He demonstrates his inner turmoil by going into con-
volusions, falling to the floor, and writhing as if in agony.)

DOCTOR: Ah, on a scale of seventy-five, this is a fifteen. This
is pitiful, sir.

MAESTRO: *(From the floor)* Oh? You think that's pitiful?

DOCTOR: Watch this.

(The DOCTOR gives his own demonstration of what inner
turmoil should look like. He moans, holds himself, and
falls to the floor.)

MAESTRO: *(Watching from a distance)* I see.

DOCTOR: *(Looking up from the floor)* You see what?

MAESTRO: Answers! You don't have 'em. Solutions! I don't
have 'em.

DOCTOR: Viennese double bologna, Maestro. Those words
come from neither the head nor the heart.

MAESTRO: Where do they come from?

DOCTOR: Maybe you're about to find out.

(With a loud crash, the DWARFS run on and DOCTOR and
DWARFS do an eccentric, spastic dance to incredibly
loud music. MAESTRO rushes out in disgust and returns
without his skirt and headdress. The music stops.)

MAESTRO: Well, now that I'm out of my fancy costume, why
has the entire medical team decided to stop their funny
dancing?

DOCTOR: I give you some big advice here, Maestro.

MAESTRO: What?

DOCTOR: Don't ask for any.

MAESTRO: Ah—thank you, Doctor. That famous "Don't ask me" piece of advice.

DOCTOR: Watch this.

(He gestures to the DWARFS, and they spin the floor cranks, which makes the MAESTRO stagger dizzily.)

Does this make you dizzy?

MAESTRO: I'm not sure.

DOCTOR: Ah—betwixt and betweening!

MAESTRO: You might be.

DOCTOR: Yah. This is called the dizziness.

MAESTRO: It's true.

DOCTOR: What.

MAESTRO: I could imagine being less dizzy than I am now— which heretofore I've considered the state of being not dizzy.

DOCTOR: Get bearings from the internal gyroscope inside me, sir.

MAESTRO: I'd rather not do that.

DOCTOR: Hey—! Have you checked your shoelaces, maybe?

MAESTRO: Not recently.

DOCTOR: Tied or untied—shoelaces?

MAESTRO: Now? If I decide on an examination—or when I put them on originally—carefully tied?

DOCTOR: Still tied?

MAESTRO: I have every reason to believe so.

DOCTOR: That means, if you walk, your shoes will not be falling off.

MAESTRO: I should think so.

DOCTOR: I, too, should think so.

MAESTRO: Pure poetry in that—

(He is sitting on the edge of the downstage table, and the DWARFS cover him with a white sheet, as if preparing for medical procedure—but they are beneath the sheet also.)

Traveling around. Shoes well secured to the feet.

DOCTOR: Yah. But you don't think checking them would be in order?

MAESTRO: *(Under the sheet)* Excuse me for a minute. *(Lifting a foot, peeking out through a hole in the sheet.)* Everything seems quite perfect.

DOCTOR: Bravo—this is provisional.

MAESTRO: I have the feeling these shoes are such that even if the laces came undone, the shoes would probably remain in place. On the foot. Oh, they might flop around a bit, but they wouldn't fall off.

DOCTOR: Then you're in good shape.

MAESTRO: *(Throwing off the sheet)* Yes I am!

DOCTOR: Shoe-wise.

MAESTRO: *(Nods)* Shoe-wise.

DOCTOR: Other wise?

MAESTRO: I say we start to revolve. One-two-three!

> *(He whirls. Trumpets sound, and he stops suddenly and looks at the others.)*

MAESTRO: I didn't say anything about stopping.

DOCTOR: This was your mistake.

MAESTRO: That's right.

DOCTOR: Then you can respond with silence if you are choosing silence.

MAESTRO: Correct.

DOCTOR: Hah! But this is not your choice.

MAESTRO: You requested silence, I responded with silence.

> *(The DWARFS frantically revolve the floor cranks and stop at a loud noise.)*

DOCTOR: What I want from you is not something so easily identifiable, sir.

MAESTRO: Is that because I'm not in control of my behavior, Doctor?

DOCTOR: Who else is controlling?

MAESTRO: *(Holds head)* Oh my God—

DOCTOR: It just hit?

MAESTRO: It certainly has.

DOCTOR: What's just hit?

MAESTRO: Can you imagine all of the things I've forgotten about myself over the course of a lifetime?

DOCTOR: *(Starts to go, then stops, disgusted)* This is not my responsibility.

(All but the MAESTRO exit.)

MAESTRO: *(Looking at the empty stage)* Thrust back on my own resources, I arrive at the theater. Light from the stage blinds me, but a curtain blocks my access to deep space and questions me—dare I penetrate this plateau of emergent sensations? And I am paralyzed in front of the not yet risen curtain, behind which I suddenly hear the sharp crack of crystal shattering as if life itself—

(DWARFS run on with the curtains on sticks, others with clapboards [the style used before shooting a scene in a movie] which they make snap to rhythmically punctuate the dialogue.)

—stopped in all of its atypical yet certainly occurring moments. My God, does the end of the real world really happen?

COLOMBINE: Where does that leave the rest of us, Maestro?

MAESTRO: No problem. I go on as before.

PIERROT: Without a world, you don't go on, Maestro.

MAESTRO: Yes I do, yes I do, yes I do. *(Steals one of the clap-boards.)*

COLOMBINE: Are you trying to be your deepest desire speaking?

MAESTRO: I'm trying to be non-stop in my own particular universe—don't you get it?

(He claps the board, and all lurch.)

My blood clots belong to me and nobody else!

(He slumps against a table.)

My God, I have no energy for this—yet—what I have is energy! How the hell do I reconcile these two options?

PIERROT: Ah. They are never reconciled.

MAESTRO: "Ah"? What does your "ah" mean?

PIERROT: Which "ah"?

MAESTRO: The "ah" that precedes an otherwise ordinary sentence.

PIERROT: *(Lifting a finger)* Ahhhhh!

COLOMBINE: I know what "ah" at the beginning of a sentence means.
MAESTRO: Do explain.

COLOMBINE: It means that in the course of things—

MAESTRO: *(Overlapping softly)* Ah—

COLOMBINE: *(Continues through)*—The meaning, or the *thrust* of meaning, is about to reverse itself, or begin again in a new direction or on some differently articulated plateau.

MAESTRO: *(Lying back on a table, his feet up in the air)* Ah. We are on a plateau.

COLOMBINE: *(Closing her eyes ecstatically)* That's why I can feel the wind blowing through my hair.

ALL: *(As they join her in collapsing ecstatically to the floor)* AHH!

PIERROT: Ah—me too.

COLOMBINE: Me too.

MAESTRO: *(Overlapping)* Excellent—an all-purpose word providing everyone with the illusion that he or she is in touch with reality once and for all.

(They stop to look at him as he bounces up from the table.)

And don't think a performer balanced between tragedy and comedy such as myself rejects such self-gratifying vocalization—but don't think, on the other hand, that an entire career can be based upon that single whoosh of verbal energy. I admit the power to bless oneself with an orgasmic feeling of self-importance—

ALL: Ahhhh—!

MAESTRO: But let's not fall into the trap, my dear children, of considering ourselves—drunk with such guttural expressiveness—the leading character in some vast psychodrama!

(They all step back to look at him.)

Oh yes! Each one of you virtuosos of the "ahhh" believes yourself the leading character in this monumental spectacle, while I of course believe I'm just here feeding you material.

PIERROT: That seems viable.

MAESTRO: Get this straight! You are not the main character. I am not the main character.

(He races to one of the blackboards and begins erasing as PIERROT and COLOMBINE toss large balls in the air.)

The world itself is the main character, ladies and gentlemen. And it effectively hypnotizes all of us to achieve its own ends.

ALL: Ahhhh?

MAESTRO: The only difference between us being: I happen to believe I am in DIRECT COMMUNICATION with this double world.

(He now steals two large balls, one gold and one black, which PIERROT and COLOMBINE had been tossing and catching.)

So when the double world wonders—as even double worlds do, ladies and gentlemen, tend to wonder about themselves—Do I really exist? Well, it tries to find out through me, through my disguises.

(He turns to face the others, holding his two balls. A loud trumpet fanfare sends the others running from the room. The MAESTRO is left holding just one of the balls, as the DOCTOR, now dressed for golf, carrying a club in one hand and a platter with a decapitated head on it in the other hand, slowly appears on the other side of the stage.)

This is heavy stuff, right?

(The DOCTOR sets down the head in position for hitting it with his club.)

Once upon a time, this cold and hostile atmosphere would have delighted me. Ah. I said "once upon a time." This must mean—now.

DOCTOR: This is never once upon a time, Maestro.

MAESTRO: Of course it is.

DOCTOR: No—

MAESTRO: See how the light bounces off the back of my hand? This is a genuine invitation, sir.

DOCTOR: Who's being invited?

MAESTRO: Not you, Doctor—but here you are.

DOCTOR: Such a frigid glare he is sweeping in my direction.

MAESTRO: Ah, what parts of the body pick up on that, Doctor?

DOCTOR: *(As the MAESTRO is blindfolded)* My eyes, apparently —but I am capable of controlling myself, and now I feel better.

MAESTRO: You're so very quick to psych things out, Doctor— I find in myself a sudden preference for the placid frigidity of total explanation.

DOCTOR: Good.

(He swings his club and sends the head flying as the MAESTRO bangs his body three times into the padded panel, which has reappeared. Music rises.)

You will now explain your motives.

MAESTRO: I don't have any.

DOCTOR: Your desires—

MAESTRO: I don't have any. Ambitions—none at all. That's why I like it here.

DOCTOR: Don't you think the time is now for shifting some gears, Maestro?

(All enter, waiting for the MAESTRO *to act. A pause.)*

Well, make something thrilling to happen with all of us, Maestro.

MAESTRO: *(Takes off his blindfold)* No.

DOCTOR: No?

MAESTRO: No.

(He turns his back on them and leaves the stage. Then the others look up towards the light. Fear enters them. They shield their eyes from the light and slowly retreat offstage. After a pause, the MAESTRO *reenters, all alone, eating from a plate with his fingers. Then he notices the audience and freezes momentarily.)*

Let's say—nothing's supposed to happen. Let's say that life is meant to be wasted, ladies and gentlemen—its potential brilliance—

(The lights flare and then darken.)

—forbidden to flower, that potential flowerlike brilliance of a life.

—My life, for instance.
Does this serve the universe's purposes?
Is this what life is truly lusting for?
Implosion?

(The others are slowly creeping back onstage.)

A sinking into itself. Yes, yes, yes.
A black hole of a life over-rich to the point of self-
consummation.

COLOMBINE: Sicko, Maestro, sicko, sicko. What happens to everything beautiful? Your answer? Down the toilet!

MAESTRO: Just what life needs, my little twitterhead. Down the toilet. And why does life need such treatment, Doctor? Because life is, at best, a proliferating cancerous growth on the beautiful emptiness of the perfect universe. Now think about it. If God had wanted—

DOCTOR: Leave God out of this.

MAESTRO: I'm just using it as a convenient term.

DOCTOR: It confuses the issue.

MAESTRO: I'll drop it.

DOCTOR: Good.

MAESTRO: I'm dropping God for your benefit.

DOCTOR: Thank you.

MAESTRO: What I mean to convey is this. What I mean to convey is this. The created universe seems to be presented to us in two ways at once.
   One view—daily life, solid objects, other persons

with personalities, the facts of the so-called world of lived experience.

Second view, laboriously arrived at through the evolution of the most rigorous scientific research—*(Leafing through a large book.)*—the world revealed as a network of high energy particles which in themselves don't really exist, except as potential factors in some grand equation of possibility. —Pure emptiness. The world—that filigree woven around nothingness—only SEEMS to arise when two nothings come into momentary conjunction. A thought entertained, but immediately inoperable.

(The others have by now fallen asleep.)

So the pinnacle of evolved scientific and metaphysical thought—the realization that everything we humans build or cognate—

(He is circling the table where they all sleep.)

—from bridges to intellectual systems to other recognizable humans with traits and proclivities—all of this in fact does not exist—mere fictions projected on a network of underlying nonexisting atomic nothings. Ghosts, like you and me, ladies and gentlemen. How perfect, then, to withdraw into that nothingness. To collaborate with what is—which is what is not—by actively preventing one's life from flowering into further illusion.

(He shouts, to awaken them.)

So call off the performance!
This sound perverse?

ALL: Yah!

MAESTRO: Not when compared to some poor fool doing the opposite, contributing to the building of a pretend world only, compounding lies.

(The music becomes jazzy, and the others are dancing behind him.)

My point is—the universe is so constituted that even the most profound of human efforts ultimately discovers the nonmateriality of all things—so to use this life to build a world, any sort of world—is to disguise reality with a mere facade built on totally imaginary foundations. All human flowering, a proliferating cancer, ladies and gentlemen—and I reject that cancer, as I reject every one of you. And, in preference, I implode. Return the self to its roots—serve the universal truth through contraction into nothingness!

(He runs out, disgusted.)

DOCTOR: *(Now leading the others in a bump-and-grind dance)* Very poetic, Maestro—but how can you be sure the universe's purpose isn't precisely the opposite? The miracle of this real world built from such nonmaterial stuff—

MAESTRO: *(Reentering at another door)* Ah—you mean the universe's purpose is to lie about itself?

DOCTOR: Oh please—one does not call it lying to transform amorphous nothing into the beautiful palaces with which we surround ourselves?

ALL: *(As they run off, transfixed by the vision sketched by the DOCTOR)* Yah!!!

DOCTOR: *(Alone with the MAESTRO)* Are you preparing your reply?

MAESTRO: I have no reply.

DOCTOR: Then I win.

MAESTRO: No. I refuse to fight.

DOCTOR: To be blunt, sir—you've given up.

MAESTRO: Yes.

DOCTOR: This is a conscious choice?

MAESTRO: For the moment.

DOCTOR: Very sad.

MAESTRO: Oh no, what it is, is not "sad."

DOCTOR: Here we have a difference of opinion.

MAESTRO: There's no such thing.

DOCTOR: These paradoxical games of mirrors are really of no interest to your doctor.

(He turns and leaves abruptly.)

MAESTRO: *(A pause)* Ah. He was here, now he's not here. I hardly notice the difference. What a perverse man I've become.—Wake up, Maestro! *(Slaps himself.)*

COLOMBINE: *(Returning from the shadows)* It won't work.

MAESTRO: What?

COLOMBINE: Try it. Slap yourself again.

MAESTRO: *(As she climbs into the coffin)* Then it won't be slapping myself, it would be responding to a beautiful lady's instructions. It would be about hypnotic behavior.

COLOMBINE: I'm good at that.

MAESTRO: Don't hypnotize me, please.

COLOMBINE: Too late.

> *(She slams the coffin doors closed on top of her, sending the MAESTRO reeling back against the tables. The she slowly reemerges, and they stare at each other. Then the MAESTRO looks away from her gaze, embarrassed, and digs out a card from his pocket.)*

MAESTRO: *(Turning to audience, reading a name from the card)* Excuse me. Is Dr. Eric Milton Fishman in the audience this evening?

COLOMBINE: Stop it! Stop that!

MAESTRO: Dr. Fishman?

DOCTOR: *(Reappearing)* Not tonight, I'm afraid.

MAESTRO: I'm talking about the real Dr. Eric Milton Fishman. Not here tonight? That puts me in an awkward position. My entire discourse is directed at making a certain impression on the distinguished Dr. Fishman—who is uniquely in a position to understand the poignancy of my self-documentation.

COLOMBINE: Maybe Dr. Fishman is here, but in disguise. Like the rest of us.

MAESTRO: *(Surveying the audience)* I'm speaking to just one of you amongst many.

> *(COLOMBINE slams the coffin shut again. He whirls at the noise.)*

Shut up! *(Then continues to the audience.)* A single one—who feels my words reverberating, as they self-evidently do not reverberate in those seated on either side of you. Look at them—heads encased in stone! Get rid of such petrified heads!

(Terrible music rises. The MAESTRO*'s head is covered in a white cloth. A sword is lifted and the head apparently chopped off.* DWARFS *run about, waving the* MAESTRO*'s head in the air. Then it's brought by* PIERROT *and placed on the top of the white cloth that still covers the* MAESTRO*'s real head, and he reaches up to hold it in place.)*

DOCTOR: Have we ever met before, sir?

MAESTRO: *(In a childlike voice, from under the cloth, as the decapitated head, which keeps falling off, only to be replaced by* PIERROT*)* Yes.

DOCTOR: Then perhaps it's a whole different aspect now manifesting itself—

MAESTRO: Funny! I don't feel different.

DOCTOR: Shall we add, he don't look different?

MAESTRO: *(Throwing away the cloth and collapsing on his back on the tables)* Don't hold me to such distinction, please—because I let feelings pour from my heart without naming them, which means I'm no longer naming anything in spite of this smile of recognition—?

DOCTOR: *(Now holding the head and studying it)* I'd like seeing such a smile.

MAESTRO: Don't ask for a mere imitation, please. It has to come from the heart.

DOCTOR: Does it come from the heart, Maestro?

MAESTRO: *(Jumping up)* Of course it does.

(He embraces the DOCTOR *and whirls him once, and the* DOCTOR *pulls away.)*

DOCTOR: Careful—You do not patronize me, sir?

MAESTRO: The furthest thing from our mind, sir.

DOCTOR: Oh?

MAESTRO: Wait a minute—you're not patronizing ME, Doctor?

(The rolling blackboards reenter.)

DOCTOR: Of course not. We all start from a basis of productive ignorance.

MAESTRO: Good, I think—

DOCTOR: *(Erasing on a blackboard)* Tell me everything about yourself.

MAESTRO: Haven't I done that?

DOCTOR: Again, please.

MAESTRO: Why?

DOCTOR: It's always different.

MAESTRO: I strive to avoid consistency.

DOCTOR: What drives you, sir?

MAESTRO: Drives me? Yes, I am driven.

DOCTOR: By what?

(Bell, and a deep voice intones: "A world, unfinished. Just like the real world." *All are terrified by the voice, and rush offstage. The stage is bright and empty for a few seconds, and then the MAESTRO sneaks back into the*

room and begins erasing on a blackboard. The DOCTOR
peeks in from the other side of the room.)

DOCTOR: What drives you, sir?

MAESTRO: I can't say.

DOCTOR: Tell me about your relation to the real world?

MAESTRO: Ah, that's the confusion—

DOCTOR: Is it confusing?

MAESTRO: A certain misunderstanding.

DOCTOR: Go on?

MAESTRO: Oh yes, go on and do go on and ON and ON!

DOCTOR: *(Overlaps)*—Explain how this is the basis of misunderstanding.

MAESTRO: People misunderstand me, Doctor.

DOCTOR: But how?

(The DWARFS have returned and are taking notes on the
MAESTRO's behavior.)

MAESTRO: I don't know how. I don't know about the inner
workings of other people—I'm a simple man.

DOCTOR: Are you really simple?

MAESTRO: You know better than myself.

DOCTOR: Why do you say that?

MAESTRO: *(As the DWARFS swivel their hips to taunt him)* The questions you ask! I can see you pulling things from my inside outside—

(He crosses away as COLOMBINE reappears from inside the coffin.)

DOCTOR: Ahh! Is that the answer of a simple man? —What drives you, sir?

MAESTRO: *(Thinks, then speaks quietly)* I want the world to continue, please.

DOCTOR: Come again?

COLOMBINE: Once is never enough.

MAESTRO: *(Climbing into the coffin with COLOMBINE)* Why did you say "come again"?

DOCTOR: It means "explain."

MAESTRO: It confuses me.

DOCTOR: Then erase it.

MAESTRO: Come again?

DOCTOR: Erase it.

MAESTRO: I can't. *(He maniacally rubs his crotch, laughing as the DWARFS come closer.)* I have no effective eraser in my repertoire.

DOCTOR: Why are you laughing, sir?

MAESTRO: All these unreal witnesses to my aberrant behavior. *(Jumps out of the coffin.)*

DOCTOR: Why unreal?

MAESTRO: You know perfectly well.

DOCTOR: No. I know nothing at all about you, sir.

MAESTRO: Really? You've been watching and listening to me night after night—

DOCTOR: I don't know what goes on INSIDE you.

MAESTRO: Whatever comes out.

DOCTOR: Yes. That we know. And we understand, of course, that what shows itself comes from an inside that does not show itself. So this we would like to see laid out before us, please!

MAESTRO: I'm not allowed to keep anything for myself?

DOCTOR: Why would you do this?

MAESTRO: Some of it is mine. *(Pause.)* I don't want to be emptied completely.

DOCTOR: What drives you: this is the thing you want to keep secret?

MAESTRO: Not really.

DOCTOR: What drives you, sir?

MAESTRO: *(A pause; he thinks)* I want the world to continue.

DOCTOR: You want the world to continue.

MAESTRO: I want the world to continue.

DOCTOR: Doesn't it?

MAESTRO: I want the world to continue.

DOCTOR: How. This is what we would like to hear . . .

MAESTRO: Well—*(Sighs.)* I want to please you, of course.

(The DWARFS make placating noises and throw him kisses.)

MAESTRO: *(Whirls toward them)* Stop it! *(Turning back to the DOCTOR.)* It's like this, Doctor. I let things I say come forward unexpectedly, in order to add . . . the unexpected, the unpredictable. Because otherwise the world locks in place, Doctor. Everybody seems to have learned how to behave—what to say—but the world needs something radically different. A little grease in the mechanism. A little . . . slipperiness—to keep it going.

DOCTOR: To keep the world going?

MAESTRO: Yes.

DOCTOR: This is your contribution.

MAESTRO: Yes.

DOCTOR: Slipperiness.

MAESTRO: Yes.

DOCTOR: How exactly?

MAESTRO: By what I say.

DOCTOR: It's in what you say.

MAESTRO: Yes.

DOCTOR: It's in your language.

MAESTRO: Yes.

DOCTOR: Slipperiness.

MAESTRO: To keep things going. Otherwise the gears lock up. Zip—I open things up. Zip—

DOCTOR: Zip—what is this zip?

MAESTRO: I keep things going. *(Pause.)* I say things that don't make sense, but now that you understand my motives, it all makes perfect sense. *(Pause; he turns away.)* God damn it—that's why I wanted to keep things to myself —because now that I've explained myself, our relationship has changed, but I liked it the way it was, when I was just your problematic object of examination! Now that I've explained myself—look!

DOCTOR: Look at what?

MAESTRO: Look at me! Suddenly cast as the wise man holding the balance of things on the tip of the tongue, while you sit beholden, waiting for me to perform my particular therapy. No! I liked it better when I had you off balance, trying to figure me out. *(Pause.)* But—what's done is done, so—

Off with the false faces! Only they weren't false, Doctor. So now when I go rattling through my language—now it's not going to work—because you think you know what's happening inside me now, which you will broadcast, dare I say it, to a vast assemblage—and then what? Things grind to a halt again.

Because whatever I say, from now on your pigeon-hole is available, your categorical box into which you zip whatever comes out of me like quicksilver—zip! Into the box—zip! Oh my goodness, look at all the little boxes lined up—help! Help! I can't move—excuse me, what I meant to say was help! Help! NOT ONE OF US is moving! *(Pause.)* Fine. Now off with the false face. *(Runs forward, and performs the ripping off of a pretend false face.)* Ah, what a relief. *(A more grotesque expression distorts his face.)* Look who's come to visit. *(Pause.)* I think this is going to hurt my facial muscles. Do I have permission to re-install my false face, Doctor?

DOCTOR: By all means.

MAESTRO: *(Relaxing his face)* Ah, thank you.

DOCTOR: No, thank *you.*

MAESTRO: That's all?

DOCTOR: This is everything.

MAESTRO: I can go back to my comfortable isolation chamber?

DOCTOR: Of course.

MAESTRO: Of course. Back in a jiffy—

> *(He runs and hits the padded panel that has reappeared, then rebounds, jumps into the coffin, and closes it.)*

DOCTOR: Continuing to study you carefully—

MAESTRO: *(From inside the coffin)* Do go on!

DOCTOR: I'm confused about something.

MAESTRO: *(Popping out of the coffin)* What?

DOCTOR: I'm not sure. But I'd like to see you leave this room and then reappear.

MAESTRO: Who would I be?

DOCTOR: Would you be—the person who enters, having not been here?

MAESTRO: *(Thinks for a moment)* I don't have time for this nonsense.

(He runs out of the room.)

DOCTOR: Self-evidently untrue. *(Calling out as he knocks on the coffin.)*—come in, please? *(Thinks to himself.)* Well, now I know. *(Turns to see the MAESTRO, who has reentered with a whip.)* Hello again.

MAESTRO: *(As the DOCTOR races for a chair to defend himself against the MAESTRO)* Don't I know you?

DOCTOR: This you have no time for guessing.

MAESTRO: Keep talking so I can remind myself.

DOCTOR: I'm finished with talking because this is specifically myself, sir.

MAESTRO: How odd.

DOCTOR: *(As a DWARF takes the chair from him)* Of course. Being nobody but myself is most peculiar and therefore of absolutely blinding intensity. Try this—if you dare. *(Points to his own nose, striking an exaggerated pose.)*

MAESTRO: Do I dare?

DOCTOR: Nobody but myself.

MAESTRO: First—I'd like to wipe my finger clean with my handkerchief—

DOCTOR: Good idea.

(They both start wiping their fingers as the DWARFS run in and start simultaneously rubbing their crotches, and somehow the DOCTOR and the MAESTRO are now doing the same. Music rises, then stops with a thud.)

Oh my God—look at it! His nose IS shining in the center of his face!

MAESTRO: That's not very desirable—for a nose.

DOCTOR: Don't worry, maybe this is just my way of speaking things.

MAESTRO: Why?

DOCTOR: Does this mean I have a private way of speaking things?

MAESTRO: Nobody else, I'm sure.

DOCTOR: Look at this. *(Points to his nose again.)*

MAESTRO: Maybe I'm supposed to look at the finger that's doing the pointing, rather than at the thing it's pointing at.

(He grabs for the DOCTOR's hand, and they arm wrestle as the music rises.)

DOCTOR: One nose too much, maybe.

MAESTRO: Is my nose still shining?

DOCTOR: There's no end to this kind of shining, Maestro.

MAESTRO: It's true. Even if the lights go out, things are still visible.

COLOMBINE: *(Entering from the side)* Maestro—did I show you this photograph taken of you years ago?

MAESTRO: Where did you get that?

DOCTOR: She can't remember.

MAESTRO: My nose is shining in this photograph.

COLOMBINE: I'll get my camera and take another for my collection?

MAESTRO: Please don't.

COLOMBINE: Why not?

MAESTRO: I don't want to deal with differences between two photographs.

DOCTOR: Understood!!

(The DOCTOR and COLOMBINE are revolving the floor cranks.)

Anticipate a resultant dizziness.

(The DWARFS run forward. They freeze, ready to do something aggressive. Then—a thud causes them to start rearranging the tables, and the MAESTRO holds his head, disoriented as their configuration changes.)

MAESTRO: I could imagine being less dizzy then I am now, which heretofore I've considered the state of not being dizzy.

DOCTOR: Get bearings from my own internal gyroscope, Maestro—

MAESTRO: I'd rather do that.

DOCTOR: Do that than what?

MAESTRO: *(Stops and thinks)* My white face, when tired. Such tiredness.

DOCTOR: But when alert, Maestro—*(Creeps up behind the MAESTRO and places the feather hat on his head.)*—such alertness.

MAESTRO: Okay. Okay. This is the story of the man who dressed extravagantly. He went into the street dressed in such a way that people stared at him.

DOCTOR: Paradise?

MAESTRO: A possible paradise.

(Curtains on tall poles appear in the rear; a white head attached to the end of a pole passes by the MAESTRO and comes to rest on a headless dummy dressed like the MAESTRO.)

DOCTOR: Self-fulfilling prophecies?

MAESTRO: No, I couldn't imagine that reality, I mean—that lack of reality.

COLOMBINE: *(Coming forward carrying a dummy dressed like the MAESTRO—but this one with a head, blindfolded, wearing a feather headdress just like the MAESTRO's)* Excuse me—when no story surfaces—

MAESTRO: *(Grabbing the dummy from COLOMBINE, circling the stage with it in his arms)* Wrong! This is the story of a man who runs out of stories, one hundred percent!

(The DOCTOR dances in from of one of the curtains, ringing a little bell and giggling. MAESTRO stops, placing the

*dummy on one of the tables, staring at the **DOCTOR**. Then he turns back to the audience.)*

. . . at which point silver bells are ringing, and a vast audience of one assembles in front of a white curtain, blowing softly in the wind.

DOCTOR: *(Ringing his little bell as the **MAESTRO** slowly bends over his dummy and embraces it on the tabletop)* Now—hold your dummy a little bit tighter. Now—take your left hand and smear some of this strawberry jam on your dummy's face.

*(**PIERROT** and **COLOMBINE** have brought a large bowl of jam with a wooden spoon.)*

More—a little more. Not too much. Now hold your dummy so he doesn't fall down—

*(**MAESTRO** and his dummy are sliding to the floor, and there they lie in a tight, passionate embrace.)*

—and speak the name of your beloved very softly.

MAESTRO: *(Whispers)* Beloved . . .

DOCTOR: —As if your dummy's done great harm to you, but you were full of compassion for that dummy nevertheless.

MAESTRO: *(Whispers)* Beloved . . .

DOCTOR: Good, good. Hold that position. Which I know is tiring.

MAESTRO: *(Whispering from the floor, dummy in his arms)* Beloved, beloved, beloved—!

*(He suddenly stops, looks up, and sees **COLOMBINE**.*

He rises and runs to her and tries to kiss her, but she pushes him away and he falls back on his dummy.)

PIERROT: *(Looking down over the MAESTRO)* The curtain rises on nothing, Maestro.

(The MAESTRO jumps up from the floor to confront them all.)

The audience beats its breast, rolling on the carpet, where one or two spectators break their eyeglasses—

(PIERROT and the DWARFS punch themselves in the eye as the MAESTRO runs off.)

Ow! When a possible actor erases lines of text from his sawdust-filled head.

(COLOMBINE has given him the dummy.)

So that coherence has the power of an unapproachable goal.

DOCTOR: Yah, to scenery with a twist, calling attention to devious plots that deem themselves the unrecognizable, so the giant theater of the world collapses.

PIERROT: Yes, to the dust which rises, touching, like perfume, the very wind, until empty seats go finally to those who truly think about things.

(The MAESTRO runs back onstage, wearing a white butcher's hat. Everyone pulls away from him in fear. For a moment, nothing happens.)

MAESTRO: Yes. To the theater of hesitations.

COLOMBINE: *(Coming forward with a white sheet in her arms)*

Sweet, the way a taste can be a musical afterthought, Maestro, balancing just long enough to make its collapse noticeable. *(Pulls the MAESTRO's head back.)*

Wherein its beauty—as if re-learned, Maestro. Such beauty—because so unnoticed, so defective—*(Kisses his lips.)*—so many missing parts, Maestro, the mechanism fails to function.

Beauty—*(Throws her sheet over the MAESTRO.)* —exactly in that. *(Pushes him to the floor.)*

Tell us another story, please—

MAESTRO: *(Coming out from under the sheet)* I already did.

COLOMBINE: Make it more powerful.

MAESTRO: Here's the premise. I forget everything I ever said, everything I ever experienced. Instead, I'm into real magic.

DOCTOR: I see very little evidence.

MAESTRO: I'm about to give you a demonstration.

COLOMBINE: Nothing is happening.

MAESTRO: *(Pause, then very quietly)*
You don't see it happening
But huge forces array themselves against me
And I fight my way back into this theater.
At best—self-destructive.
At worst—amassing fragments of scenery and torn curtains,
Till I arrive, finally, on stage—

(He jumps on one of the tables and, carrying a knife now, mimes cutting his throat.)

Pouring forth blood, which fools nobody.

DOCTOR: We don't see the blood.

MAESTRO: Imagine the blood.

COLOMBINE: Then it's unreal.

MAESTRO: Yes and no.
> The pretense has to be made, however.
> Bandages applied to everything visible
> So food for thought is provided.
> But certain critical minds, proclaim
> "False premise! False premise!"

DOCTOR, COLOMBINE and PIERROT: False premise!

MAESTRO: Those wounds so bound, nonexistent.
> Those developments that follow?
> Non-justifiable.
> As tears, false prophets,
> Chase us from the theater.
> Is it right to cry?
> Is it wrong to preach mental rigor?
> Yes and no.

(DWARFS run forward and dress the MAESTRO in his skirt and feather hat.)

> Helpful for some—mental rigor—
> Self-limiting for others;
> But the distribution of advantages and disadvantages can be
> Transcribed and evaluated by no known methods.
> So mystery is truly at work,
> Clothed in the bauble-laden dress of this magical occasion.
> Ladies and gentlemen. Do we notice anything out of the
>   ordinary?

(The DWARFS start manipulating a variety of disks.)

Vulgar surprises—
Rolling amidst us suddenly—
The wounded eye, singular
Of the storm—

*(Disks are hit with large drumsticks; a crash, and the
others fall to the floor as loud music rises.)*

—Closing now!
Ah, that's what should have performed the destructive act;
Some nonhuman,
Visible machine
For the destruction of the visible.
That giant eyelid
Beholden to no one.
Seeing and swallowing whatever is seen.
Hiding the seeable
So important work can truly begin—

*(All have risen; there is a "ping," and all freeze as the
music stops.)*

—Elsewhere.
And the theater: serves its function,
which is to go up in flames.

(Everyone else runs from the stage as the lights dim.)

Destroyed—
By the very moment in which our true hero
Mounts, finally—

*(He jumps down from the table and staggers upon the
small stage at the rear of the room.)*

With what effort,
With what long, disastrous
Blathering—

The sinking, ladies and gentlemen,
"Stage" itself.
*(All hell breaks loose. DWARFS run in with large mirrors,
PIERROT and the DOCTOR have curtains on tall poles, the
music explodes, and as lights blind the eyes, everyone
seems to be dancing and exchanging props in manic
defiance. The DWARFS do high kicks like a line of music-
hall entertainers. Suddenly, everything stops. In silence,
the MAESTRO jumps down from the stage.)*

So—?
Does it really happen—this destructive finale?
It depends who asks.
It depends who answers.

*(The mirrors surround him and he comes down to
speak to the audience.)*

But YOU, YOU, YOU, YOU, YOU, YOU, probably don't
want to suffer a MIND attack!
You want YOUR mind, ladies and gentlemen,
To remain invulnerable.
The most intimate part of yourself—
Am I right? Perfect.
Okay.
You will now suffer a mind attack!
Theaters across America
Will feature, tonight, inner details of YOUR mind.
People will view, if not your thoughts,
At least your associative tendencies.
And you WILL, to say the least, be humiliated.

*(A headless dummy in a chair is being placed behind
the MAESTRO.)*

It is not happening at this moment, not yet, but the
minute this apparatus is attached to your head—

(He places a strange box on the dummy's neck.)

—it will start happening.
MIND attack!
MIND attack!
MIND attack!

(The others try to hide.)

But—here's the GOOD news.
I have decided to save "you"
From mind attack,
By offering—my own mind instead.
And all you have to do to make this happen is to say
Thank you. Maestro.
Thank you for offering to save me, to save ALL OF US—
From mind attack,
By offering your own mind
As the object of this mind attack.
But you do not even have to say thank you
With your verbal mechanism,
Nor even kneel down in gratitude before me.
All you have to do is to think, in the privacy of your
own mind—
"Thank you."
And I believe you think, "Thank you."
That is my desperate belief.
And I am revealing my belief, here in public,
Which is the very first example of the way I offer MY
OWN mind
To save your own mind
From mind attack.
    This being the very first time I have ever offered my
own mind to protect other minds—the question must
be asked—why tonight, of all nights?

*(COLOMBINE has given him the blindfolded dummy
which he had previously embraced. He stares at it.)*

Is it because I love you?

(He hands it back to COLOMBINE *without looking at her, and she runs to the coffin and climbs inside, hugging the dummy.)*

Or is it perhaps because I don't love each one of you in
   particular—
But just one of you,
I won't say who,
Who sits there in the darkness in front of me,
Whom I have looked at, seen, registered in my heart
   secretly,
And loved.
   This means of course that the rest of you—strangers to
me—are beholden not only to me, but to the one my love
has secretly selected—though that one, that "other," has no
idea that "he" or "she" is the one chosen by my love.

(He is wandering about the stage, and COLOMBINE *lifts up from the coffin, but he refuses to return her gaze.)*

And so each of you may well wonder, is it me? Am I the
beloved so chosen?
You can't know, of course.
But could be.
It could be.
It's true.
   I dare not speak openly, but one of you—or rather,
I should speak directly and say "YOU!"—without look-
ing in the appropriate direction, of course—

*(He starts whirling, pointing to different actors and dif-
ferent members of the audience.)*

YOU!
YOU!
YOU!

(His whirls send him falling dizzily to the floor.)
In fact—even
I don't know if I really "love" you.

(He jumps up and smacks the box of the headless dummy in the chair, sending it to the floor.)

—MIND ATTACK?
All this broken heart of mine needs is a few good friends to talk to sometimes. Reflectors only. A life spent in search of a mirror. Now—here's a mirror.

(He grabs a mirror, hands it off, and grabs the DOCTOR.)

But why is a human being so much better than a mirror? Because you can't see yourself as you REALLY are, in another human being—all you can see is yourself disguised as who you'd like to be—

    Especially if you CHOOSE your friends carefully, and for that reason—don't we all?

(Wandering around, he ends up facing the audience.)

Do I like you? Don't like you? —Well, what kind of a MIRROR are YOU?
—Mind attack?

(The others scream and shrink away as he jumps up on a table again.)

Of course you're frightened—
Because I believe myself to be so much more intelligent Than the rest of you—you know why?
Because I know so much more about my OWN life!
—You have to admit that.
The question is, do you accept my idea of intelligence?
You say no—but seen from your own point of view—
If you see what I mean—

Don't you think I'm right?
—Mind attack!
Here are ten words plucked from my brain.
I didn't do the plucking, and if you're not interested, remember—
This is all to save all the rest of you from mind attack!

(The DWARFS run on carrying large white cards with an appropriate word printed on each, but they immediately stumble, and the cards go flying. They scramble to collect them and run offstage.)

Doubt.
Coincidence.
Rigor.
Traveling.
Snow.
Hopeful.
Gap.
Slippery.
Ten.
Error!
—Call that my personal pantheon, which is why I've been able to produce those words so quickly.

(He runs down to the audience.)

They come up onstage—all these words to stand in for that very handleable me who's made himself available for so many years—handled to great public acclaim, almost—because the total illusion contributed to the fiction that what happened onstage was my own personal effort on your behalf—being all okay.

(He stops, and his face registers disgust.)

But it was only . . . being "handled," that happened to me. And now—to shock myself—

The handling gets . . . dematerialized.
And what looks like withdrawal from the scene of action
Is really
Plunging into the real action someplace else
That of course has no scene at all.

(Smoke starts rising. The DWARFS surround him, holding up wooden paddles to hide from his anticipated fury.)

—Dematerialized.
—Ready to begin.
    That's what it doesn't look like, when you see the curtain come down in front of your eyes and you ostensibly go to sleep so that something else wakes up and gets down to REAL work—and the false face—burning—
LOOK AT IT!
—Covers itself in its own smoke—!

(He grabs a paddle and starts hitting himself in the head as the music explodes, the lights flash, and the DWARFS also smash their own heads with paddles. Then the MAESTRO collapses and screams out.)
Hold it right there—!

(The music stops, and the others run from the stage.)

Enough said.

DOCTOR: Are you ready for the experiment?

MAESTRO: What goddamn experiment?

DOCTOR: I do appreciate it as a personal favor to me.

MAESTRO: Promise it won't hurt.

DOCTOR: Not at all. You'll feel a slight tingling on the skin, but it won't be pain.

MAESTRO: Okay—

(He smacks himself again with his paddle as a small guillotine appears onstage.)

OW!

DOCTOR: *(Whirls, startled)* Mein Gott!! What hurt?

MAESTRO: Nothing yet.

DOCTOR: *(Calming down, seeing the guillotine)* Of course not. What is here is simply a machine to make thought more fluid.

MAESTRO: The devil's work?

PIERROT: *(Appearing at the rear with the DWARFS, who are tinkling small handbells)* Perhaps the devil's work, Maestro.

MAESTRO: Stop now, please. *(As they advance towards him, he shouts)* Leave the stage, every last one of you!

COLOMBINE: *(Entering)* You've ruined the play, sir.

MAESTRO: Not at all.

COLOMBINE: You've ruined the play by interrupting it.

MAESTRO: Did I interrupt it?

DOCTOR: You have brought things to a halt.

(The MAESTRO puts his head in the guillotine. With a loud thud, it falls and cuts off his head. He emerges, and his own head is tossed to him.)

MAESTRO: *(Staring at his head)* I am ready to begin again.

DOCTOR: Too late.

(All but the MAESTRO exit.)

MAESTRO: Ah. Everybody was here. Now nobody's here. I hardly notice the difference.

(He tosses his head away.)

What a perverse man I've become.
Everybody come back, please!

(They do. All the DWARFS now wear feather headdresses, just like the MAESTRO. They start to ask something, but he silences them.)

—Shhh!

(They step back.)

Ask nothing. Mysteries should never be solved. Dance to the music of that commandment, please. Everybody! *(He cracks a whip, and the DWARFS start doing a chorus-line dance, calling out their steps in falsetto.)*

—At least make it look like dancing!

(As they hop to each step, he jumps on the center table and starts to dance, when suddenly a large black horse, with the MAESTRO DUMMY heroically astride its back, appears from the shadows and, as the music suddenly fades, gallops across the stage and vanishes. Everyone has stopped moving, and the MAESTRO looks wistfully after the disappearing image of his own lost dreams.)

THE END

OF T H ET I M E?C

PARADISE
HOTEL

Paradise Hotel. Produced by the Ontological-Hysteric Theater at the Ontological Theater at St. Mark's Church, New York City. January–April, 1999. Written, directed, and designed by Richard Foreman.

JULIA JACOBSON: Juliana Francis
TOMMY TUTTLE: Tom Pearl
KEN PUSSY PUSS: Jay Smith
TONY TURBO: Tony Torn
GIZA VON GOLDENHEIM: Gary Wilmes

A large dark room, walls covered with a multitude of tied-back fringed drapes and curtains, punctuated by small paintings of amorous scenes, painted targets, and clusters of gold-leafed cupids—a complex mélange, muted in shadows. Chandeliers and, incongruously, hanging industrial lights provide dim illumination. A giant frosted lightbulb also hangs low into the room. Two tables are upside down on the floor. Along the walls hang many coats and bathrobes, some with aged human skulls peeking over the collar. Music is heard— a tiny fragment of twenties jazz with a decidedly tart flavor, repeating again and again—and a complex web of such bittersweet music underlies the entire play, forty or fifty tiny riffs, each one looped so it repeats and repeats every two seconds or so—sometimes surging into deafening climax, and otherwise underscoring the dialogue—fading just for brief moments to isolate a few words or a sentence or two in sudden silence.

In addition, the dialogue is continually underscored and punctuated by a series of high-pitched pings, cymbal crashes, drum thuds, and deep resonating gongs. On occasion, the lights flash—as if in a cosmic thunderclap of sexual energy—and all cry out and hold their eyes. In addition, throughout the play, as the music rises, a loud "Wheee!" of excitement is heard over the loudspeakers, and the extras jump up and down in tremendous glee.

As the play begins, one of these music loops rises in volume, and a nasal male voice sings, "I'm happy, you're happy, I'm happy, you're happy," but that singing is overpowered by other music, as the entire cast runs onstage—principals and an equal number of extras (all dressed as potential hotel guests)—to dance in line in front of the footlights: a frantic Charleston, but with their faces frozen in anxiety—and GIZA VON GOLDENHEIM, with a superior air, prances before them, waving a baton.

GIZA VON GOLDENHEIM: *(Over the music)* Well, hello everybody. Swing and sway the old-fashioned way!

(Then a deep, powerful VOICE interrupts over the loudspeaker, and the music stops.)

VOICE: Ladies and gentlemen, ladies and gentlemen—attention, please!

(The cast stops dancing; there is a flash of light and a loud gong, which makes everyone whirl in pain from the noise—then recover and run offstage—but GIZA shouts after them, "Get the fuck back in here," and they reverse direction to reform their line as the music rises again and a "Wheee!" of excitement is heard over the loudspeakers. They again dance. But immediately the VOICE is heard, interrupting the music, and again they run offstage. Now the stage remains empty.)

VOICE: This play *Paradise Hotel* must be preceded by an announcement that may well prove disturbing to certain members of this audience—

(TONY TURBO, always anticipating the worst, peeks out from behind an arch, a worried expression on his face.)

But while no one desires to offend, this risk must be taken. All audiences must now be informed that this play, *Paradise Hotel* is not, in fact, *Paradise Hotel*, but is, in truth, a much more disturbing, and possibly illegal, play entitled—"Hotel Fuck"!

(Music rises and GIZA *runs out, the music lowers and* GIZA *smiles at the audience and whispers, "Hello there!")*

We do apologize, ladies and gentlemen—but rather than being disturbed at this revelation, we urge you, please, redirect your understandable distress—towards an even more potent threat—posed—by yet a third—much LESS provocatively titled play, entitled "Hotel Beautiful Roses."

This third play threatens to replace, in the near future, the much more provocatively titled "Hotel Fuck"—which is now filling the stage in front of your very eyes—

(Everyone returns and dances in line, worried looks on their faces.)

—trying desperately to hold on to its proper and genuine self—in the face of such terrible adversity—forever and forever and forever—HOTEL FUCK! HOTEL FUCK!

TONY TURBO: *(The music is loud now, and he shouts over it to quiet things down)* Do you know what this means, everybody? It means we're in big trouble, all of us—

KEN PUSSY PUSS: What kind of trouble, Tony Turbo?

TONY TURBO: Look, definitions of trouble are elusive, agreed? Let's try to experience this—emotionally.

JULIA JACOBSON: *(A lady of more elegance than the others)* But—I don't feel emotional.

TOMMY TUTTLE: *(A tough guy)* Me neither. I don't feel emotional, so fuck you.

TONY TURBO: *(Taken aback for a moment, then recovers)* Well, fuck you.

KEN PUSSY PUSS: *(A nervous type)* Well, fuck YOU, Tony Turbo!

*(Everyone surrounds **TONY**, poking at him and laughing as the music rises, and most of them quickly leave the room.)*

TONY TURBO: *(Still wobbling from the attack)* Are they all blind, for Christ's sake?

GIZA VON GOLDENHEIM: Maybe.

TONY TURBO: Hey, what about these terrible "sexual emotions" that victimize every fucking one of us?

JULIA JACOBSON: *(Lurking in the background)* Oh my God— you're right, Tony Turbo. *(Turns to call to the next room.)* Come back, listen to this everybody, come back!

GIZA VON GOLDENHEIM: This is no big revelation, Tony Turbo. We're all victims of sexual emotion. We have no control over ourselves—so what's the difference?

TONY TURBO: The difference is—try!

TOMMY TUTTLE: *(Entering, buttoning up his fly)* Try what, Turbo?

TONY TURBO: Let's try having a little control over our sexual emotions—

TOMMY TUTTLE: Oh come on, that's not possible!

KEN PUSSY PUSS: *(Entering)* Here's what I say, fellas. If control is impossible . . . let's pack up those sexual emotions that are getting us in such big trouble and head straight for the Hotel Fuck!

JULIA JACOBSON: *(From the rear, where she has been lurking)* Okay, boys—

KEN PUSSY PUSS: *(Whirling in surprise and embarrassment)* Oh-oh! There's a lady in the room, fellas!

JULIA JACOBSON: —what will we do when we get to the Hotel Fuck?

KEN PUSSY PUSS: *(Hesitates, then blurts out)* Fuck our brains out, possibly!

(They all laugh, as the singing tape rises: "I'm happy, you're happy, I'm happy, you're happy.")

JULIA JACOBSON: Wait a minute. I don't understand what you're saying. Can't we fuck right here, boys? Where we are?

TOMMY TUTTLE: Oh, Julia Jacobson is so naive—

KEN PUSSY PUSS: Excuse me, lady. What I've heard is—it's much better fucking if you're inside the real Hotel Fuck.

JULIA JACOBSON: But why?

KEN PUSSY PUSS: *(Irritated)* Why? It's better, that's all!

TOMMY TUTTLE: Then it's settled, isn't it?

TONY TURBO: I hope so.

TOMMY TUTTLE: Ready, boys?

TURBO AND KEN PUSSY: Yeah!

(They all run to small cranks on the walls, or on thin pillars that surround the room, and start revolving the cranks to the music in a way that suggests sexual anticipation.)

TOMMY TUTTLE: We're all headed to the Hotel Fuck, sooner or later.

JULIA JACOBSON: Okay. I agree with Tommy Tuttle in principle. But instead of just talking about it, how do we get to the Hotel Fuck?

(A loud gong signals the return of the singing—"I'm happy, you're happy, I'm happy, you're happy"—and GIZA enters with a large dildo, striped black and gold, protruding from his pants.)

GIZA VON GOLDENHEIM: That's where I can be of assistance, ladies!

(One of the extra guests runs a taut string from the wall to the tip of his dildo. These taut strings which occur throughout the play are facilitated by hidden fishing reels with an automatic rewind mechanism built into the reel.)

I will point my significantly erect member towards the public bus stop, where we can all catch the number thirteen bus straight to the Hotel Fuck itself.

KEN PUSSY PUSS: *(As all the others enter)* He's right! I remember a bus stop right around the corner—let's go, everybody—let's go to the Hotel Fuck!

(All but GIZA run out excitedly, but somehow smash into the walls and fall back with a crash to the floor as the tape rises: "I'm happy, you're happy, I'm happy, you're happy . . .")

GIZA VON GOLDENHEIM: Is there a problem, Julia Jacobson?

JULIA JACOBSON: *(Rising from the floor)* Hmmm, no problem—

GIZA VON GOLDENHEIM: Yes, there is a problem, Julia Jacobson, can you deal with the fact that the Hotel Fuck itself threatens a voluntary self-transformation into that boring, boring, boring rival play—"Hotel Beautiful Roses"?

JULIA JACOBSON: Oh my GOD, that does sound like a boring play!

TONY TURBO: *(Running in, wearing a dress and a bonnet)* Be reassured, dear friends! I, Tony Turbo, promise—

GIZA VON GOLDENHEIM: *(Interrupting)* Why are you wearing that dress?

TONY TURBO: *(Stops, worried, thinks—)* Well, it's my party dress. *(Whirls once, then readdresses the serious matter at hand.)* And I promise that this play, "Hotel Fuck," will never be allowed to become some less desirable play—including that terrible one called "Beautiful Roses." This will not happen!

TOMMY TUTTLE: *(Running into the room, waving a pistol)* What the fuck—can I believe what I'm hearing about a rival hotel?

(The other guests scream and try to take cover.)

JULIA JACOBSON: Oh SHIT! Tommy Tuttle heard everything!

TOMMY TUTTLE: Yes, I did, Julia Jacobson.

KEN PUSSY PUSS: Put down that gun!

TOMMY TUTTLE: And I am very, very upset that the play "Hotel

Fuck" could EVER turn into an insipid play like "Beautiful Roses." I am so fucking upset at this possibility that I think—

GIZA VON GOLDENHEIM: What do you think, Tommy Tuttle?

TOMMY TUTTLE: I think I'm going to shoot myself in the head.

GIZA VON GOLDENHEIM: Shoot yourself in the head for a hotel, Tommy Tuttle? That's really not necessary.

TOMMY TUTTLE: However, that's exactly what I'm going to do.

(He puts the gun to his forehead and pulls the trigger— but nothing happens.)

Hey, are there any fucking bullets in this gun? I don't think so.

TONY TURBO: *(Entering, waving his own gun around, as the others again scream and take cover)* That's because—I took all the bullets for myself.

TOMMY TUTTLE: Every fucking bullet?

TONY TURBO: Every fucking bullet, because I need every fucking bullet for myself! *(Places his own gun to his forehead.)*

TOMMY TUTTLE: Tony Turbo is a selfish bitch who takes every fucking bullet for himself!

TONY TURBO: *(Gasps with a shock of self-recognition)* Maybe —I am selfish.

JULIA JACOBSON: *(Entering with yet another gun)* Here, Tommy Tuttle—try this substitute gun, with lots of bullets.

TONY TURBO: *(Irritated)* Where did THAT come from?

TOMMY TUTTLE: *(Taking the offered gun)* Selfish bitches—

> *(As music rises, he slaps* JULIA JACOBSON *and puts the new gun to his forehead.)*

—this one's mine!

> *(He again pulls the trigger, but this time there is a shot, and he falls to the floor as the singing rises: "I'm happy, you're happy, I'm happy, you're happy . . .")*

KEN PUSSY PUSS: Oh, what an unfortunate accident—but this is unclear to me. Did this happen because Tommy Tuttle could no longer stand living in a world of selfish bitches like Tony Turbo? Or did this happen because this play was about to turn into that boring play, "Hotel Beautiful Roses"?

> *(*TOMMY TUTTLE *suddenly twitches and rises up—all the others gasp and fall to the floor around him in shock.)*

JULIA JACOBSON: Oh this is fuck fuck fuck—that is an amazing resurrection.

GIZA VON GOLDENHEIM: Did that happen by itself, Tommy Tuttle? Or did you receive help from higher sources?

KEN PUSSY PUSS: What the fuck are higher sources?

JULIA JACOBSON: *(As all kneel in reverence)* I don't think he'll tell us that.

TOMMY TUTTLE: Well, all I have to say is, thank God I'm not fucking dead permanently.

KEN PUSSY PUSS: *(Running to* TOMMY TUTTLE, *brushing him off)* Right. What really matters is, now we don't have to change plans, and with renewed enthusiasm, we can head straight for the Hotel Fuck.

(TOMMY TUTTLE tries to pull away.)

Oh, I know, an apparent miracle is always a little unsettling—

TONY TURBO: It sure is—

KEN PUSSY PUSS: —but as soon as we get to the Hotel Fuck, all is forgotten and forgiven, right?

(A crash, and in a moment of loud music, everyone but TOMMY TUTTLE manages to clump together in a giant, undulating hug.)

TOMMY TUTTLE: Wait one good goddamn fucking minute, please! Why do I feel like I'm already inside the Hotel Fuck?

JULIA JACOBSON: *(Breaking away from the group.)* What you claim is impossible, Tommy Tuttle, we still haven't taken the bus.

TONY TURBO: There's the bus.

(They all run a few steps to the imagined bus, then stop in confusion.)

Where's the bus?

(A gong sounds as the lights flash, and they all whirl, holding their eyes.)

KEN PUSSY PUSS: No problem! We're gonna perk up fast, because where are we headed, bus or no bus? Straight to the Hotel Fuck, right?—bye-bye, everybody!

(The music rises as cheers are heard over the speakers, and all run from the room except KEN PUSSY PUSS, who

has become entangled in a string from one of the pillars, which is pulled taut to his groin. He freezes, and the music stops.)

KEN PUSSY PUSS: Oh, this is terrible. For some reason I'm stuck in one place. Could it be my memories are a problem? They are all one hundred percent sex memories, of course.

(TOMMY TUTTLE enters, holding a stick with a white ball on one end.)

Except—what the hell makes me nervous about the possibility that I have FORGOTTEN lots of those important sex memories? That must be the explanation, right?

TOMMY TUTTLE: *(Mocking him)* Right.

(He takes his stick and reaches up to make contact with the giant lightbulb, producing a flash of light as the music rises and all the women, including JULIA JACOBSON, tumble into the room holding aloft threatening badminton rackets.)

KEN PUSSY PUSS: Listen, up till now, I'm certain I was full to the brim, me, with such great sex memories—so it's understandable I'm a little worried, because what do I have left—

(The women swing their rackets with a swish, and KEN PUSSY PUSS screams and protects his crotch.)

—if I've lost all my sex memories?

JULIA JACOBSON: I don't have that problem—because me, I have three—

*(Another swing from the women, and a scream from
KEN PUSSY PUSS.)*

—or four—

(Another swing.)

—wonderful sex memories that I can remember.

TOMMY TUTTLE: I'll bet you do—Selfish Polish or something—
bitch.

*(He again hits the light with his stick, producing a flash
and a surge of music as all whirl in pain.)*

JULIA JACOBSON: Those sex memories get me in lots of trouble,
that's for sure!

TOMMY TUTTLE: Sure—

KEN PUSSY PUSS: Oh sure!

TOMMY TUTTLE: —and Julia Jacobson is so confident about
every one of her fucking sex memories.

JULIA JACOBSON: Well, certainly more self confident than
Mr. "Might-As-Well-Shoot-Myself-in-the-Head" Tommy
Tom Tuttle.

TOMMY TUTTLE: Okay, that's the difference between us—I'm a
human being who's not convinced of anything one
hundred percent—which is why occasionally I have to
shoot myself in the head.

JULIA JACOBSON: Okay, but this time, instead of shooting ourselves in the head again and AGAIN—

*(Now KEN PUSSY PUSS has the stick and hits the bulb,
with similar results.)*

—can we please go to the Hotel Fuck?

TOMMY TUTTLE: That's the idea, lady.

JULIA JACOBSON: So I can get deliciously fucked by the two of you at one time?

(She has positioned herself inside one of the upside-down tables, with her bare legs up in the air, provocatively revealing her panties. Three other women come and stretch taut strings to the point between JULIA JACOBSON's legs.)

KEN PUSSY PUSS: *(Hesitates, confronted with this tableau)* The two of us at once? No way, lady.

TOMMY TUTTLE: That is not possible.

JULIA JACOBSON: Why the fuck not?

TOMMY TUTTLE: Listen, it doesn't mean we wouldn't like to fuck you individually—

KEN PUSSY PUSS: —as an individual thing—absolutely.

TOMMY TUTTLE: We do find Julia Jacobson absolutely fuckable.

KEN PUSSY PUSS: But fucking you simultaneously, that's something we could not permit ourselves.

JULIA JACOBSON: Why not, please?

TOMMY TUTTLE: Now come on—you figure it out, lady!

JULIA JACOBSON: I can't figure that out.

KEN PUSSY PUSS: *(As he and TOMMY TUTTLE embrace, buddy-*

style) Fucking you simultaneously is one thing bosom buddies do not share, Julia Jacobson. This is appropriately compartmentalized.

TOMMY TUTTLE: That's a fucking necessary precaution!

JULIA JACOBSON: But it's such a drag!

TOMMY TUTTLE: Oh Jesus—if we both fuck you at once—it's obvious. Mixed-up fucking like that, we could end up losing our individual body orientation.

KEN PUSSY PUSS: *(Pulling away from TOMMY TUTTLE)* Hey!—I almost did that.

JULIA JACOBSON: *(Rising as the tableau dissolves)* But that would be so BEAUTIFUL—!

TOMMY TUTTLE: No, that would be one rotten stinking idea!

JULIA JACOBSON: *(Knocking him down with a karate chop)* Okay, I've lost interest in both of you stinky guys at once!

TOMMY TUTTLE: *(As JULIA JACOBSON turns her back and exits)* Selfish, selfish, selfish, what a selfish world!

GIZA VON GOLDENHEIM: *(Entering with his big dildo, which is immediately carried off by one of the women)* You gentlemen realize, of course—there is never immediate resolution to a complex web of superimposed appetites.

(Other girls are lined up behind him and begin wiggling to the music.)

KEN PUSSY PUSS: Giza von Goldenheim is right, Tom Tuttle— here we are like two assholes waiting for something big to happen that never happens to me. *(Looks at the girls shaking their asses.)*

Is that dancing? Stop dancing. Stop dancing. Stop dancing!

(The music rises as the girl who has taken GIZA's big dildo returns now with it strapped onto her body in the appropriate place. She dances across the stage to the loud music, using a whip to lash the dildo as if she were urging on a racehorse. With each whip, the others scream and twitch violently. As she disappears, GIZA recovers.)

GIZA VON GOLDENHEIM: Such things happen, gentlemen—more than any of us would like to imagine. Guess where?

(The girl with the dildo reappears, holding aloft two large tickets.)

TOMMY TUTTLE: What's that?

GIZA VON GOLDENHEIM: Two bus tickets to Hotel Fuck.

TOMMY TUTTLE: Wait a minute—real bus tickets?

KEN PUSSY PUSS: Hotel tickets, maybe—

GIZA VON GOLDENHEIM: It's the same thing. Special hotel, special bus.

TOMMY TUTTLE: Oh yeah? Well—I never fucked on a public bus.

(The girls scream delightedly and surround TOMMY TUTTLE.)

KEN PUSSY PUSS: *(Shocked)* Do people do that?

TOMMY TUTTLE: But just in case, I'm gonna need a few more tickets.

KEN PUSSY PUSS: *(Grabbing the tickets away)* Oh selfish, self-ish Tommy Tuttle—

(All the others are entering.)

GIZA VON GOLDENHEIM: How many tickets do we propose for the inexhaustible Tommy Tuttle?

TOMMY TUTTLE: Ten, twenty, a hundred maybe—!

TONY TURBO: *(Gliding in from the rear)* Plus! One more very big ticket for me, please?

TOMMY TUTTLE: Why not? A hundred and one tickets for the Hotel Fuck. Because if you don't have enough tickets, you don't get as many fucks.

(The music stops. JULIA JACOBSON pushes forward.)

JULIA JACOBSON: Oh my God! Better not to live in a world of such selfishness.

(She has a gun, which she brings to her forehead to shoot herself.)

Wait a minute, how do I know there are bullets in this thing?

GIZA VON GOLDENHEIM: Oh? You want bullets?

JULIA JACOBSON: Of course. I have a right to my own bullets!

TONY TURBO: Selfish, selfish Julia Jacobson.

JULIA JACOBSON: *(Stunned by the accusation)* I suppose I am.

(She turns to the others, who wave threatening fingers at her.)

Do you suppose I really, truly am?

(She again lifts the gun, shoots herself in the ear, and falls to the floor. The others bend over to look and, as the music rises, break into cheers. Then TOMMY TUTTLE runs forward and takes the gun.)

TOMMY TUTTLE: *(Excitedly, doing a little dance, gun to his head)* Now it's my turn!

(He shoots himself and falls. More cheers as KEN PUSSY PUSS runs forward to take the gun.)

KEN PUSSY PUSS: That was pretty good. But now it's my turn.

(He beats his chest like an excited gorilla, shoots himself, and falls as the others cheer. TONY TURBO runs forward.)

TONY TURBO: Now it's finally my turn.

(He shoots himself, all cheer and start dancing to the music, including those on the floor who rise to join the dance.)

GIZA VON GOLDENHEIM: *(Amidst the swirling dancers)* My God, is this the way things are supposed to happen, boys and girls? We all start twirling like fairies in firelight—all the most ravishing people, totally on fire, ravishing people ready to die for such—RAVISHING people—I do hope against hope against hope!

KEN PUSSY PUSS: My God, I realize this could all be true, except—one most beautiful person is the person I am trying to imagine for myself—!

JULIA JACOBSON: Oh do tell us Ken Ken Kitty Kat—which is the most beautiful person imaginable to little Kitty Ken Kitty Puss Puss Puss—

(The music rises, and we hear the VOICE *demanding,* "Let's do that again, please!"*)*

ALL: *(Singing to the music)* Hey, ho, let's go—

TOMMY TUTTLE: *(Stepping forward with a hand mike)*—That's the way they dance in France.

ALL: Hey, ho, let's go—

TOMMY TUTTLE: —Wearing tight and shiny pants.

ALL: Hey, ho, let's go—

(After each sung phrase, a few fall to the floor.)

TOMMY TUTTLE: —Watch them wiggle. Watch them prance.

ALL: Hey, ho, let's go—

TOMMY TUTTLE: —Thoroughbreds with no real chance.

(By now, everybody except JULIA JACOBSON *is on the floor. She steps through the field of bodies.)*

JULIA JACOBSON: Oh shit—why does everybody keep falling to the floor like dead people?

TOMMY TUTTLE: Hey lady—cut the crap. We're on the floor trying to get fucked.

TONY TURBO: *(As everybody rises)* But first, let's decide who is the most beautiful, okay?

TOMMY PEARL: *(As* JULIA JACOBSON *whirls to the music)* The most beautiful—is the lady inside the Hotel Fuck.

TONY TURBO: Guess again, smart-ass—as of yet, nobody's found out how to get inside the fucking front door of the fucking Hotel Fuck!

JULIA JACOBSON: Ohh!—big-time mistake!

GIZA AND KEN: Knock, knock, knock!

(The music stops.)

TONY TURBO: *(Complaining)* Hey, listen, lady—I've been damn well trying!

GIZA VON GOLDENHEIM: Maybe Tony Turbo hasn't been KNOCKING the proper way.

VOICE: Let's do that again, please?

(The music is rising, and three girls with big three-foot-long, striped dildos appear and dance across the room, quickly disappearing.)

TONY TURBO: *(Shocked)* Nobody here knocks more than I knock.

GIZA VON GOLDENHEIM: But exactly how hard does Tony Turbo knock, when he knocks?

(Music rises again as the three girls with dildos make another pass through the room as TONY, GIZA, and KEN pull a string taut from one of the pillars—doing a high-kick accompaniment—but tumbling back onto each other as a telephone is heard ringing.)

TONY TURBO: HELLO! Is this the phone call I been waiting for my whole fucking life?

VOICE: I don't know about that, Tony Turbo—but I CAN tell you the Hotel Fuck is now ready to receive visitors.

And rooms are now available for the whole world inside the Hotel Fuck. The really big—Hotel Fuck!

*(The music again becomes very loud as a baggage cart appears, loaded with suitcases, on top of which sits a small model of the Hotel Fuck. The girls jump up and down, cheering, as **TONY TURBO** approaches the little hotel.)*

TONY TURBO: This may be a problem, everybody. The Hotel Fuck is ready to receive millions of visitors, but I can never believe the entire Hotel Fuck fits into this relatively tiny apparatus.

*(**TONY TURBO** has the little hotel placed over his head and shoulders as the **VOICE** intones—"Let's do that again, please." The girls and **KEN PUSSY PUSS** line up behind him and cross the stage in a conga line behind the hotel-covered **TONY TURBO**. **TOMMY TUTTLE** appears in a rabbit hat and hops about excitedly carrying his big stick and munching on a carrot. As the line crosses the stage, **TONY TURBO** momentarily lifts one side of the little hotel and calls out.)*

TONY TURBO: Hey! How is this possible? I don't see how everybody can fit in here.

*(He disappears inside again as the music surges and they reach the side of the room, then all collapse against one another, running themselves between the legs as **GIZA** runs into the room, talking into a telephone receiver and massaging himself between the legs with an oversize white handkerchief.)*

GIZA VON GOLDENHEIM: Oh my goodness—Mr. "Look-on-the-Dark-Side" may turn out to be right after all—because—sorry to report at this time—oh, oh—we are previously occupied with—oh, guess what happened—just a little—ohhh!

(As he collapses in orgasm, TOMMY TUTTLE hits the light-bulb with his stick. Accompanied by a flash of light, the loud music changes radically as girls run off carrying the little hotel; then the music softens.)

TOMMY TUTTLE: Okay, something happened downstairs, you little bunny rabbits, a little un-premeditated, but I say we shouldn't feel wiped out about this, because we are still in control of our major emotions.

KEN PUSSY PUSS: Which are the major emotions, Tommy Tuttle?

TOMMY TUTTLE: All we need is a mental adjustment.

(He swings his stick, and the others duck.)

POW! Let's imagine—being inside the Hotel Fuck right now. What would that be like?

(A gong sounds, and as the VOICE intones—"It is now: Twelve o'clock Hotel Fuck Time," a baggage cart enters with suitcases, against which stands a partially naked woman [JULIA JACOBSON] with her head covered in a black hood.)

TOMMY TUTTLE: Jesus Christ—who is this beautiful, almost naked, lady arriving coincidentally with all of our crappy baggage?

KEN PUSSY PUSS: My God—don't you recognize her, Tommy Tuttle? It's the beautiful woman from the Hotel Fuck.

TOMMY TUTTLE: This is close to impossible. We better verify this—

KEN PUSSY PUSS: I don't think we should touch her physically.

TOMMY TUTTLE: It's time to touch somebody physically!

GIZA VON GOLDENHEIM: *(As JULIA JACOBSON slowly crosses the room and disappears down a brightly lit corridor)* That might be necessary, gentlemen. Because if nobody does no touching, and if nobody does no rubbing up against, and if nobody does no licking and fucking and sucking—then there will be no touching, evidently. No fucking, evidently. No refucking, multifucking—

KEN PUSSY PUSS: Remember what that beautiful woman said to us?

TOMMY TUTTLE: We don't want to remember.

KEN PUSSY PUSS: It's interesting to remember such things!

(He grasps TOMMY TUTTLE's stick and hits the lightbulb; bright lights and a gong make them whirl in pain.)

She wanted to fuck, only with multiple partners—me and Tommy Tuttle, specifically.

GIZA VON GOLDENHEIM: Sounds quite radical, boys.

TOMMY TUTTLE: Oh yes—she's a radical selfish bitch. We were looking her straight in the eye when she said that.

GIZA VON GOLDENHEIM: No kidding?

(Behind them, two large white disks have appeared, one above the other, forming a sort of solid figure eight, behind which someone is hiding.)

TOMMY TUTTLE: What the fuck is that?

GIZA VON GOLDENHEIM: I think it's a warning, gentlemen.

TOMMY TUTTLE: Warning what in particular?

GIZA VON GOLDENHEIM: Let's put it this way—

TONY TURBO: *(Interrupting)* No, I'll handle this. *(Holds a large drumstick and prepares to hit the lower disk, as if hitting a gong.)*

TOMMY TUTTLE: *(Brandishing the light-stick)* I wanna help.

> *(Still in his rabbit hat, he takes a little hop, and he and* ***TONY TURBO*** *both prepare to strike the disk. But before they can do so, a loud gong sounds.)*

—What the hell was that?

GIZA VON GOLDENHEIM: OK, Tony Turbo, it's time.

TONY TURBO: Time for everybody to get undressed?

> *(One of the disks has rolled off, and the other, held by someone to cover the upper half of the body, advances downstage with a pair of naked legs showing beneath.)*

VOICE: Let's do that again, please!

> *(Another gong sounds, and the disk is taken away by a girl, revealing* ***JULIA JACOBSON*** *behind it, with her skirt tucked up into her belt.)*

TOMMY TUTTLE: Here's a better idea.

KEN PUSSY PUSS: Are you sure it's better?

TOMMY TUTTLE: *(Indicating* ***JULIA JACOBSON*** *and* ***TONY TURBO***, *still in his skirt and bonnet, as he will remain until the end of the play)* Yes I am. Because we leave these two beautiful bitches alone in this room, and then they just

work everything out between themselves—you know—
EVERYTHING?

(Everyone but TONY TURBO and JULIA JACOBSON leave the room.)

TONY TURBO: Hey—Don't leave me alone with this bitch!

JULIA JACOBSON: *(Wrapping TONY TURBO in a strip of fabric)* I never would have guessed it, Tony Turbo, but you must be one of those two beautiful bitches everybody seems so worked up about. So tell me—are you fuckable like I'm fuckable?

TONY TURBO: You know I don't like talking to myself.

JULIA JACOBSON: Of course—

(She pulls the fabric, making TONY TURBO spin free, he staggers to a wall.)

—Because that would be one BAD conversation.

TONY TURBO: Just like this conversation.

JULIA JACOBSON: Notice? My table is well spread, bitch. How about yours?

TONY TURBO: My table is well spread, bitch. Read my mind to find out about it—

JULIA JACOBSON: Not much of a turn-on, bitch. *(She starts to exit.)*

So read MY mind first, and come up with something more interesting?

(She ducks offstage, then whirls back with a large sledge-

hammer, which she crashes onto TONY TURBO's *foot. As he howls in pain,* KEN PUSSY PUSS *runs on with a sledge-hammer, yelling "Sledgehammer" as* TONY TURBO *grabs it from him and waves it in the air.)*

TONY TURBO: How's this for interesting, bitch!

(He slams JULIA JACOBSON's *foot; she howls in pain.)*

KEN PUSSY PUSS: If Tony Turbo could really read minds, bitch, total catastrophe!

JULIA AND TONY TURBO: Right now, bitch. Right now!

(They each smash a sledgehammer on the other's foot.)

TOMMY TUTTLE: *(Enters, excited, holding a sledgehammer)* God damn it! Look at this big bopstick, everybody! Does this mean we're inside the fucking Hotel Fuck right fucking NOW?

JULIA JACOBSON: Of course we are in the fucking Hotel Fuck for as far back as I can remember, fuckhead!

(New music rises, and she cocks her head to listen.)

What a crazy song—

(Now they all have sledgehammers, and they line up and sing and dance—manipulating their sledge-hammers—while the other guests jump up and down excitedly.)

ALL: If you like your baby, like you like no babies.
If you like your baby, like you like no babies.
If you like your baby, like you like no babies.
If you like your baby, like you like no babies.

KEN PUSSY PUSS: Wait a minute, please—how did we get to the Hotel Fuck without even riding the number thirteen bus?

GIZA VON GOLDENHEIM: That answer should be obvious. Everybody can read everybody else's mind.

KEN PUSSY PUSS: You mean even ME—?

(Suddenly, he bumps into TONY TURBO by accident and whirls away, now with the end of a string in his hand, the other end pulled taut by TONY TURBO.)

I hope not quite—

TONY TURBO: Nobody reads my mind past page one!

(A web of additional strings are pulled by guests to various foreheads.)

GIZA VON GOLDENHEIM: *(Ducking the strings)* Tony Turbo's mind . . .

TONY TURBO: No!

GIZA VON GOLDENHEIM: Ken Pussy Puss Pussy's mind—

KEN PUSSY PUSS: No!

GIZA VON GOLDENHEIM: Julia Jacobson's mind—which I am reading right this minute by the way.

JULIA JACOBSON: *(Holding her forehead where the string makes contact)* I don't think so, please—

GIZA VON GOLDENHEIM: —Because Julia Jacobson is riding on a fucking bus.

JULIA JACOBSON: Stop reading my mind, Giza von Goldenheim, because I have private memories—

GIZA VON GOLDENHEIM: I know that, sweetie, because when you're riding that fucking BUS—the destination is obvious.

JULIA JACOBSON: Wrong, Giza von Goldenheim—your own fucking memory is reading itself in a mirror.

GIZA VON GOLDENHEIM: Totally true. Of course.

JULIA JACOBSON: *(Quiet, as* TONY TURBO *crosses so that the string he holds, with* KEN PUSSY PUSS *on the other end, captures* JULIA JACOBSON *around the neck. She pulls against it gently, as if to choke herself, leaning forward like the figurehead on the prow of an ancient sailing ship.)* Could I be alone, please?—My head visits strange neighborhoods when I read minds—and sometimes it hurts—

(The music—now classical piano and violin music—rises.)

It hurts. It hurts. It hurts.

(The music stops.)

GIZA VON GOLDENHEIM: Make sure that pain is accurate, my dear. Because it COULD be somebody else's life story.

JULIA JACOBSON: That makes it hurt even more and more and more and more.

(The music has returned, ever changing.)

Pull harder, boys, harder, much harder!

KEN PUSSY PUSS: *(Whispering as he strains to tighten the string against which JULIA JACOBSON's neck is pulling)* My God, Tony Turbo, this girl really knows what she's doing.

JULIA JACOBSON: Of course, because what I'm really GOOD at—is reading the mind of little Giza von Geek—

GIZA VON GOLDENHEIM: *(Upset, regressing to his childhood self)* No!

JULIA JACOBSON: . . . Goldenheim! All alone and scared on the big bus all alone downtown where one tiny little boy is looking out the window of the great big bus—

(She is chasing him around pillars, into shadowy corners.)

—at the houses that go zipping by—zip! And the big apartment houses zipping by—zip, zip! And the windows in all those big houses, zip—zip—zip—what's behind those windows where the pretty curtains are pulled tight?

GIZA VON GOLDENHEIM: I know what's behind those windows, God damn it—

(He pushes her to the other side of the stage.)

JULIA JACOBSON: Of course he does, because all those big grown-up people are hiding right behind those windows—is that possible?

(The music is rising, and she runs to revolve one of the cranks.)

Are they fucking, fucking, fucking, fucking, fucking, fucking!

(Deafening music and a loud gong make her fall away

from the crank, but she recovers and returns as the music shifts and is quieter.)

Sun comes up, daddies go to Daddy's office. Sun goes down,
Mommies are making dinner. Sun comes up again—bye-bye!

Off to the factory to do big jobs—but my God, when the sun goes down again—back to fucking, fucking, fucking, fucking, fucking, fucking!

(The music again becomes deafening as many guests run in holding small red curtains in front of their faces. JULIA JACOBSON whirls away from the cranks, and the music quiets down.)

Is this right? Can this possibly be happening?

GIZA VON GOLDENHEIM: *(His face appears above one of the red curtains, but he has grown a large protuberant nose and is disguised in a bushy black beard. His voice is suddenly hoarse with age and degeneracy.)* A little sweetie pie is riding on the bus—

JULIA JACOBSON: No she's not!

GIZA VON GOLDENHEIM: Riding on the bus, when cute little curtains blow open for just a minute—

(He runs to a crank and starts revolving it, and the people with red curtains run to the wall and, still hiding their faces, start to massage themselves between the legs.)

And behind cute little curtains, oh my God—the whole world is fucking, fucking, fucking, fucking, fucking, fucking—

(The music becomes deafening, a gong rings out, the music changes, and JULIA JACOBSON sings operatically and defiantly—)

JULIA JACOBSON: —I have more important things to think about!

(She dances out of the room.)

GIZA VON GOLDENHEIM: Of course—there are other things to look at when she's riding on the bus. There are houses with cute little curtains, and big tall buildings made of dirty redbrick—

(He runs to the people against the wall, touching and tickling them.)

And bridges with shiny cars that are green and red and purple, and big thick books for smart people with shiny black hair, and old people with soft gray hair, and important people with big tummies. . . .

(JULIA JACOBSON has returned, and upon seeing GIZA touching the others, she is overcome with frustrated desire and throws herself upside down inside one of the upside-down tables and starts touching herself in front of GIZA.)

—and mothers and fathers and fucking and fucking and fucking and fucking and fucking and fucking!

(The music is deafening. GIZA staggers forward as it quiets down.)

—Oh my God, let an old man catch his breath for all that fucking and fucking and fucking and fucking and fucking and fucking!

(The music changes, and he is suddenly standing over her and waving his fists like an old-fashioned minister preaching hellfire and damnation.)

And fucking and fucking and fucking!

(A gong rings and, as the music changes again, all but GIZA *and* JULIA JACOBSON *run from the room.* GIZA *changes back into a degenerate old man licking his lips and slobbering loudly at* JULIA JACOBSON. *Then he dashes off and immediately returns with a large bouquet of red roses, which he thrusts on the stunned* JULIA JACOBSON. *Once more he slobbers loudly, then runs from the room. She starts to dash after him, as if to get rid of the flowers, then turns back in a daze and looks at the flowers.)*

JULIA JACOBSON: *(Horrified)* What am I holding in my arms? This isn't something I should be holding in my arms.

TONY TURBO: *(Running into the room with the others, grabbing the flowers away from her)* Bitch!

JULIA JACOBSON: I'm sorry!

TOMMY TUTTLE: Hey! You must be totally nuts, Julia Jacobson.

JULIA JACOBSON: I'm sorry, I must be crazy—

KEN PUSSY PUSS: This is the Hotel Fuck!—Not the Hotel you-know-what-we-don't-want-to-say-it!

JULIA JACOBSON: Really?

KEN PUSSY PUSS: Really!

JULIA JACOBSON: Say "Hotel Fuck" again, convince me—

(A guest comes whirling into the room, carrying more roses.)

TOMMY TUTTLE: *(Running to attack the roses)* The Hotel Fuck! Hotel Fuck! Hotel Fuck! Hotel Fuck!

(Another comes and zips the flowers on top of a six-foot-tall pedestal, where they are immediately hidden by a small white panel carried by another guest running in.)

Hey! What happened to the flowers?

JULIA JACOBSON: —My God, I am imagining such an incredible alternative reality!

TONY TURBO: Why's the selfish bitch holding her head?

JULIA JACOBSON: *(As a guest runs with a string to her forehead)* I'm holding my head because I feel—so much PRESSURE!

KEN PUSSY PUSS: Of course, because the Hotel Fuck stands in for everything totally OPPOSITE to the Hotel Beautiful Roses—

TONY TURBO: Don't even mention that name!

KEN PUSSY PUSS: Oh, the name must be spoken! Because there is a real suspicion in my head that Julia Jacobson has led us in a totally wrong direction—straight into the Hotel Beautiful Roses.

TONY TURBO AND GIZA VON GOLDENHEIM: No such thing! No that's impossible!

TOMMY TUTTLE: *(Racing into room, carrying a big bunch of roses)* Who did this?

JULIA JACOBSON: *(Aghast)* I'm sorry.

> *(She grabs them to hide behind her back. Other guests bring her more flowers, and more, and she spins dizzily, trying to get rid of them.)*

TOMMY TUTTLE: You better be sorry!

JULIA JACOBSON: I'm sorry!

TONY TURBO: Prove it!

ALL: Prove it!

JULIA JACOBSON: *(Trying to organize her defense)* Look—

TONY TURBO: Bitch!

JULIA JACOBSON: Can a sneaky, stinky idea—

> *(She holds her head and swoons to the floor as guests run in rear, carrying an assortment of white disks and panels which they vibrate in the air—as if to stand in for JULIA JACOBSON's turbulent unconscious bad ideas.)*

GIZA VON GOLDENHEIM: *(Screaming above the music)* Oh my God she fell down!

> *(A gong rings. GIZA is frantic.)*

Oh my God—get up, Julia Jacobson! Try! Try!

JULIA JACOBSON: *(Struggling to her feet)* Look, can a sneaky, stinky idea which is not being thought by anybody on purpose—

> *(She runs to the side and grabs a string, then runs back, holding it taut to her forehead, center stage in front of the quivering white shapes.)*

Can such an unwelcome idea be said to exist in a human brain?

GIZA VON GOLDENHEIM: Sad to say it's possible. Pulling us towards very naughty places.

TONY TURBO: Naughty? Then we are obviously still inside the Hotel Fuck.

(A guest runs in with a covered tray, topped by a little statue of a naked lady, and TONY TURBO's eyes light up.)

Well, am I right?

(The tray is uncovered, revealing a mass of additional roses. Everyone screams in horror.)

TOMMY TUTTLE: *(Rushing forward)* Don't think about roses! Think about the one thing that's gonna be PROTECTION against ROSES!!!

(He is attacking the guest with the roses, and they somehow end up on another pedestal, again immediately covered with a small white screen held in front. TOMMY TUTTLE, chasing the flowers, tumbles back onto the floor at the shock of the white screen.)

—Hey! What happened to those flowers? All we should think, from this moment on, is Hotel Fuck! Hotel Fuck!

JULIA JACOBSON: I agree—Hotel Fuck. C'mon boys, Hotel Fuck!

ALL: *(Lifting their fists for the battle)* Hotel Fuck. Right!

(They all charge forward and crash into the wall of the hotel. They fall back in pain and regroup around one of the tables and sing, bellowing together—)

Hotel Fuck!

(Fists in the air, which plunge down and hit themselves in the groin, at which they howl in pain, but then recover to bellow again to the loud music—)

Hotel Fuck!

(The process is repeated—but this time as they bellow "Hotel Fuck!," the music fades and someone appears rear, hiding behind a giant bouquet of roses lifted in the air. Instead of hitting themselves in the groin, they are overcome with the need to sneeze from the powerful fragrance. They all sneeze powerfully and whirl to see the roses. There is a stunned silence. Then TOMMY TUTTLE screams in terror and runs from the room. The others turn to one another, upset.)

KEN PUSSY PUSS: *(As TOMMY TUTTLE reappears from another entrance)* Look, there he is!

TOMMY TUTTLE: *(Breathing heavily)* A goddamn door!

KEN PUSSY PUSS: What door?

TONY TURBO: I don't see a door.

TOMMY TUTTLE: —A fucking door is opening in my brain— because all my fucking clothes are on fire? With ROSES! *(Grabs the big bunch of roses and clutches them to his body.)* With blood pouring from a hundred holes in my body where those roses HURT me! I mean—they really HURT me! How is this possible—my fucking teeth slicing my tongue like pieces of raw meat—

KEN PUSSY PUSS: Sad to say, that's what the human body is, tongues included—raw meat, Tommy Tuttle.

TOMMY TUTTLE: Raw meat, huh? And what is my poor raw tired-out asshole that shits out a million dried-up words and words and words—

(He dashes across the room, holding the rose aloft as the other guests surround him and the music rises. As the mass of people and roses whirl in place, TOM TUTTLE escapes the melee, and the others speed the roses from the room. The music is quiet now.)

—piled up like shit under this giant rosebush—until my whole body is one giant turd, of one great big sticky flower.

JULIA JACOBSON: Oh, just uguhhh—

TOMMY TUTTLE: I'm sorry, but I think it was necessary for me to have that powerful visionary experience. Because now—being Tiger Tommy Tuttle—I am hearing with my own two ears what a certain dangerous Hotel called "Beautiful Roses" is whispering into the back door of my skull.

GIZA VON GOLDENHEIM: Question. Roses powerful enough to make people a little bit topsy-turvy?

TOMMY TUTTLE: Topsy-turvy? Not me, buddy!

(The music rises, and KEN PUSSY PUSS whirls into the room covered with roses, including even a crown of roses on his head. The others run from the room at the sight, then creep back in slowly. TOMMY TUTTLE is now wearing a red bellboy hat.)

KEN PUSSY PUSS: *(Giddy, eyes spinning in his head)* Look at me, look at me, look at me! *(Pause.)* Festooned with roses, am I not?

TOMMY TUTTLE: Enough roses to feed the fucking toilets till Christmas!

KEN PUSSY PUSS: *(Coming down from his high)* Okay, okay, I

won't insist my own flowers take precedence—though I do hope you won't treat them badly.

JULIA JACOBSON: We'll stuff them into one great big giant rose-bush.

GIZA VON GOLDENHEIM: Why not, please? At certain critical moments, the human nervous system itself—flips into emergency mode—emergency mode!

ALL: *(Scream and run to the walls)* Help!

GIZA VON GOLDENHEIM: *(Calmly)* But that's okay. Because if roses turn into human beings, then human beings counterwise start smelling like roses, until that wonderful stench gets so overpoweringly powerful, that first one human being—

TOMMY TUTTLE: *(Rubbing his crotch, he runs to a crank)* That's me!

GIZA VON GOLDENHEIM: And then another human being—

TONY TURBO: *(Rubbing himself)* That's me! *(Runs to a crank.)*

GIZA VON GOLDENHEIM: And then another and another, all screaming through the tops of heads—that now, now, now is the appropriate moment to stop talking like normal human beings! To click into a much more appropriate mode.

KEN PUSSY PUSS: Ohhhhh—this is it, please!

(There is a gong, and the other guests appear, ready to fly into action.)

Well, let's get the furniture arranged for some serious fucking.

TOMMY TUTTLE: *(As the furniture is rearranged)* What's your problem? It's fucking! Not furniture—

KEN PUSSY PUSS: Listen, Tuttle, fucking without good furniture means bad fucking.

TOMMY TUTTLE: Furniture isn't important for fucking.

JULIA JACOBSON: Hey! Are you people crazy?

TOMMY TUTTLE: You too, lady!

JULIA JACOBSON: Hey, what do you fuck on, fuckhead—or shouldn't I ask?

TOMMY TUTTLE: *(As a gong rings and the tape loop is heard singing "I'm happy, you're happy. I'm happy, you're happy")* C'mon, ask me, ask Tuttle what he fucks on, Tuttle will tell you!

(A conga line follows TOMMY TUTTLE out of the room, but TONY TURBO spins off and falls onto one of the tables.)

JULIA JACOBSON: *(Quietly)* It's to be expected around here. Instead of delightful sofas with soft pillows, these pathetic assholes make do with hard, ugly tables. Ya?

(She has placed a little target on TONY TURBO's behind, his collapsed position on the table making that possible. One of the guests runs in with a little bow and arrow, wearing a red bellboy hat, and takes aim, Cupidlike, at TONY TURBO's bottom.)

TONY TURBO: *(After a pause, head still down, ass up)* Well? What the fuck is everybody waiting for? I plop myself down on this table in order to support myself while being penetrated. So c'mon. goddamn it! Come on!

(The others run into the room and then, seeing the pre-sented tableau, retreat a bit.)

KEN PUSSY PUSS: You go first, Tommy Tuttle.

TOMMY TUTTLE: I'm not going first, you go first!

TONY TURBO: *(Shouting from his prone position)* You don't know what's involved here? *(Straightens up, and now appears ready to cry.)* My possible happiness is involved here, that's all. That's the one little, teenie, weenie, tiny, itzy, bitzy—

TOMMY TUTTLE: Oh, c'mon now. Is this the Hotel Fuck or the Hotel Fuck You?

TONY TURBO: You say that, but you don't care. You don't really care.

(The singing is heard again—"I'm happy, you're happy. I'm happy, you're happy." All look offstage and see something!)

—Oh my God.

(A totally transformed GIZA enters, on high cathorni making him a foot taller than he is, dressed like Louis XIV, embroidered coat with lace, a tall white wig topped with a tiny crown. He is holding an eight-foot-long staff, and controlling on a leash a big black-and-gold-striped dildo that emerges from his pants. Someone else holds a big white disk up behind his head, like a giant halo.)

GIZA VON GOLDENHEIM: Well, hello there, everybody! After a glorious reign of fucking on demand—what I need now, ladies and gentlemen, is for you to bring a fucking chair so I can set down my tired fucking ass.

TONY TURBO: We have chairs, Your Majesty.

JULIA JACOBSON: *(Lifting a golden chair)* Like this one!

KEN PUSSY PUSS: But please sit on us. We're human people . . .

GIZA VON GOLDENHEIM: I don't sit on people. What I do with people?—I fuck people.

KEN PUSSY PUSS: You hear that, fellas? Fuck people. Like us!

(The singing of "I'm happy, you're happy" rises, and all but GIZA do a frantic Charleston, lifting their arms and shouting, "We fuck people! We fuck people!" A gong stops the music, which shifts to a happier tune.)

It must be that we zip tick-tock backwards in time, because for hundreds of years it's true the Hotel Fuck has been very important to civilized society.

TOMMY TUTTLE: Congratulations! But who amongst us is scared shitless to utter the name of a hotel even more civilized?

(Someone has rolled into the room a cart loaded with vases stuffed with roses, and the others attack it.)

TONY TURBO: Will somebody get those fucking ROSES outta here once and for all!

GIZA VON GOLDENHEIM: *(Over the hubbub)* I still want my fucking chair just because I'm so much bigger than the rest of you and I get tired when I—*(Sees JULIA JACOBSON, who is acting girlishly in his presence.)* Well, hello there little one.

JULIA JACOBSON: Do you like roses, Your Majesty?

GIZA VON GOLDENHEIM: Roses? Well, I uh . . . er . . .

JULIA JACOBSON: Fucking can always be better with better decoration. Am I right?

GIZA VON GOLDENHEIM: The evidence is standing before you, my dear. *(Pounds the floor with his staff and calls out)* More freshcut flowers for better fucking. Flowers for fucking, flowers for fucking!

TONY TURBO: *(As guests enter wearing rose hats, carrying flower boxes)* Oh. Shit!

KEN PUSSY PUSS: Maybe it's true! If there were a just few more roses—you know—for the ambiance?

TOMMY TUTTLE: Any MORE ambiance—this fucking hotel turns over in its grave for us to jump in and FUCK this, this, this play about a Hotel Up-its-fucking-rear-end!

GIZA VON GOLDENHEIM: Sorry—You can't fuck a play, darling.

ALL: Oh?

(The music rises, and all form a line, dance, and sing.)

La, la, la, la
Do, re, mi, fa
In a Hotel, Jack and Jill fell
On their fannies
That's the plan he's
Found a big hole
That's the real goal
In a Hotel
Do, re, mi, fa
La, la, la, la

GIZA VON GOLDENHEIM: Come to think of it, you can't fuck hotels, even. This is tragic, in a way.

JULIA JACOBSON: You know what I think? It's too bad there aren't enough cute little roses in the Hotel Fuck so it could simultaneously be the Hotel Beautiful Roses.

(Others object.)

Yes! Yes! Because if it were more beautiful, then everybody would feel so good—they'd start FUCKING all over the place.

KEN PUSSY PUSS: Wait a minute—everything Julia Jacobson says makes me think to myself—which of two rival hotels—

TONY TURBO: *(Interrupting as JULIA JACOBSON jumps on a table upside down and waves naked legs in the air invitingly)* —THIS Hotel, Ken Puss-Puss.

KEN PUSSY PUSS: But wait a minute—how do we know this hotel isn't behind our backs—

(He has backed into the table, and JULIA JACOBSON captures him in her legs.)

TOMMY TUTTLE AND TONY TURBO: Behind our backs!

KEN PUSSY PUSS: *(Screaming and pulling free)* Turning into that rival hotel—!

GIZA VON GOLDENHEIM: You want proof, baby boy?

(He lifts his staff like a thunderbolt as lights flash and a loud gong rings.)

—Follow the leader, because this big bitch is always in heat!

KEN PUSSY PUSS: Now wait just a minute, Giza von Geek!

VOICE: Let's do that again, please!

TOMMY TUTTLE: Something's weird with Goldenheimer—

KEN PUSSY PUSS: Look at those great big giant dirty feet!

JULIA JACOBSON: Oh my God—those big dirty feet covered in dirty muck.

(They are all examining GIZA's dirty cathorni; overcome with disgust, they fall back on the floor and roll away from him.)

TOMMY TUTTLE: Yeah, fucking dirty shoes.

GIZA VON GOLDENHEIM: I understand completely. But to properly apportion one's justifiable disgust, cast those same suspicious eyes down to your own filthy footwear, my little partners-in-sticky-stuff.

TONY TURBO: *(As they examine their own shoes)* What kind of dirty degenerates are we? Whatever we do, people—don't lick 'em!

GIZA VON GOLDENHEIM: Oh, please, please, gentlemen—

KEN PUSSY PUSS: Maybe we LIKE them—a little bit mucky?

TOMMY TUTTLE: No we do NOT! Either we each clean up privately, or we're gonna have to choose partners—

(A guest pulls a rope that rings a bell, and the others scream out in fear and trepidation—"Partners? Partners!?"—as others run forward with big brushes at the end of long handles—first hitting TONY TURBO and KEN PUSSY PUSS and TOMMY TUTTLE, forcing them to bend down and watch as they go to work very aggressively on their shoes. A loud VOICE on tape screams over the

excitement—"I won't do it! I won't do it! I won't do it!"
*GIZA presides from on high, shaking rhythmically as
others work on his big shoes.)*

BOYS: Lick 'em, lick 'em, lick 'em!

TOMMY TUTTLE: These shoes need a lot of work, I guess.

GIZA VON GOLDENHEIM: Get a load of that! SOME people like
sticking their asses up in the air for no reason what-so-
ever.

TONY TURBO: *(Popping up)* That's not the reason!

KEN PUSSY PUSS: Bend back down like the rest of us, Turbo!
Bend over!

TONY TURBO: That's not a problem!

*(He turns to see JULIA JACOBSON, poised near the bell
rope.)*

But I got somebody else in mind to do dirty work down
below.

JULIA JACOBSON: Not right now I'm afraid.

(She rings the bell.)

GIZA VON GOLDENHEIM: Bellboy please!

(A gong rings and everybody scatters.)

Let's have official bellboys to do a better job on these
filthy shoes!

KEN PUSSY PUSS: *(On all fours, searching under furniture)* If I
remember, there is shoe polish here someplace—

TOMMY TUTTLE: *(Kicking KEN PUSSY PUSS)* Finding new ways to use old shoes—why not? I bet you like that.

KEN PUSSY PUSS: No, I don't like that, Tommy Tuttle!

(One guest in a bellboy hat is following TOMMY TUTTLE carrying a large dirty sack, with a rigid circular opening on top, and it keeps nudging up against TOMMY TUTTLE.)

TOMMY TUTTLE: Hey! What's with this irritating sack following me around the room!

GIZA VON GOLDENHEIM: I beg your pardon sir, that's my dirty giant garbage eighteenth-century shoe sack.

TOMMY TUTTLE: Yeah, that's a genuine eighteenth-century shoe sack?

TONY TURBO: Get it outta here!

GIZA VON GOLDENHEIM: Not yet.

(Other female guests come strutting through the room with little targets attached to their ankles and circle around through the scene, stepping to the eccentric music.)

As a kind of group activity in the wonderful Hotel Fuck, you will all step with dirty shoes inside this giant shoe sack. Where once inside—

(TOMMY TUTTLE, TONY TURBO, and KEN PUSSY PUSS shout their objections.)

—you will all take a giant collective step in the direction of your choice.

(He turns and storms from the room.)

TOMMY TUTTLE: Hey, I hope he's not kiddin' about this?

KEN PUSSY PUSS: No, we are left alone with one smelly garbage sack, Tommy Tuttle, which we are all supposed to climb into like a barrel of dirty monkeys.

JULIA JACOBSON: Well, I think I can handle this, boys?

(She steps into the sack, the music rises, and there is a loud cheer as the other guests jump up and down excitedly.)

Oh my God, this thing stinks!

TOMMY TUTTLE: Oh yeah? Well I'd like to verify that for myself, thank you very much. *(Steps into the sack.)*

KEN PUSSY PUSS: Hey, I don't want to be left out of this daredevil stuff, please!

(He tries to get inside but fails. The music rises, the others dance, and JULIA JACOBSON and TOMMY TUTTLE start shaking inside the sack.)

TOMMY TUTTLE: Okay. I don't like to say this—but this Hotel Fuck garbage sack is getting really smelly—

TONY TURBO: *(Dancing with a big stick)* Yeah!

KEN PUSSY PUSS: That is the truth, Tommy Tuttle—

TOMMY TUTTLE: Plus—my feet that are inside this garbage sack—

TONY TURBO: Yeah!

TOMMY TUTTLE: —are starting to swell up or something—

TONY TURBO: Yeah!

TOMMY TUTTLE: 'Cause it really hurts!

TONY TURBO: Yeah!

TOMMY TUTTLE: It hurts!

TONY TURBO: Yeah!

TOMMY TUTTLE: It hurts!

> *(The music has become deafening, and TONY TURBO reaches up to the big lightbulb with his stick. As he touches it there is a flash of light and everyone recoils in pain as the music cuts and the VOICE is heard amidst silence—)*

VOICE: Let's do that again, please!

> *(The music returns, and the female guests begin doing high kicks with their target-covered feet.)*

TOMMY TUTTLE AND JULIA JACOBSON: *(In spasms inside the sack)* It hurts! It hurts! It hurts!

> *(GIZA explodes into the scene, no longer dressed as Louis XIV, but now with his black beard and carrying two big clubs with which he starts beating those inside the sack as the women kick higher and the music grows deafening and the lights fade to black. The music stops suddenly. There is a gong, and the lights come up on a dim nighttime scene as everyone runs from the stage and TONY TURBO explodes in from the side, carrying two suitcases—stumbling and falling to the floor, cursing.)*

TONY TURBO: *(Getting back on his feet, all alone in the darkened room)* Why am I always arriving too late to finish things that could only begin if they weren't fucked up by a lot of beginners? Loaded down with

heavy baggage that probably doesn't even belong to me!
Hello, please!

VOICE: Just one minute, Tony Turbo. Hotels may effect one's
outward behavior, but they must never be allowed to
interfere with that personal sense of self that protects
even you, Tony Turbo, against a world that resists your
pathetic pleas for true and lasting happiness.

TONY TURBO: *(Defiant, lifting a fist)*
—Guess who's come to visit?
Stuffed to the brim
With raucous rumbles
Of rectoid ruckus?
It's ME—ME!
All-boy in his runt
The way I likes it best!

*(GIZA has snuck into the room, in the shadows at the
side, wearing a red bellboy hat and carrying suitcases.)*

GIZA VON GOLDENHEIM: Hello there!

(TONY TURBO whirls, fists up to fight.)

No, no, no—before the expected affectionate greeting,
Sir Tony, tell me—which do you find more upsetting?
My personality, or my bellboy hat?

TONY TURBO: Well, your personality stinks.

GIZA VON GOLDENHEIM: *(Pauses to consider)* Okay. I apologize
for my personality. But I'll never apologize for my hat.

*(Everyone else has gradually appeared behind GIZA,
each carrying two suitcases.)*

TONY TURBO: *(Sarcastically)* Look everybody, one remarkable
bellboy hat.

GIZA VON GOLDENHEIM: Well—

(He comes to TONY TURBO and recites a limerick.)

Dressed like a bellboy,
Red hat on my head
Though I carefully take off that hat
Before snuggling into somebody's bed.

(Leans forward and whispers.) Okay? *(Rapidly tiptoes from the room.)*

TONY TURBO: I bet that fucking bellboy is getting fucked a lot more than the rest of us are fucking.

JULIA JACOBSON: This is one fucking bellboy with an attitude problem.

GIZA VON GOLDENHEIM: *(Popping in again)* Excuse me, I heard that, but—*(Another limerick:)*

A bellboy's agenda
Can never be known.
Though its depths can be fathomed
Through lunges and twitches
Expressing its hunger
For fabulous bitches.

(He pops out of the room again.)

TOMMY TUTTLE: Oh fuck fuck fuck fuck fuck!

KEN PUSSY PUSS: I bet that lucky bellboy is getting fucked a lot more than the rest of us are fucking.

TONY TURBO: Plus, now we have to carry our own heavy baggage.

JULIA JACOBSON: Wait a minute. How do we remember which is our own baggage if they all look the same?

(As the music rises, all the suitcases lift into the air and clump together as everyone shuffles center stage, as if bewitched by their suitcases—crying out in fear—)

ALL: Help, help!

TOMMY TUTTLE: Everybody let go! Drop them, drop them!

(All the suitcases come crashing down.)

Jesus, look at all those suitcases.

KEN PUSSY PUSS: All that dirty baggage on the floor, do we still think "bellboys have more fun"?—or is it just that fucking red hat?

GIZA VON GOLDENHEIM: *(Suddenly runs back into the room, wearing only his bellboy hat and a large stuffed diaper)* Ready for a surprise, please? *(Poses like a muscle man as the others shrink back in disgust.)* Bellboys remain bellboys, even when a uniform gets lost in the dirty laundry.

JULIA JACOBSON: I don't like looking at naked bellboys, and I don't like thinking about dirty laundry!

GIZA VON GOLDENHEIM: *(Twirling and posing)* And sometimes, sometimes!—that famous baggage just happens to be private bellboy baggage—

(As the others exit with bags, he picks up two suitcases and rubs them against his body.)

—the allure of fine leather against muscles that stress and strain.

JULIA JACOBSON: Oh, shut up that know-it-all bellboy!

BOYS: Right!

*(They chase him from the room as a **VOICE** comes over the loudspeakers.)*

VOICE: Julia Jacobson, paging paging Julia Jacobson—

JULIA JACOBSON: God damn it! I don't like being identified in public—

(She whirls and sees someone holding a tray with a folded piece of paper on it.)

Oh my God—am I getting a private message right in the middle of the Hotel Fuck?

VOICE: Ken Pussy Puss, paging Ken Puss Pussy—

KEN PUSSY PUSS: *(Running onstage as someone else enters with a second tray and message)* Fuck! I'm getting a message here in the Hotel Fuck too—how come ME, of all people?

JULIA JACOBSON: I'm getting a message here in the middle of the Hotel Fuck.

(They both read and crumple their messages.)

I am really, truly, getting a crazy message—

VOICE: Paging Tom Tom Tommy Tuttle. Tom Tom Tommy Tuttle—paging Tom Tom Tommy Tuttle. Tom Tom Tommy Tuttle—

TOMMY TUTTLE: *(Entering and overlapping the **VOICE**, a new message is delivered to him)* This is my fucking message, huh? Sooner or later I knew I'd be getting a fucking message.

TONY TURBO: *(Grabbing **TOMMY TUTTLE**'s message)* No, I got a message—me! Me!

(They all start shouting, "I got a message. Me—me—! I got a message!" as the music rises, and GIZA is heard shouting offstage.)

GIZA VON GOLDENHEIM: Outta the way, everybody, I got a big package here!

(He rushes onstage, his head peeking over a large cut-out, heavily decorated heart he is carrying—with a message scrawled on the front: "Guess where I've been?" Upon sight of this apparition the others cover their eyes in fear and whirl, screaming out, "one-two-three-four-five-six-seven-eight-nine-ten!" Then GIZA croaks in a gravel voice.)

Ah, words from the whirlwind, my friends—

(All again scream and count to ten, whirling.)

Words, words, words, from the whirlwind of the world on fire!!

(The music rises, and two guests carry in a large folded letter sealed with a heart. As GIZA leaves the stage with the heart, they open the letter revealing the message "I used to love you!" It rocks back and forth to the loud music, and the others scream, and lifting some of the drapery, start to erase on blackboards that are scattered about on the walls half-hidden by the drapes. The music is overcome by a loud nasal VOICE singing, "Never kissed a girl, never kissed a girl, never kissed a girl.")

ALL: *(As they erase)* Oh, fuck, fuck, fuck, fuck, fuck, fuck—

(The singing fades.)

TONY TURBO: Hey, wait a minute, what kind of message is that? One single word, over and over and over?

KEN PUSSY PUSS: Four words: I—used—to—love—oh fuck! Five words.

TOMMY TUTTLE: Oh, fuck you.

JULIA JACOBSON: I don't think I'm satisfied if I just get one word over and over.

TOMMY TUTTLE: What's the matter with you people? What's the fucking problem?

JULIA JACOBSON: Ah, now that we've finally made it here in the goddamned Hotel Fuck, Tuttle Titty hasn't got a problem?

TOMMY TUTTLE: Watch that language, bitch.

GIZA VON GOLDENHEIM: *(Has entered with two hats, one on top of the other, and a covered tray, and is dancing about the room)* Remember me? Hotel—? Now what the hell was the name of that hotel? "Majestic Splendid . . . Fuck?"

TOMMY TUTTLE: *(As the others laugh and dance)*—Because I'm the one fucking person in this hotel without a problem.

GIZA VON GOLDENHEIM: Well, congratulations, Tommy Tuttle.

TOMMY TUTTLE: Fucking congratulations is right.

TONY TURBO: Congratulations for what?

TOMMY TUTTLE: For getting the dope on all those fucking messages in the Hotel Fuck.

(Another girl arrives with a paper on a tray, and he tosses away her message.)

So, fuck you.

JULIA JACOBSON: Now wait a minute. Does Tommy Tuttle believe, all of a sudden, for no logical reason, that the Hotel Fuck is speaking to him personally?

TOMMY TUTTLE: Yeah. Maybe.

KEN PUSSY PUSS: A hotel speaking like a person?

TONY TURBO: That's impossible.

GIZA VON GOLDENHEIM: As impossible as this?

(He whisks the cover off the tray to reveal a crown.)

It's not a hotel, maybe, but it's here for the taking.

KEN PUSSY PUSS: *(As TOMMY TUTTLE seizes the crown)* Careful, Tommy Tuttle. Nobody said that belongs to you.

TOMMY TUTTLE: Oh yeah? Well, who do you think was getting all those messages personally?

(Guests run in holding little red curtains in front of their faces, and form a ceremonial line behind TOMMY TUTTLE.)

KEN PUSSY PUSS: Tommy Tuttle?

TOMMY TUTTLE: A certain hotel must think so. *(Puts the crown on his head, over his bellboy hat.)* Follow the leader!

(He runs from the room and the others chase him—he comes back from another door and the red curtains revolve as he pushes through to the front of the stage.)

Where did everybody go?

JULIA JACOBSON: *(Following him through the curtains)* Okay, is the Hotel Fuck still speaking personally to Tommy Tuttle?

TOMMY TUTTLE: Hey, maybe it is.

(A jazzy riff, like a fanfare, makes the curtains part, revealing TONY TURBO, KEN PUSSY PUSS and GIZA, linking arms and leaning forward towards TOMMY TUTTLE.)

GIZA VON GOLDENHEIM: *(Mockingly)* Well, hello there, Your Highness.

TOMMY TUTTLE: *(Still holding the crown on top of his hat)* Watch that hiney stuff, Geekheimer.

JULIA JACOBSON: And what does the Hotel Fuck say to Tommy Tuttle when the Hotel Fuck speaks personally to Tommy Tuttle?

TOMMY TUTTLE: That's a little hard to explain.

KEN PUSSY PUSS: *(Exasperated)* Fuck fuck fuck fuck—

TOMMY TUTTLE: It's more complicated than fuck, fuck, fuck, fuck, fuck!

JULIA JACOBSON: No! It's not complicated—because after all this time if the Hotel Fuck were saying something, it wouldn't be saying something to Tommy Tuttle—it's ME!

(She explodes in jealous rage as the others back off and exit, and the red curtains start shaking like crazy, and then she also runs off.)

ME! ME! ME! ME! The Hotel Fuck is speaking to me! Me personally!

TONY TURBO: *(Peeking in at a doorway)* Oh sure, and if we

believe that, at this late date, we believe the big sign at the end of the corridor that says "Break down this heavy door and get to lick my lollipop till lunch time!"

(He stops, realizes the opportunity is still there—and hurries off excitedly.)

JULIA JACOBSON: *(After a pause)* Okay. Something's wrong. Now that twenty-seven assholes are not babbling all at once, I no longer know if I still believe that something like a hotel—the Hotel Fuck in particular—

(She runs to the side and pulls a string from the wall taut to her forehead, center stage, as others enter and hold up white disks as the evocation of secret "Hotel Fuck" sources of energy.)

Can a hotel as crazy as the Hotel Fuck—talk to me!

TOMMY TUTTLE: *(Entering as others run in repositioning furniture)* I don't know what you think you're listening to, bitch, except a lotta furniture and other stuff—getting moved around the Hotel Fuck.

JULIA JACOBSON: Listen, don't blame me if I'm the one person making an effort around here.

GIZA VON GOLDENHEIM: *(Grabbing the string from her and returning it to the wall)* Everybody stop TALKING!

(Music stops, there is silence.)

Now—crazy as this may seem—before running from this hotel screaming and tearing one another's hair out by the roots—
(The others silently twist from imagined pain of hair being pulled, and run out of the room.)

—we all listen to secret messages from the Hotel Fuck.

(He looks about the deserted room. He goes and puts his ear to the wall.)

Like this.

KEN PUSSY PUSS: *(Sneaking back into the room)* What's he doing?

JULIA JACOBSON: *(Returning, along with TOMMY TUTTLE and TONY TURBO.)* This is crazy.

GIZA VON GOLDENHEIM: Do it.

(All but JULIA JACOBSON join GIZA in listening to the walls.)

JULIA JACOBSON: No.

GIZA VON GOLDENHEIM: Do it.

JULIA JACOBSON: No.

GIZA VON GOLDENHEIM: Do it!

JULIA JACOBSON: No!

GIZA VON GOLDENHEIM: *(Bellowing)* DO IT!!!!

JULIA JACOBSON: *(She to goes to listen, then turns away)* Oh, this is crazy.

Hey—?

(A phone rings in the distance.)

TOMMY TUTTLE: *(Looking up, wondering)* Yeah. I hear the telephone.

GIZA VON GOLDENHEIM: Be patient, Tommy Tuttle.

(There is a deafening gong, then Loud Voices chanting to a musical beat—"WE'RE HERE! WE'RE HERE! WE'RE HERE!" *Another gong silences the chant, but the others have all jumped clear of the walls, stunned.)*

GIZA VON GOLDENHEIM: *(As soft music busily oscillates in the background)* Well? What more does it take to convince this collection of Hotel Fuck assholes that this hotel is definitely, now—speaking for itself?

KEN PUSSY PUSS: *(Worried)* Speaking for itself? But what does it say? It's just a hotel.

VOICE: *(Booming out)* Here I am! Oh, here I am!

KEN PUSSY PUSS: *(Scared)* Guess what. I'm outta here right now!

(All but JULIA JACOBSON run from the room, yelling, "Me too!")

JULIA JACOBSON: *(All alone comes downstage)* Okay, now I'm listening all by myself.

VOICE: Ladies and gentlemen, the Hotel Fuck is ready to receive visitors.

(A gong, and the music gets louder.)

The really big Hotel Fuck, the really big Hotel Fuck.

JULIA JACOBSON: *(Pacing angrily)* Big Hotel Fuck? This is not enough for me—and that makes me so frustrated—

(She runs to a table and rips off one of its legs. Then she throws it on the floor and starts stamping on it in rage, as the music crests, then fades low.)

TONY TURBO: *(As the men peek back into the room)* Trying to cause trouble with the furniture, bitch?

JULIA JACOBSON: *(Controlling herself with steely calm)* Trouble? Not me, boys. I was just treating this extra table leg the way I dream of treating a couple of missing penises. You know what I mean?

(All the men are now seen to be carrying table legs.)

KEN PUSSY PUSS: Somebody using a table leg for a penis—there's a prescribed punishment.

JULIA JACOBSON: What kind of punishment?

KEN PUSSY PUSS: I don't know, but I can imagine some bad kinds.

JULIA JACOBSON: *(Pause)* Funny, but I can no longer imagine what to do with my extra table leg.

KEN PUSSY PUSS: Now that you mention it—I don't know what to do with my table leg either.

TONY TURBO: I've got a table leg—but what the fuck do I do with it?

TOMMY TUTTLE: Guess what, geniuses. Having a table leg instead of a penis, that's a problem.

KEN PUSSY PUSS: *(Very upset)* That's not my problem, because I don't have a penis problem!

TOMMY TUTTLE: If this isn't a penis problem, fuckhead, then what the hell kind of problem is it, huh?

VOICE: *(As several white screens are carried across the stage to make a white wall at one side.)* Here I am! Oh, here I am!

TOMMY TUTTLE: I'll tell you problems! Once upon a time—this is a problem—I wanted to fuck somebody so bad.

KEN PUSSY PUSS: My God, Tommy—I have the same problem!

TOMMY TUTTLE: No! You don't have the same problem. Me—I wanted to fuck somebody so bad—

JULIA JACOBSON: *(Peeking out from behind one of the screens)* That's okay, Tommy Tuttle. You can fuck me later.

TOMMY TUTTLE: When? When is later?

JULIA JACOBSON: *(Peeking from behind a second screen)* Just later.

TOMMY TUTTLE: But when? When? When? When is later!

JULIA JACOBSON: Not right now, I'm afraid.

(The screens are now recrossing the stage like a little train to chugging music, and JULIA follows them, exiting as the screens reposition themselves behind a table.)

TOMMY TUTTLE: Not right now? Not right now? *(Races across to start revolving one of the cranks.)* No! Right now! Right now! Right now!

VOICE: LATER, PLEASE! MUCH LATER!

(A gong sends TOMMY TUTTLE running from the room and charging back in from another door as the music crests. He is hurled against a wall as the music softens.)

TOMMY TUTTLE: I wanted to fuck somebody so bad. And it kept on not happening and not happening and not happening and not happening! And in total frustration, I threw myself onto my empty bed with a feeling—that's it, if I'm not getting fucked, then I give up I give up forever.

(The music rises and he shouts—)

That's it for me!

(He goes and throws himself onto a table as the white screens come forward and surround the table. The music softens to a soprano voice sustaining one clear note, and TOMMY TUTTLE slowly appears, standing on the table, looking out over the enclosure of the white screens.)

But at that moment of giving up forever—Jesus! As if a switch had been thrown at the bottom of my consciousness—as if giving up all hope of sexual fulfillment—I'd suddenly fallen into an ocean of white light, where, painlessly, I was burned empty of all anxiety and suffering.

(Someone wearing an "Old Man" mask appears from behind the table—as if a white-bearded and ancient God were approaching. He holds a pure white ball between his hands and lifts it up towards TOMMY TUTTLE.)

And this . . . total emptiness. Sheer bliss inside everything that had kept me heretofore in turmoil. And this was accompanied by a feeling of joy and light and happiness. Happiness that had no equal in my entire fucking life.

(He takes the globe from the Old Man, and the white screens quietly drift away, gathering behind the table.)

But then, alas—that wonderful feeling started to go away, and I slept a little.

(The music has changed—a faint jazzy dance tune is heard.)

And when I woke up, I could remember having had that heavenly experience I remembered. But I could no longer remember—what did it REALLY FEEL like?

(The Old Man takes the ball back and carries it away, and TOMMY TUTTLE is back on the floor.)

This I could no longer remember. So okay. Once again, I try it—I give up!

(He throws himself back onto the table, and the jazz tune gets louder. He springs up from the table, and the music softens.)

It didn't work! No white light, no happiness.

(He gives it one more try, throwing himself onto the table and screaming over music once again, loud—)

I give up, I give up, I give up!

(The screens part and TONY TURBO is revealed, charging forward with a large dildo strapped to his dress, whipping it with all his might as he charges around the room.)

TONY TURBO: Back to the real world I'm afraid—!

TOMMY TUTTLE: *(Rising from the table)* Wait a minute—I give up! I give up!

(The others whirl into the room, GIZA and JULIA JACOBSON dancing a frantic waltz, as the VOICE cries out—)

VOICE: Oh never never again, oh never never again, oh never never again!

(TOMMY TUTTLE has been blindfolded by a group of lady guests. A large white disk halo is held behind his head.)

GIZA VON GOLDENHEIM: Oh, never again, my friend?

TOMMY TUTTLE: Never again.

(The women lean forward to touch him, one kissing him on the cheek.)

GIZA VON GOLDENHEIM: *(Bowing in mock seriousness)* Well hello there, Mr. "Hole" in the Hotel Fuck!

TOMMY TUTTLE: *(Blindfolded still)* No, no, no, the pleasure is all mine, Madam—"Hole" in the Hotel Fuck.

JULIA JACOBSON: Okay, you pathetic bundle of beanbags without balls. What this lady thinks with her head screwed on tight like a good fuck in the rumble seat of a revved-up refurbished roadster! What she thinks is this.

(She runs to crash into a side wall. The music cuts. She staggers back and calls out artificially—invitingly—)

Owww!

(The others look at one another, then all run and crash into walls, and are thrown to the floor by the impact.)

Don't you get it?

GIZA VON GOLDENHEIM: *(As everyone staggers back to their feet, holding their heads in pain)* Yeah, we get it.

JULIA JACOBSON: Oh, I know what you're thinking about me.

GIZA VON GOLDENHEIM: You know what we're thinking about Julia Jacobson?

JULIA JACOBSON: And I know what you're thinking about the Hotel Fuck.

GIZA VON GOLDENHEIM: You know what we're thinking about the Hotel Fuck?

JULIA JACOBSON: Don't think that! And never, never, never think that—about the Hotel Fuck!

(She races out of the room angrily, and GIZA pulls the bell rope to produce a loud "boing"—at which JULIA JACOBSON runs back into the room and screams—)

Why did you ring that bell behind my back?

GIZA VON GOLDENHEIM: *(Shrugging)* I don't know why I rang that bell behind your back.

JULIA JACOBSON: I know why! I know why! *(Grabs one of the detached table legs and starts whirling it like a furious propeller attached to her crotch.)* Because there is a brand-new kind of understanding that a thing like a hotel can have of people outside of a hotel who are thinking about fucking, fucking, fucking!

(Women strut across the stage, little baby dolls perched on their heads, but baby dolls with skulls instead of normal baby heads.)

What kind of understanding can a stupid GIRL like ME!—have of the fucking Hotel Fuck?

TONY TURBO: —between a human girl and a hotel believe me everybody—

(The baby dolls fly from the women's heads to perch onto TONY TURBO's big dildo, to a "whee!" of excitement over the loudspeakers.)

—there is no possible comparison. So bye-bye!

(He waves and dances off with dildos and dolls as JULIA JACOBSON seizes a sledgehammer and runs towards them.)

KEN PUSSY PUSS: Oh! Don't hit the babies!

TOMMY TUTTLE: *(Grabbing the sledgehammer from JULIA JACOBSON)* WRONG! WRONG! WRONG! Julia Jacobson. Some things are wrong, no matter how many times you try making them right! *(Turns to the others.)* Am I right?

GIZA AND KEN PUSSY PUSS: Maybe.

(TOMMY TUTTLE touches the lightbulb with the sledgehammer. There is a flash, and all recoil in pain.)

KEN PUSSY PUSS: Oh please! I think this. I think we should reconsider the Hotel Beautiful Roses.

TOMMY TUTTLE: Roses of DEATH my friend! Death roses—

GIZA VON GOLDENHEIM: *(Dancing to piano music)* Hotel Pie in the Sky? Hotel Turn Your Back on Tomorrow? Hotel Fuck Me, Fuck Me, Fuck Me? Because who wants to get fucked after all?

KEN PUSSY PUSS: Don't I want to get fucked?

GIZA VON GOLDENHEIM: Oh, you've been fucked, my friend, so let's dance.

KEN PUSSY PUSS: *(As the music rises)* No dancing!

(A gong; they all stagger, and the music shifts.)

GIZA VON GOLDENHEIM: Why not? Hotel Fuck!

KEN PUSSY PUSS: Hotel Fuck? Hotel "Help Me." Hotel Help Me! Hotel Help Me! Help me! Help me!

(KEN PUSSY PUSS keeps screaming "Help me," and the others turn to him mockingly and dance around him,

taunting him, imitating his "Help me, help me, help me!" A gong interrupts, and the music gets even louder as the others run in and throw KEN PUSSY PUSS *against a wall and then line up behind him, pressing him flat against the wall as all grind their hips against the body in front of them.* KEN PUSSY PUSS, *almost squeezed to death, pulls away and grabs a vase filled with roses with which he threatens those who chase after him. All freeze as he lifts his vase in the air, and the* VOICE *intones—)*

VOICE: Let's do that again, please!

KEN PUSSY PUSS: *(Frozen with his flowers over his head, he sings softly)*
"If I was the only boy in the world
And nobody found me a girl?"

TOMMY TUTTLE: You want girls? I'll show you girls.

(The music returns, and all run to throw KEN PUSSY PUSS *against the wall and sexually violate him. He escapes and is recaptured as the* VOICE *is heard over the music—*
"Here I am! Oh here I am! Oh here I am!" *After a second escape and recapture, all fall to the ground in agony, and at that moment, a naked* TONY TURBO *appears at the rear.*
He is in radiant light, in a feather headdress, resembing a vision of a Blakean innocent babe. In his outstretched hand, he carries a basket of eggs.)

TONY TURBO: Don't—!

(The music suddenly becomes soft, and he speaks softly, with a radiant smile on his face.)

—say a word. Nobody says a word, because I know— nobody expects real happiness at this late date. But look at me. I have a surprise.

KEN PUSSY PUSS: A surprise? After all this time do you have real, bone-crushing happiness, Tony Turbo?

GIZA VON GOLDENHEIM: It does seem impossible, but maybe the impossible—is possible?

TONY TURBO: *(Smiling, eyes wide)* It HAS to be possible, that's my understanding of things. So right now, everybody—

(The music starts to sound more ominous, and at the same time, TONY TURBO's attitude starts to change, becoming quietly threatening.)

Take off your clothes, please. Because what I want to see surrounding me now is naked, voluptuous flesh!

(The music is frightening now, and so is TONY TURBO. After each of his angry phrases, the others lurch forward, as if their bodies were being torn by greedy hands.)

That's the one thing that interests me! And if this doesn't happen immediately—I will express my rage and frustration—by tearing at every one of you with my long fingernails—exploding in frightening ways from every hole in this turbulent body of quivering expectation! Be forewarned!

(TONY TURBO rips at his own body, and the others quiver in pain as the music climaxes. But then the VOICE is heard over the music, which quiets, then ends.)

VOICE: *(Triumphant)* Here I am! Oh, here I am again! For the hundredth time, just doing my thing.

(In the shadows at the rear, a giant bleeding heart appears, tiny pinpricks of light framing it in a tangled halo.)

Just doing my real true thing, for the hundred-millionth time! Again and again and again!

*(As the **VOICE** has been speaking, all except **TONY TURBO** cower and leave the stage, trying to hide from the **VOICE**.)*

TONY TURBO: *(All alone now, speaks softly, almost crying)* You know what I really say? I say—please, no more fucking, please. *(Hides his face.)* Please, please, no more fucking.

JULIA JACOBSON: *(Slowly returning with the others)* Oh God, me too.

KEN PUSSY PUSS: *(Crying softly)* Me too, me too.

JULIA JACOBSON: No more fucking.

TOMMY TUTTLE: Okay. No more fucking is what I hear . . . but me—I seem to have no choice in the matter. So what I say, because I can't think of anything else to say is— Hotel Fuck.

(Jazzy music returns, and he shouts out defiantly.)

Hotel Fuck! Hotel Fuck!

*(The music is loud now, and the others twitch convulsively, as if controlled by forces from elsewhere, and **TOMMY TUTTLE** runs rearstage and starts jumping up and down like a jumping jack, shouting as the lights fade.)*

Hotel Fuck! Hotel Fuck! Hotel Fuck!

*(As soon as the lights are out, the music switches to the nasal voice singing, "I'm happy, you're happy. I'm happy, you're happy. I'm happy, you're happy." The lights come on again, and everyone is seen dancing a frantic Charleston to that singing—desperate looks on their faces—except for **TOMMY TUTTLE** who still bounces up and down in the rear shouting, "Hotel Fuck! Hotel Fuck!" The lights go out again, and the music stops.)*

THE END

ADDENDUM

In Europe *Paradise Hotel* was titled *Hotel Fuck*. For those who choose to produce the play under that name, an alternative opening speech is provided:

VOICE: *(Interrupts dancing)* Ladies and gentlemen, ladies and gentlemen—attention, please! This play, *Hotel Fuck* must be preceded by a potentially disastrous announcement. While no one desires to cause confusion or disappointment, this risk must yet be taken. All audiences must be informed that the play *Hotel Fuck* has not, in fact, one hundred percent guaranteed continued existence as the play *Hotel Fuck.*

At this very minute, ladies and gentlemen, a second, much less provocative play entitled—"Hotel Beautiful Roses"—is threatening to replace the much more provocatively titled—*Hotel Fuck*—which is now filling the stage in front of your very eyes—trying desperately to hold on to its proper and genuine self—in the face of such adversity—forever and forever and forever— HOTEL FUCK! HOTEL FUCK!

ADDITIONAL PRODUCTION NOTES

It may be useful to know that in many of my plays, in my own productions, many of the actors use foreign (or sometimes regional) accents. This gives another layer of aural complexity which I find relevant to my aesthetic concerns—plus, it serves as a valuable, almost Brechtian "distancing" device applied to the language itself. It is obviously up to individual producers whether or not they want to use accents—and/or if they want to use accents other than the ones I chose for particular actors in my productions. As information only, therefore, I provide the following list:

THE UNIVERSE: Mary—Middle European accent
BENITA CANOVA: Madame—Middle European accent
Christina—California "Valley Girl" accent
PEARLS FOR PIGS: Doctor—German accent
PARADISE HOTEL: Julia Jacobson—Middle European accent
Ken Pussy Puss—Spanish accent
Tommy Tuttle—Brooklyn accent